W9-CJN-509

ENGLISH VERSE SATIRE 1590-1765

English Verse Satire 1590-1765

RAMAN SELDEN

Department of English, University of Durham

London
GEORGE ALLEN & UNWIN
Boston   Sydney

First published in 1978

© George Allen & Unwin (Publishers) Ltd, 1978

British Library Cataloguing in Publication Data

Selden, Raman
    English verse satire, 1590–1765.
    1. Satire, English – History and
    Criticism   2. English poetry – Early
    modern, 1500–1700 – History and
    criticism   3. English poetry – 18th century –
    History and criticism
    I. Title
    821'.07   PR508.S27

ISBN 0-04-827016-4

Typeset in 11 point Bembo by Northampton Phototypesetters Ltd
Printed in Great Britain at the University Press, Cambridge

Acknowledgements

Much of the spade-work for this book was done some years ago in the course of research for my doctoral thesis. I should like to take this opportunity of thanking Professor Harold F. Brooks for his warm-hearted and meticulous supervision. I am only sorry that my book is not a more fitting tribute to him. I should also like to record my thanks to Professor T. S. Dorsch, Peter Lewis, Peter Malekin, Derek Todd and Professor Gavin Townend for reading parts of the book and giving me helpful advice. I am especially grateful to Mr Graham Blyth for reading through the entire manuscript. My thanks also go to the University of Durham Research Fund Committee for financing work in the British Museum.

Raman Selden
University of Durham

Contents

Acknowledgements   *page* 7

1   The Roman Verse Satirists and their
Reputation   11
*Horace – Juvenal – the reputation of the Roman satirists
during the Renaissance*

2   The Elizabethan Satyr-Satirist   45
*The survival of 'Complaint' – the 'sour and crabbed
face' of Juvenal – formal satire of the 1590s*

3   Commonwealth and Restoration Satire   73
*Heraclitus' tears – the neoclassical Horace – Cleveland
and Oldham: extremists vs extremists – Butler and
Rochester: low-style satire – Dryden: mock-heroic,
heroic and fine raillery*

4   The 18th-Century Horace: Pope and Swift   119
Good-humoured satire: Young's Love of Fame –
Pope and Swift

5   The 18th-Century Juvenal: Dr Johnson and
Churchill   153
Dr Johnson's imitations of Juvenal – Charles Churchill

Notes and References   176

A Reading List   186

Index   187

Chapter 1

The Roman Verse Satirists and their Reputation

The following account of Latin verse satire is almost exclusively devoted to Horace and Juvenal. The fragments of Lucilius and the five satires of Persius do not require full treatment because they were not used directly as models by the English Augustan satirists, despite the fact that Lucilius was the founder of formal satire, and Persius was an important model for the Elizabethan satirists.

The contrast between Horace and Juvenal was translated, in different periods, into distinctions between malignant and benign laughter, between a snarl and a smile, between vituperation and ridicule, between 'railing' and 'raillery'. It is, in essence, an ethical distinction projected into a fictional form. Throughout the period of this study (1590–1765), English verse satirists adopted a version of one or other of these voices, modified and transformed by psychological, historical, social and literary factors. The labels 'Juvenalian' and 'Horatian' were a convenient shorthand for the extreme ends of a spectrum of possible satiric voices. The transformations of the voices have been numerous, and yet the demarcation between the two contrary voices remains useful as a means of establishing the outline of a typology.

There has been a tendency in the past to construct a unitary ideal type of the 'satirist', with a view to establishing a normative or prescriptive model by which a writer's work is judged. This approach (normal in periods of classicism) inevitably represents certain types of satire as deviant or peripheral. A model built upon an antithesis is to be preferred, because it encourages an exploratory or heuristic approach rather than a prescriptive criticism. It is unfortunate that two of the most influential recent theorists of satire have characterised the genre in terms of a single type. Alvin Kernan suggests that the typical 'satirist' is 'proud, fiery, intolerant and irascible'. After making a half-hearted qualification ('the degree of indignation varies with the man, and the satiric conventions of his time'), Kernan tries to answer the objection, that

the satire of Horace, Erasmus, and Ben Jonson is too mild to con-
form to his definition, by appealing to a covert Freudian explana-
tion. The Juvenalian satirist, he argues, is the essential type: 'Such
writers, by carrying to extremes the private personality of the
satirist, bring into relief the tendencies of all satire, tendencies
which are repressed in the gentler types.'[1]

There is a common tendency among theorists to establish a
clear boundary between comic and satiric genres. Northrop Frye
argues that satire is 'the seamy side of the tragic vision', and that
'to the extent that a comedy is satiric it possesses a more than
comic seriousness'.[2] The definition of the 'satirist' as malcontent
or Iago-like detractor is taken to an extreme by one critic who
regards the essential characteristic of satire to be its motiveless
sadism.[3] Even in the Elizabethan period (Kernan's period), the
Horatian voice can be heard as an undertone or suppressed intona-
tion.

Ronald Paulson's reflections on satire culminate in a useful
generalisation.[4] Horace's world is inhabited by fools, whose folly
is signified in the fact that they bring punishment down upon
their own heads. Juvenal's is inhabited by knaves, whose knavery
consists in the damage they do to others. A knave's victim is
usually a fool. Alternatively, in Juvenal's satires folly inevitably
results in knavery: the man who foolishly pursues wealth incites
the murderer and the thief. One might add that Horatian satire
tolerantly regards most moral and social deviance as folly, while
Juvenal's satirist sees the lineaments of knavery even in mere
foibles and eccentricities. In general, it is the tone and stance of the
satirists that differ and not the objects of satire. The theme of
the decline of hospitality, for example, is treated by both satirists:
Horace's view of Nasidienus (Satire II, viii) is tolerant and amused;
Juvenal's treatment of Virro (Satire V) is bitter and savage.[5]

Although one cannot expect that the traditional antithesis
between Horace and Juvenal will be capable of providing the basis
of a complete theory of satire, it has the useful simplicity of the
classic contrasts between Plautus and Terence, Richardson and
Fielding, Lawrence and Joyce. In addition, the labels 'Horatian' and
'Juvenalian' serve as short-hand terms for certain combinations of
style and tone which are used for various purposes by a wide
variety of writers. The labels have the kind of general usefulness
which is associated with pairs of philosophical terms like 'idealist'
and 'materialist', 'subjective' and 'objective'. In calling a satirist
'Horatian' or 'Juvenalian', one is not establishing a very precise
description even of the writer's general characteristics, and one is
certainly not making a generalisation about the writer's entire
work. Pope is generally 'Horatian', but uses material from all

three Roman satirists in his imitation of Horace's first satire of the second book.[6] Charles Churchill is the eighteenth-century Juvenal, but, at the same time, he is often 'romantic' in a quite unclassical manner. Nevertheless, the labels have a value in locating certain satiric 'voices', strategies, topics, stances and styles, which are redefined and redeployed throughout the history of English verse satire.

One of the most lucid descriptions of the traditional contrast between Horace and Juvenal was written in the early eighteenth century by Pope's arch-enemy John Dennis, who distinguishes between the cloistered 'Tragick Eloquence of *Juvenal*' and the urbane and polite 'Comick' satire of Horace.[7] But before we briefly trace the history of these stereotypes in the Renaissance period, we must examine the Latin satirists in detail through modern eyes in order to establish a perspective which will permit us to see more clearly in subsequent chapters the manner of the English satirists' transformation of the classical traditions. For example, the commonly held seventeenth- and eighteenth-century view that Juvenal is a 'serious' and even 'tragic' writer is probably a misconception, but must have weighed heavily with Dr Johnson when he came to imitate Juvenal's tenth satire. To delineate a modern interpretation of Juvenal's satiric manner has the effect of highlighting the historical relativity of Dr Johnson's interpretation.

HORACE

Horace's appeal to the English Augustans is understandable: like them, Horace stood for 'rational' order, plainness, moderation, social quiescence and 'good humour'. John Dennis praises Horace's satire in social terms: 'And above all things, must it not be most agreeable to a Polite Court, where that dexterous Insinuation, that fine good Sense, and that true Pleasantry, which are united in the *Horatian* Satire, are the only shining Qualities which make the Courtier valuable and agreeable?' (p. 219). There is little doubt that in those dangerous years after the Civil Wars, when Augustus was laying the foundations of the *Pax Augusta,* the genial and delicate irony of Horace the satirist was profoundly 'valuable and agreeable' to the regime. The satires of Samuel Butler played a similar role in the period immediately after the English Civil War. In his rather un-Horatian tetrameters, Butler consistently undermined the idealists of the Parliamentary party, notably the Puritans and the religious enthusiasts. Horace's turn of mind was less sceptical than Butler's, but his cultural significance is similar: his qualified rejection of Stoic idealism in favour of the moderation

of the Epicureans, and his gently aristocratic denigration of 'demo-
cracy' *(odi prophanum volgus)* was no less potent in the post-
revolutionary period. Horace's 'charisma' was enhanced by his
avoidance of any servile dependence upon the Court. Despite the
fact that he owed a great deal to the good offices of Maecenas (and
Virgil) in securing the favour of Augustus, and that he was at a
psychological disadvantage in having fought for Brutus against
the future emperor at Philippi, Horace retained his independence
both in his writing (except in a few patriotic odes) and in his life
(he rejected the offer of the post of secretary to the emperor). The
gift of the Sabine farm which guaranteed Horace's real indepen-
dence of Rome justified the occasional panegyric line in praise of
his benefactor *(Maecenas atavis edite regibus)*, but did not render
spurious that Horatian tone of 'easy familiarity' which the English
Augustans so much affected (compare Swift's letters to Harley).
The independent stance signified cultural stability, while the ease
of social discourse indicated an achieved cultural unity (or con-
formity). This combination of independence and conformity is
characteristic of both the English and the Roman 'conservative'
satire, which on the one hand rejects all philosophical or ideological
commitments, and on the other hand confidently bases its judge-
ments upon certain well-defined cultural values. Horace owes
allegiance to no philosophical school and will not be 'bound over
to swear as any master dictates' *(nullius addictus iurare in verba
magistri).* On the other hand, there is nothing of the corrosive
and disrespectful nonconformity of *Private Eye* or *Oz* in Horace's
satiric portrayals. He is the conservative satirist *par excellence,*
ridiculing any deviation from norms of restraint and 'common
sense'. The fact that Horace confines his attention exclusively to
abuses in the realms of literature and private morality does not
diminish the wider cultural significance of his conservative role.
There is nothing in Horace's satires which approaches the tragic
vision of the end of civilisation to be found in the final book of
The Dunciad, but Horace shares with Pope the same pattern of
social, ethical and literary values.

Some of the general characteristics of Horatian satire can be
quickly established by an examination of Horace's views on
Lucilius, the father of Latin hexameter satire. By choosing to follow
the model of Lucilius rather than the model of Menippean satire
(Ennius and Varro), Horace was furthering tendencies towards
formal unity rather than formal variety, without, however,
abandoning the spirit of improvisation which is associated by
Livy with primitive satire. In rejecting the medley (the original
meaning of *satura*)[8] of prose and verse, Horace was not rejecting
the informal 'negligence' which is suggested by Lucilius' term

for his own satire (*schedium*, an improvised raft). An effect of casual spontaneity is achieved through style, form, narrative method and persona. The style is firmly grounded on the informal yet sophisticated norms of conversation *(sermo)*. The satires are loosely structured, giving the impression of spontaneous and un-premeditated composition. But the impression is an achievement of great artistic labour. One of Horace's main criticisms of Lucilius is that his work lacked polish and careful revision: 'Herein lay his fault: often in an hour, as though a great exploit, he would dictate two hundred lines while standing, as they say, on one foot' (I, iv, 9–10).[9] It is, of course, a general feature of Augustan 'classicism' that it regards 'naturalness' as an effect of labour and not of romantic self-abandon. But the desire for 'correctness' of language and prosody does not inhibit the development of the satirist's persona.

Indeed, Horace's satires are remarkable for their richly auto-biographical narrative voice. Horace's admiration for the open-ness and self-revelatory nature of Lucilius' satires can best be understood in relation to the conventions of the classical plain style. Roman rhetorical theories about plainness appear to have first dominated literary culture in the time of Lucilius, and particularly in connection with the almost mythical Scipionic Circle, a group of aristocratic leaders of taste, a kind of Roman Falkland Circle or Bloomsbury Group. Horace appears to have followed a later and more refined version of their theories as they were developed by the 'Atticists' of Cicero's day in Horace's boyhood. At the level of language, the Atticists advocated a subordination of style to content (*verba* to *res*) in the tradition of Socrates. In the *Ars Poetica,* Horace argues that the good writer will derive his content from the writings of the Socratic school *(Socraticae chartae),* and that once the content is established, the style will follow without difficulty (310–11). To achieve its function of subserving the subject-matter of a work, the style must be simple, concise and refined. While Horace evidently found Lucilius' work lacking in refinement,[10] he admired Lucilius' adherence to the second require-ment of the plain style: self-revelation and self-irony.[11] Lucilius places his whole life before us open to view like a votive tablet (*votiva . . . veluti descripta tabella*). Just as the polished comedy of Terence is the 'mirror' of life, so the plain-style satire is the mirror of the self, or at least this is its 'claim'. The Horatian satirist is the devotee of the 'Honest Muse'. The finest exposition of this view is to be found in Ben Jonson's *Discoveries:*

Language most shewes a man: speake, that I may see thee. It springs out of the most retired and inmost parts of us, and is the Image of the Parent of it, the mind. No glasse renders a mans forme or likenesse so true as his speech.[12]

Horace's satires are full of self-revelation, self-scrutiny and self-irony. He does not present himself as a remote and self-righteous preacher, but rather as a familiar and fallible everyman. He presents himself as a rather plump, bald, bleary-eyed and slightly self-indulgent freedman's son, who, after a rather inglorious military career, was driven by poverty to scribble. On the other hand, he relates with pride the moral education imparted to him by his father, who taught him his respect for experience above theory and his commitment to moderation in all things. Horace's closing remarks in the fourth satire of the first book are full of delicate irony and unegotistical introspection:

> Thanks to this training I am free from vices which bring disaster, though subject to lesser frailties such as you would excuse. Perhaps even from these much has been withdrawn by time's advance, candid friends, self-counsel; for when my couch welcomes me or I stroll in the colonnade, I do not fail myself: 'This is the better course: if I do that, I shall fare more happily: thus I shall delight the friends I meet: that was ugly conduct of so and so: is it possible that some day I may thoughtlessly do anything like that?' Thus, with lips shut tight, I debate with myself; and when I find a bit of leisure, I trifle with my papers.
>
> (129–39)

Two characteristically Horatian features stand out here. The first is the apparently effortless and spontaneous presentation of the satirist's inner life, a quality not usually associated with classical poetry. The second is the relativism of Horace's ethical stance: not all human errors are of equal seriousness. In this, Horace is firmly opposed to the Stoics' absolutism, which he ridicules in a number of places. This ethical relativism is the basis of Horace's 'good-humoured' attitude to his satiric victims.

Horace admired the freedom *(libertas)* with which Lucilius 'rubbed down the city with much salt' (I, x, 4), but had reservations about the virulence of his attack. The Earl of Rochester's imitation of this passage in 'An Allusion to Horace' conveys the point well:

> But within due proportions circumscribe
> Whate're you write, that with a flowing tide
> The style may rise, yet in its rise forbear
> With useless words t'oppress the wearied ear.

Here be your language lofty, there more light:
Your rhetoric with your poetry unite.
For elegance' sake, sometimes allay the force
Of epithets: 'twill soften the discourse.
A jest in scorn points out and hits the thing
More home than the morosest satyr's sting.[13]

If we adopt the 'classical' view of the development of verse satire as an art form and see it as a progressive humanisation of violent primitive instincts or as the taming of a predatory animal, then the satires of Horace would represent the high point of civilisation and pacification. The venom of the wild satirist has been removed and replaced by a harmless nettle. Occasionally in the satires we glimpse the potentially serious repercussions of libellous and defamatory satire, for example, in the first satire of the second book, when Horace asks the advice of Trebatius, a famous jurist of the day, about his literary career. Throughout this oddly ambivalent poem Trebatius constantly advises Horace against writing satire, especially of the libellous kind. Although Horace at no point openly declares his intention to follow such a course, Trebatius concludes his advice with a firm warning: 'But for all that, let me warn you to beware, lest, by chance, ignorance of our sacred laws bring you into trouble. If a man write ill verses against another, there is a right of action and redress by law' (80–3).

Horace playfully and wittily dissolves the potentially serious implication of Trebatius' warning in a pun which confuses the legal terminology with the aesthetic: 'To be sure, in the case of ill verses. But what if a man compose good verses, and Caesar's judgement approve? If he has barked at someone who deserves abuse, himself quite blameless?' 'Good' carries both moral and aesthetic significance: a satire ceases to be libellous when it is morally justified and when it is mollified by the correctness and elegance of its style. We know from the three 'programme' satires (I, iv; I, x; II, i) that Horace considered that Lucilius wrote 'good verses' in the first sense but not in the second sense. Horace saw his role in the history of satire in the context of a general process of cultural amelioration. In his account of the civilising of Roman taste under the influence of Greece (*Epistles*, II, i), Horace describes the degeneration of the primitive Fescinnine verses until innocent rural jest turned into cruel and violent abuse requiring the institution of a law 'forbidding the portrayal of anyone in abusive verse' (*malo . . . nollet carmine quemquam describi*). In civilising the satiric spirit, Horace believed he was transforming the satirist from a savage and bloodthirsty predator into a benign and innocent moralist. The writing of 'good' poetry is a sign of cultural advance in both art and ethics. If satire is no more than abuse, then 'I should have to admire the [farcical and grotesque] mimes of Laberius as pretty poems' (I, x, 6).

Horace's commitment to the plain style reinforces his rejection of vituperation *(acre)* in favour of jest *(ridiculum)*. The attributes which Horace wishes to temper belong to the grand style *(genus grande)*[14] and to that branch of the *genus* which relates to oratorical invective. The *Rhetorica ad Herennium* (II, 13, 23) divides the genus into *contentio* and *amplificatio,* the former for the stimulation of violent passion, the latter for the evoking of lofty passion; the effect of the former is acerbity, and of the latter luxuriance. When, in the first programme satire (I, iv), Horace relinquishes all claims to the title of *poeta,* he is evidently dissociating himself from the *genus grande*:

> Nor would you consider anyone a poet who writes, as I do, lines more akin to prose. If one has gifts inborn, if one has a soul divine and tongue of noble utterance, to him grant the honour of that name. Hence some have questioned whether Comedy is_ or is not poetry; for neither in diction nor in subject-matter has it the fire and force of inspiration. (41–7)

Thus Horace recognises that his satiric writings belong to the *genus tenue* ('plain kind') which avoids both *amplificatio* ('the tongue of noble utterance') and *contentio* ('fire and force') in favour of a style approaching ordinary speech *(sermo)*. It is this commitment to the normative value of *sermo* which lends Horace's satires their most distinctive tone.

In all Horace's best satires there is an avoidance of direct invective. Although he often uses the sermon-like form of the diatribe, all the harshness and asceticism which had characterised early cynic diatribes have gone. The moral tone is delicate, reasonable and amused. The tone of the satires is that of a familiar and conversational appeal to common sense rather than of preaching or of moral rebuke. Several narrative strategies are employed which succeed in creating an effect of rational distance or indirection. The use of a dialogue form is Horace's favourite device for avoiding direct moral reprehension. In his use of dialogue as a mode of argument, Horace resembles Plato: the direction of the argument is never in a straight line, but rather follows an alternating rhythm of thesis and antithesis. The method of argument is undogmatic and exploratory, although sometimes the dialectical subtlety leaves some doubt about the author's real position in the argument. For example, in satires three and seven of Book II, in both of which Horace is subjected to a diatribe by a social inferior, we are left uncertain as to Horace's own sentiments about the Stoic philosophy which Damasippus and Davus preach. In both satires, Horace loses his temper in a manner so uncharacteristic that we are forced to question the formal labels 'Davus' and 'Horace' (in the case of II, vii). The Stoic argument put forward by Horace's servant Davus, that 'only the wise man is free', culminates in a description of the wise man which expresses an idealistic conception which Horace himself could not have expressed in his own person without abandoning the role of self-amused and only-too-human satirist:

> Who then is free? The wise man, who is lord over himself, whom neither poverty nor death nor bonds affright, who bravely defies his passions, and scorns ambition, who in himself is a whole, smoothed and rounded, so that nothing from outside can rest on the polished surface . . . (83–7)

Occasionally in the *Odes*, where a more elevated style is appropriate, Horace rises to this kind of Stoic idealism (for example, in *Iustum et tenacem propositi virum*), but never in the satires. In any case, Davus' attack on Horace is full of inconsistencies which highlight his dogmatic tone. At one point he argues that it is only the risk which prevents Horace from becoming an adulterer ('set aside restraint, and Nature will spring forward, to roam at will'). Twenty lines later, in lines which are heightened by a Platonic metaphor, Davus argues that Horace has a master *(dominus)*, his passions, who plagues his soul and drives him on unmercifully against his will. It might be possible by clarifying the psychological implications of the metaphor to reconcile the two statements, but what is evident is the violent idealism of the arguments which Horace directs against himself and which are not characteristic of his normal conversational satire. It is significant that Horace's simulated anger at the end of the satire is no less uncharacteristic and immoderate:

Horace.	Where can I find a stone?
Davus.	What's it for?
Horace.	Or arrows?
Davus.	The man's raving, or else verse-making.

Thus, on the one hand, Davus proposes the rigid and dogmatic tenets of Stoicism, while on the other, Horace rebuts these arguments with an (ironically) unreasoning violence. Horace subjects himself (dramatically) to moral recriminations which imply a characterisation of his own persona which is quite at odds with

his own declarations elsewhere in the satires. Damasippus, the re-
formed bankrupt, accuses Horace of aping the wealthy in his
building projects, and of living beyond his means, while Davus
paints a picture of Horace as a jaded glutton: 'Why, that feasting,
endlessly indulged, turns to gall, and the feet you've duped refuse
to bear up your sickly body.' What, then, is the satirist's purpose
in these dialogues? It seems to be to combine ridicule of the
cruder forms of Stoicism (notice that the Stoic sages themselves,
Stertinus and Crispinus, are presented indirectly through their
rather naive and socially inferior disciples) with some delicate
and witty self-criticism. However, the effect is neither one of total
rejection of Stoicism nor of serious self-doubting.

The ill-tempered rebuttal of the Stoic philosophy is successful
as a satiric ploy only because the reader knows that the ill-temper
is merely assumed. We know that the satirist is a benevolent and
tolerant critic of himself and of others. Horace rarely presents
his own 'philosophy' directly in the satires, but in the third satire
of Book I we are presented with a clear indication of the funda-
mental principles of Horace's plain-style satire. Here Horace re-
jects the ethical absolutism of the Stoic in favour of an Epicurean
appeal to expedience and utility:

> Those whose creed is that all sins are much on a par are at a loss
> when they come to face facts. Feelings and customs rebel, and
> so does Expedience herself, the mother, we may say, of justice
> and right . . . If you will but turn over the annals and records
> of the world, you must needs confess that justice was born of
> the fear of injustice. Between right and wrong Nature can draw
> no such distinction as between things gainful and harmful, what
> is to be sought and what is to be shunned; nor will Reason
> ever prove this, that the sin is one and the same to cut young
> cabbages in a neighbour's garden and to steal by night the sacred
> emblems of the gods. Let us have a rule to assign just penalties
> to offences, lest you flay with the terrible scourge what calls for
> the strap. (96–8, 111–9)

Horace was never a consistent Epicurean, and one cannot extract a
systematic theory from his explicit 'philosophical' statements.
Indeed, his tolerance and refusal to adhere to the teachings of
any school are an essential part of his satiric stance. This relativistic
and tolerant attitude towards moral faults constitutes the under-
lying ethical tone of Horatian satire. The reader's acceptance of this
stance is assumed throughout, so that the Stoic diatribes of Davus
and Damasippus require no direct criticism from Horace; the
criticism is implicit in the Horatian satiric stance. The amusing

indirection of Horace's pretended anger is transparent to the reader because he is assumed to be a confidant of the urbane and playful satirist. All the nuances of Horatian satire stem from this plain-style stance of 'rational' moderation. The slightest departures from the norm warn the reader that irony is around the corner. For example, we are made aware that Horace's deference toward Catius in the fourth satire of Book II is ironic by the slight exaggeration in Catius' opening remarks about the lecture he has just attended on the culinary art: 'I have no time to stop, so keen am I to make a record of some new rules, such as will surpass Pythagoras, and the sage whom Anytus accused, and the learned Plato.' The slightly absurd enthusiasm of Catius for his culinary mentor warns us that his Epicurean interest in food is not to be identified with the mild indulgence of Horace. Horatian satire undermines with irony all pretensions and assertions of self, including those of the satirist himself.

An examination of three of Horace's most perfect satires will enable us to survey rapidly the general features of his satiric manner. The account in the fifth satire of Book I of Horace's journey to Brundisium on Maecenas' diplomatic mission from Octavian to Mark Antony in 38 BC is modelled on a poem by Lucilius. Horace dwells not upon affairs of state, which would have been incompatible with his conception of the stylistic level of satire, but upon the relatively trivial incidents of the journey itself. The satire is very close to the informal travelogue with its chatty anecdotes and its diary-like form.

The satire is stylistically exuberant and extremely varied. However, the underlying plain-style perspective determines the reader's understanding of the variations. There is an amusing mixture of low and high style which lends the satire its peculiar vivacity. Horace begins his second paragraph with the playful epic formula: 'Already night was beginning to draw her curtain over the earth and to sprinkle the sky with stars.' This is immediately followed with a lively description in naturalistic style of the life of the canal-side at Appii Forum in the vein of Roman comedy:

Then slaves loudly rail at boatmen, boatmen at slaves: 'Bring to here!' 'You're packing in hundreds!' 'Stay, that's enough!' (11–13)

At a later stage in the journey, Horace describes in formal mock-heroic style, after the manner of Plautus, the battle of wit between two buffoons which took place in the comfortable villa of Cocceius: 'Now, O Muse, recount in brief the contest of Sarmentus the jester and Messius Cicirrus, and the lineage of the two who engaged in the fray.' The account closes with an elegantly plain description of the social tone of the occasion: 'We prolonged that dinner exceedingly agreeably' *(prorsus iucunde cenam producimus illam)*. In this way Horace indicates to the reader that the mock-heroic passage does not aim to castigate the combatants or to present them in a demeaning light, but rather to present an amusing spectacle in the context of a witty and sophisticated (but unpretentious) dinner party. When Horace ridicules the pretentiousness of the local chief official at Fundi, the tone of benign amusement is clearly registered: 'Fundi, with its "praetor" Aufidius Luscus, we quit with delight, laughing at the crazy clerk's gewgaws, his bordered robe, broad stripe, and pan of charcoal' (34–6). A similar subject (a praetor's absurd pomp) is treated in Juvenal's tenth satire, not with benign amusement but with sardonic irony and bitter scorn.

The satire's tone acquires its most distinctive note from the continued introduction of plain-style self-revelation, especially in the form of a playful self-depreciation. In the very first paragraph, Horace describes in bantering mock-heroic fashion the effects of the bad water on his digestion: 'I declare war against my stomach, and wait impatiently while my companions dine.' Later, in Campania, both Horace and Virgil take an afternoon nap to nurse their sore eyes and dyspepsia. Finally Horace suffers the indignity of staying awake half the night for a girl who doesn't turn up, only to end the vigil with a messy wet dream! However, the self-depreciation is that of a writer who is not only sure of the appropriateness of his reader's reaction but also is confident of his social role in the society of his betters; the self-depreciation is like the modesty of a virtuous man.

Horace provides us with the fullest account of his entry into high society in the sixth satire of Book I where he describes his introduction to Maecenas:

> Fortunate I could not call myself as having won your friendship by some chance; for 'twas no case of luck throwing you in my way; that best of men, Virgil, some time ago, and after him Varius, told you what manner of man I was. On coming into your presence I said a few faltering words, for speechless shame stopped me from saying more. My tale was not that I was a famous father's son, not that I rode about my estate on a Saturnian steed: I told you what I was. As is your way, you answered little and I withdrew; then, nine months later, you sent for me again and bade me join your friends. (52–62)

A number of features associated with the classical plain style[15] appear in this account: a concern for truthfulness (inner reality and true nobility rather than outward appearances), a stance of modesty and simplicity, and an implied high valuation of reserve, of economy of utterance and of conciseness. The perfect control of the familiar plain style found in passages like this make it easy to understand why Horace was to provide the literary model of the relationship between poet and patron in the late seventeenth and early eighteenth centuries. The poet's social role requires the maintenance of a delicate balance between warm friendship and deference, and between enthusiastic pride and modest reserve. A social tact and control of language is evident in Horace's careful avoidance of a potentially offensive contrast between his father's lowly origins and the high birth of the nobility. The contrast does not depend upon a valuation of low birth above high birth, but of true nobility above the mere appearance of nobility (as suggested by the 'Saturnian steed'). In this way, the reserved and unostentatiously aristocratic Maecenas is indirectly admired for his moral discrimination. Horace's enthusiasm for friendship is that of a man of good sense *(sanus)* and not of a wild idealist or of a cynical calculator. In the ninth satire of Book I he launches a brilliant satiric attack on the bore, who turns out to be something of a cynical calculator.

The satire is a first-person account of a boring socialite, who introduces himself to Horace on the Sacred Way and refuses to be shaken off. The theme of the client-patron relationship is subtly introduced when the bore's trivial chat gradually leads up to a request for an introduction to Maecenas. The bore represents values which Horace wishes to attack, especially those associated with self-seeking and place-seeking. The bore tries to ingratiate himself with Horace by trying to adopt the correct social tone and values: 'How stands Maecenas with you, a man of few friends and right good sense? No one ever made wiser use of his luck [*fortuna*].' The aristocratic elitism of 'few friends' and 'good sense' hits the right Augustan note, but the insinuation that Horace owed his position in Maecenas' circle to luck and not to ability and virtue reveals the bore's social and moral inferiority. As we saw in the sixth satire, Horace owed his friendship not to luck *(nulla etenim mihi te fors obtulit)*, but to his own qualities as a man. All this is done without a word from Horace: the bore's shortcomings are satirized by the general context and assumed values which the reader shares with Horace (Horace's ideal reader, that is). The bore goes on to suggest that he might work for Horace's interests in Maecenas' entourage, but Horace immediately rejects the implied picture of cunning and intrigue:

We don't live there on such terms as *you* think. No house is cleaner or more free from such intrigue than that. It never hurts me that one is richer or more learned than I. Each has his own place.

Once again, the values of true friends and the company of like minds are asserted together with a recognition of due hierarchy and social order. Here, as elsewhere, Horace expresses distaste for the pusher, the social climber and the vulgar upstart. Horace offers the perfect recipe for social order and complaisance, which was no doubt well received by Augustus' trusted minister of state.

The 'bore' resembles the 'character' of the relatively harmless windbag found in Theophrastus and elsewhere in Horace (in *Satires,* II, v, for example), who is insensitive to the *norms* of rational behaviour accepted by the culturally dominant elite. He exposes his crass and blundering vulgarity as soon as he opens his mouth. The use of this type of 'character' is common in English Augustan satire and comedy. The rustic oafs of comedy and the bourgeois scribblers of satire are pilloried for their lack of social awareness and orthodoxy. They are deviants from what are felt to be civilised and civilising norms.

As in the fifth satire, the controlling plain-style rationality of the narrative voice enables the reader to interpret the stylistic variations correctly. The occasional heightened metaphor or image is introduced to convey the poet's suppressed irritation and comic despair. The tone, unlike Juvenal's, is mock-serious rather than caustic: 'To think so black a sun as this has shone for me.' Horace asks the bore to finish him off and fulfil the 'sad fate' prophesied by the Sabine witch. The narrative method is a subtle combination of first-person narrative and dramatic dialogue. The silent prayer 'finish me off' is both a comic inner exclamation and part of the dialogue.

The satire usually known as 'The Town Mouse and the Country Mouse' (II, vi) is probably the best constructed of the satires and the most subtle in its style and dialectic. The poem is divided into a celebration of the country life (lines 1–76) and the fable proper (lines 77–117). The first part is itself structured in the manner of a triptych composed of three settings: morning in the country, day in the city and evening in the country. In the second part the contrast between the peaceful country and the restless city is allegorised in the fable of the town mouse and the country mouse.

The style and tone of the opening twenty-five lines are remarkably elusive. In a modest prayer addressed to Mercury,

Horace expresses his ideal of simple self-sufficiency. He contrasts his own modest wishes with the obsessive ambitions of others. The passage is a fusion of conversational and elevated idioms (religious and epic), molded into a unified tone. Sometimes the collocations of different styles are unexpected. After the slightly self-amused opening prayer for a modest country retreat, Horace celebrates his 'castle in the hills' in 'the Satires of my prosaic Muse' *(Musa pedestri)*. Having reminded us of the lowly status of the satirist in the poetic hierarchy, he goes on: 'Here no wretched desire for honour destroys my peace of mind, nor leaden sirocco, nor unwholesome autumn, that brings employment to hateful Libitina.' This dignified and almost ornate poetry is immediately followed by a ritual address to the Janus: 'O father of the dawn, or Janus, if you prefer, from whom men take the beginnings of the work and toil of life – be thou the prelude of my song' *(tu carminis esto principium)*. The slightly incongruous use of *carmen,* a term more appropriate to the productions of the *poeta,* is more noticeable after the reference to the satirist's prosaic muse. There is certainly nothing irreligious in the tone here: the assimilation of both colloquial and sublime idioms is achieved without disturbing the central tone of rational poise and polite elegance. Above all things, Horatian satire is an achievement of perfectly controlled *tone*. The great German scholar Edward Fraenkel has shown us the full complexity of Horace's use of various ritual formulae,[16] but his scholarship tends to draw attention away from the normative plain-style speaking voice. Reuben Brower's description is worth quoting here, since it captures this normative quality precisely:

> The tone and movement are remarkable and characteristic: we come on the poet talking to himself, half-praying, in language that varies little from familiar Latin prose in order and vocabulary. Rhetorical emphasis and diction are kept at the most moderate level of intensity, although *magnus* and *hortus* and *fons* and *auctius* are thrown into sufficient relief to suggest an inner warmth of feeling . . . The impression of the arrest and flow of casual speech and thought are reminiscent of Robert Frost in his most 'speaking' poems . . .[17]

The brief but vivid description of the bustling city once again affords an opportunity for Horace to establish his easy familiarity with Maecenas:

> The seventh year – or rather nearly the eighth – will soon have passed since Maecenas began to count me among his friends,

but only as far as treating me as one he would like to take in his carriage when on a journey, and entrust with trifles like this: 'What's the time?' 'Is the Thracian Chicken a match for Syrus?' 'The morning frosts are biting now if people are not very careful', and other remarks which are safely dropped into a leaky ear. For all these years, every day and hour, yours truly has been more and more the object of envy. He has just watched the games, or played ball in the Campus with Maecenas, and everyone cries 'Fortune's favourite!' Does a chilly rumour run from the Rostra through the streets? Whoever comes my way asks my opinion: 'My good fellow, you must know – you are in so much closer contact with the gods: you haven't heard any news about the Dacians have you?' 'None, whatever.' 'How you will always mock us!' But heaven confound me if I have heard a word! . . . When I swear I know nothing, they marvel at me as, forsooth, the man of all men remarkably and profoundly reticent. (40–57)

The familiar yet modest tone established in the opening lines is undercut delicately by the mock self-devaluation (Maecenas only entrusts him with trivial chat, which can be communicated without fear of political leaks). Horace's enjoyment of the reputation of tight-lipped confidant is counterbalanced by his implied low valuation of the world of political intrigue. Between the trivial chat and the high affairs of state we sense an area of realised human intimacy, hinted at when a by-stander suggests that Horace has got Maecenas too much on his mind, which elicits the rejoinder: 'That gives pleasure and is like honey, I'll not deny.'

The fable is one of Horace's best pieces of dialectic. He avoids presenting us with a simple contrast between the happy man *(beatus)* of the country and the careworn *(sollicitus)* city-dweller. The identification of Horace and the country mouse has little more justification than the identification of Swift and the Houyhnhnms. His description of the country mouse is finely balanced:

asper et attentus quaesitis, ut tamen artum solveret hospitiis animum. (82–3)

(He lived roughly, frugal of his store, yet could open his thrifty soul in acts of hospitality.)

Asper has connotations of rudeness which reinforce those of *rusticus*[18] as opposed to *urbanus,* and at the same time, as a description of moral qualities, is often associated with the austerity of

Stoicism. Similarly, *artum* can be read as 'thrifty' or as 'severe' (denoting self-restraint). Such a mouse can hardly be identified with the satirist who celebrates the leisure of the countryside in such Epicurean tones in the first part of the poem. The obliqueness and ambivalence of Horace's presentation of the country mouse is reflected interestingly in the variety of interpretations of the two lines quoted above; the following versions[19] were all published in the year 1767 in England:

> A good plain Mouse our Host, who lov'd to spare
> Those Heaps of Forage he had glean'd with Care;
> Yet on occasion would his soul unbend,
> And Feast with Hospitality his Friend . . .
> > (Francis Fawkes)

> This mouse was blunt and giv'n to thrift,
> But now and then cou'd make a shift
> (However rigid or recluse)
> With open heart to give a loose . . .
> > (Christopher Smart)

> Pleas'd with his Lot, and happy with his Spouse,
> With simple Diet, at his Frugal Board,
> Once entertain'd the Chaplain of a Lord.
> > (Edward Burnaby Greene)

In Fawkes, the mouse is the 'happy man' whose plain fare is an attribute of his Epicurean moderation; in Smart he is a Stoic recluse; in Greene's imitation he becomes a complacently self-sufficient cleric.

The fastidious and rather supercilious town mouse preaches a simple and conventional Epicureanism to which his host is promptly converted. The journey to the town, the sumptuous dinner of scraps, and the final catastrophe when their feast is rudely interrupted by Molossian hounds, are narrated with great rapidity and with the interpolation of playful mock-heroic touches similar to those in the fifth and ninth satires of Book I. Such is the wit of Horace's presentation that we are left in no doubt that the country mouse's final words are not to be taken too seriously as the poem's moral: 'No use have I for such a life, and so farewell: my wood and hole, secure from dangers, will comfort me with modest vetch.'

To conclude, Horace is a plain-style satirist, a description which denotes his adherence to classical norms of 'rational' discourse (that is, appealing to 'clarity', 'common sense', 'moderation', and 'sincerity'). This does not mean that his style is undeviatingly plain in its idiom, but that stylistic variations (vulgar, colloquial, mock-heroic, mock-Stoic) are always *controlled* by a normative plain-style rationality which gives the reader the key to an interpretation of the variations. Satire of this type is usually, as in the case of Horace, conformist and politically quiescent. The satirist sees himself as an improver of the tradition in which he is working; Lucilius was the vigorous founder of Roman satire, but he lacked 'correctness' and civilised culture. Horace aims to *combine* rhetorical invective *(contentio)* with disarming and benevolent laughter, thus taming the wild beast of primitive satire. The cultivation of a familiar and 'negligent' style is related to the satirist's self-conscious and highly developed social sense. A habit of witty self-depreciation and modest self-revelation is combined with a fine sense of social tact. The social role of model client requires both an aristocratic elitism and a deferential self-restraint. Finally, Horace is the master of dialectical reasoning, preferring the interplay of dialogue and the exploration of nuances to the crudeness of blunt assertion and the absolute judgements of the Stoics.

JUVENAL

Near the end of the seventeenth century, before the vogue of Horace was established, Dryden wrote a comparison of Juvenal and Horace in terms which were not to be repeated again in the Augustan period:

> . . . granting Horace to be the more general philosopher, we cannot deny that Juvenal was the greater poet, I mean in satire. His thoughts are sharper; his indignation against vice is more vehement; his spirit has more of the commonwealth genius; he treats tyranny, and all the vices attending it, as they deserve, with the utmost rigour: and consequently, a noble soul is better pleased with a zealous vindicator of Roman liberty than with a temporising poet, a well-mannered Court slave, and a man who is often afraid of laughing in the right place; who is ever decent, because he is naturally servile.[20]

The account is thoroughly misleading,[21] since Augustus never set up a court in the manner of the later emperors, and Juvenal's attacks on Domitian's reign were not written until at least fourteen years after Domitian's assassination. Horace was never a 'court slave' and Juvenal never showed much interest in the political reform or abolition of the principate. Nevertheless the account does point to a real difference in social stance between the two satirists. While Horace's benign and undogmatic satire is founded upon a sense of achieved social order and personal satisfaction, Juvenal's indignant and authoritarian satire is based upon a sense of social disorder and personal dissatisfaction. He himself probably experienced disappointment of his hopes of advancement in both the military and the civil spheres. At a time of great social mobility, when the barriers of Roman citizenship were broken down in the empire, Juvenal saw the rise to high office of foreigners and social upstarts, while men of good birth (like himself) were overlooked and subjected to indignities at the hands of social inferiors. Thus Juvenal's social attitudes are those of the reactionary idealist and the small-minded chauvinist. His angry denunciations of the miserly patron, the ill-bred foreigner, the degenerate aristocrat and the unscrupulous social climber are all coloured by a tone of resentment and a sense of personal injustice. But the biographical approach does not take us far towards an understanding of the nature of Juvenal's qualities as a satirist.

Juvenal's reputation as the indignant satirist, the *vir iratus,* is based particularly upon the programmatic assertions of the first satire where he declares that he cannot sleep for thinking about the vices of contemporary society: 'Though nature say me nay, indignation will prompt my verse.' Here we detect a characteristic claim of the Juvenalian satirist, who argues that he writes straight from his feelings and not from poetic ambitions. The times are so vicious ('all crime is at its acme') that one cannot help speaking out and exposing flagrant wrongdoing. In the eighteenth century, Charles Churchill adopts this stance of indignant and careless spontaneity:

> Nothing of Books, and little known of men,
> When the mad fit comes on, I seize the pen,
> Rough as they run, the rapid thoughts set down,
> Rough as they run, discharge them on the Town.
> Hence rude, unfinish'd brats, before their time,
> Are born into this idle world of rime . . .
> (*Gotham,* II, 171–6)

We only find an inconsistency in the fact that Churchill was a well-read and polished poet if we confuse the 'man' with the 'satirist'.

Juvenal regrets that he cannot emulate the freedom of expression of the old satirists, but is forced through fear of persecution to attack the vices of the previous generation. This qualification of the satirist's powers might seem inconsistent with the apparent immediacy of the opening lines of the satire (and with much that follows):

What? Am I to be a listener only all my days? Am I never to get my word in – I that have been so often bored by the Theseid of the ranting Cordus? Shall this one have spouted to me his comedies, and that one his love ditties, and I be unavenged?

Juvenal confesses that, when he sees a eunuch marry, a woman act like a man, an ex-barber become a millionaire and a rich Egyptian parvenu show off his wealth, he finds it 'hard *not* to write satire'. But we need not inquire whether Juvenal's victims are contemporaries or 'buried along the high roads', whether they are real or fictional. The impression of *immediacy* is achieved and is an essential feature of Juvenal's satiric 'voice'. Only by separating 'Juvenal' from his satiric 'voice' are we able to do justice to his artistry and to define his contribution to the literary world of satire.

The briefest acquaintance with the sixteen satires makes it clear that the stance of indignation is radically modified, at least after the ninth satire. In Satire I, Juvenal repeatedly describes his tormenting rage (his heart 'burns dry with rage'), but in the thirteenth satire we find Juvenal delivering a sermon in which he advises Calvinus against immoderate anger. The latter has been defrauded of a large sum of money and cannot contain his anger. The satirist argues against the very emotions which the satirist of Satire I indulged in so violently:

A man's wrath should not be hotter than is fit, nor greater than the loss sustained. You scarce are able to bear the very smallest particle of trivial misfortune; your bowels foam hot within you because your friend will not give up to you the sacred trust committed to him. (12–16)

The Stoicism enjoined here comes strangely from the mouth of the *vir iratus*. It is tempting to accept W. S. Anderson's argument[22] that in the early satires Juvenal indulges in the rhetoric of indignation in a manner which is inconsistent with his appeal to rationality, but that in the later satires Juvenal rectifies this inconsistency by adopting the rational stance of the Senecan philosopher and by creating 'a new satirist in close conformity with the Senecan ideal', a satirist who rebukes man's irrationality without himself resorting to irrational anger *(ira)*. On this view, Juvenal is converted to the 'saner attitude of the ironic satirist': the *vir iratus* becomes the Democritean satirist whose laughter is detached, if bitter. Two important qualifications are needed if Anderson's argument is to be made acceptable. First, we must beware of the biographical critic's temptation to identify the 'real' Juvenal with the more 'rational' later satirist and to regard the earlier indignant satirist as a mere 'mask' or pose. A writer (whether dramatic or poetic) is always making or remaking his 'voice' or 'voices', which bear a relationship to his inner life that must remain to a large extent unknown. Secondly, the 'rationality' of the later satirist is by no means consistently evident.

The modified satirist in Satire XIII often seems uneasy in the role of detached Stoic philosopher. He recommends moderate anger on the grounds that vice has become so much the norm that toleration is the only reaction possible. His rejection of the emotion of vengeance, which some have regarded as a noble pre-Christian utterance, is spoiled by a characteristic satiric side-kick: 'For vengeance is always the delight of a little, weak, and petty mind; of which you may straightway draw proof from this – that no one so rejoices in vengeance as a woman' (189–92). But nothing does more damage to the Stoic role of the 'rational' satirist than the closing lines of the satire when Juvenal consoles Calvinus with the thought that wrongdoers go from bad to worse and finish up enduring the pangs of hell-torture: 'You will exult over the stern punishment of a hated name, and at length admit with joy that none of the Gods is deaf . . .' Gilbert Highet's comment is the only one open to the biographical critic:

> This from the man who has just delivered a warning against the petty pleasures of revenge! Yet it is of a piece with Juvenal's character. He was vindictive and hateful himself, as we see from the venom with which he pursues his dead enemies . . . Satirists are not happy, noble, well-balanced men. They are twisted because their world is out of joint.[23]

This explanation is more satisfactory than Anderson's in so far as it recognises the inconsistency of stance. One might conclude that, however 'Stoical' and detached the philosophy which Juvenal adopts in the later satires, his satiric stance remains that of the *vir iratus*. A sense of inconsistency is inevitable.

Some of the inconsistencies in Juvenal's satiric voice are reflected in the traditional ambivalence of his reputation. Even in the medieval and early Renaissance periods, two quite different pictures of Juvenal were painted. The pro-Horatian critics emphasised his ill-mannered roughness, while the pro-Juvenalian critics emphasised his moral sublimity which was thought to justify his acerbity. There is no doubt that the latter view was the prevailing one and has remained so except during the romantic period.

In the late Roman empire and after there was a general tendency to Christianise Juvenal's pagan philosophy. Lactantius (*fl.*

AD 315) was the earliest to stamp the conclusion of Satire X with a mark of Christian approval.[24] In the Renaissance, Petrarch wrote, in a manner which anticipates the later neoclassical attitude, of Juvenal's essentially moral insight: 'It is experience which speaks to us, . . . it is Truth which speaks to us . . . but, if you ask the name of the mortal author, these words are spoken by Juvenal, a man of great experience who has a profound knowledge of human nature.'[25] Aeneas Silvius is able to say, in 1450, that Juvenal 'showed himself a man of such deeply religious feeling, that he appears to be inferior to none of the teachers of our faith'.[26]

This tradition of Juvenal's moral sublimity was sustained in England, particularly in the Augustan period. The translators of Juvenal varied a good deal in their versions of the satires, but were unanimous in their approval of Juvenal's ethical qualities: 'Such as have scaped the Preacher, may fall upon the Satyrist, and then, no doubt but they will reforme, if not for Christian duty, yet for the shame to be thus divinely reproved by a Heathen.'[27] According to Henry Higden, the tenth satire is 'by All approved for the Gravest and most *Phylosophical,* both for Argument and Matter, of all our Authors'.[28] Thomas Shadwell, Dryden's arch-enemy, calls the satire 'one of the *wisest,* and *noblest,* in the Book; wherein any man may perceive the difference between the *Wisdom* and *Dignity* of *true Roman Satyr,* and the *Levity* and *baseness* of false English Libells'.[29] John Harvey follows Dryden in alluding to the Bishop of Salisbury's (Burnet's) recommendation that the tenth satire should be used as a common-place book for sermons.[30] While most editors and critics recognised that there were many unsavoury passages (and entire satires) in Juvenal's works, they were confident that, for the most part, he was a thoroughly noble and enlightened moralist.

For the apologist of pagan satire a belief in the satirist's moral seriousness is necessary, not only to justify the satirist's pagan ethics but also to justify his self-righteous and indignant tone. We can only accept the *vir iratus* if he is also a *vir ethicus.* But, in the last twenty years, critics have begun to see a different Juvenal from the bitter but essentially noble satirist of tradition. The greatest controversy has centred upon the tenth satire, the closing lines of which Highet called 'this noble treatment of a tragic theme'.

The tenth satire describes the disappointment of every aspiration and ambition conceived in the heart of men. Desire for wealth or power always ends in disaster: the rich man is poisoned; the great general is finally defeated ignominiously. Juvenal declares: 'What grandeur, what high fortune, are worth the having if the joy is overbalanced by the calamities they bring with them?' The traditional interpretation of the satire suggests that the satirist regards the disastrous outcome of men's ambitions as a tragic or at least pathetic story. But it is hard to sustain such a view when one considers passages like the following in which the statues of the politicians (including that of Sejanus) are symbolically destroyed:

> Down come their statues, obedient to the rope; the axe hews in pieces their chariot wheels and the legs of the unoffending nags. And now the flames are hissing, and amid the roar of furnace and of bellows the head of the mighty Sejanus, the darling of the mob, is burning and crackling, and from that face, which was but lately second in the entire world, are being fashioned pipkins, basins, frying-pans and chamber-pots. (58–64)

A potentially tragic effect is totally destroyed in the demeaning and derisive particularity of the last lines. If one were in any doubt about the satirist's tone, it is only necessary to examine an earlier passage where Juvenal commends the wisdom of two Greek philosophers, Democritus, the laughing philosopher, and Heraclitus, the weeping philosopher. Juvenal plainly rejects a tragic view in favour of a bitterly comic view when he says, 'To condemn by a cutting laugh comes readily to us all; the wonder is how the other sage's eyes were supplied with all that water' (32–3).

The closing paragraph of the poem seems to offer some grounds for regarding the satire as at least partly animated by moral sympathy for man's plight. We are enjoined to entrust our destinies to the gods who know what is best for us, and to confine our prayers to a simple petition for health of mind and body *(mens sana in corpore sano)*, for courage in the face of death, and for calm passions and simple desires. But a closer look at the following passage leaves us in some doubt about the tone:

> Impelled by strong and blind desire in our hearts, we ask for wife and offspring; but the gods know of what sort the sons, of what sort the wife, will be. Still, that you may have something to pray for, and be able to offer to the little shrines entrails and prophetic little sausages from a white piglet, you should pray for a sound mind in a sound body. (350–6)

It is significant that Juvenal condemns the mere desire for a wife and children, not the desire for a fatally beautiful wife, which might justify a warning voice and a serious moral tone. Presumably, the gods know that the wife will turn out like the wives of Satire VI ('The bed that holds a wife is never free from wrangling and mutual bickerings'), and the sons like the degenerate sons of Satire XIV. Juvenal here displays his fondness for a *cynical wit* rather than his reputed moral seriousness. Several critics have had difficulty in giving a credible account[31] of the demeaning and irreverent description of the suppliant's sacrifice. A convincing interpretation of the passage would not attribute to it a tone of moral seriousness. The repeated diminutives *(sacellis, candiduli, tomacula)* are characteristic of Juvenal's satiric manner: even the most pious human activity is subjected to derision. There is only scornful laughter, no sympathetic tears.

The greater part of Satire XIV is concerned with the education of the young and with the instruction of fathers in their responsibilities as guides and examples. However, Juvenal appears to be unable to resist the temptation of deriding men's follies at large, for there is an abrupt transition at line 256 to a general survey of mankind's restless folly:

> I am showing you the choicest of diversions, one with which no theatre, no show of a grand Praetor can compare, if you will observe at what a risk to life men increase their fortunes, become possessors of full brass-bound treasure-chests, or of the cash which must be deposited with watchful Castor, ever since Mars the Avenger lost his helmet and failed to protect his own effects. (256–62)

Mankind's absurd greed stirs no moral indignation in the satirist, but merely provides an enjoyable spectacle and food for bitter scoffs. The robbing of a temple (like the sacrifice in Satire X) is presented with comic particularity ('lost his helmet') and with amoral wit.

Juvenal is often portrayed (and the picture is not entirely false) as an indignant conservative idealist, who presents us with a horrifying picture of contemporary moral turpitude against a backcloth on which is depicted the ideal world of old republican Italy, when men's desires were kept in bounds, social classes knew their places and family life was seemly and chaste. Thus we are presented with thesis and antithesis: the ideal and its corruption. However, it is rare to find Juvenal presenting the ideal past without a hint of comic deflation. It is true that the description of the simple fare of rural republican Italy (in Satire XI) and of the modest farms in which the veteran republican army were settled (in Satire XIV) are without irony or deflation, but, in Satire VI, the account of female degeneracy is prefaced by a brief sketch of the

innocent family life of olden days, a sketch which does not pro-
ceed far before the romantic bubble is burst with a vulgar piece of
comedy, when the faithful wife is depicted as 'one whose breasts
gave suck to lusty babes, often more unkempt herself than her
acorn-belching husband'. With a single word *(ructante)* the image
of noble simplicity is replaced by one of rustic vulgarity.

Particularly in the early satires, one looks in vain for a moral
perspective. More often, the direction of a particular piece of
invective is determined not by moral considerations but by the
requirements of wit and rhetoric. In the second satire the attack on
hypocritical moralists soon develops a rhetorical momentum, and
heaps up hypothetical examples for purely witty purposes:

> Let the straight-legged man laugh at the club-footed, the white
> man at the blackamoor: but who could endure the Gracchi
> railing at sedition? Who will not confound heaven and earth,
> and sea with sky, if Verres denounce thieves, or Milo cut-
> throats? If Clodius condemn adulterers, or Catiline upbraid
> Cethegus . . . (23–7)

The passage is evidently unsatisfactory if one is looking for the
application of normative moral ideals. Why, one asks, should it
be easier to accept the straight-legged man's laughter at the
cripple than the hypocrisy of the notorious villain? Evidently
Juvenal is not primarily interested in the degree of moral turpitude
involved in each particular case, but in the opportunities afforded
for witty incongruity. The brilliant compression and ingenious
word order of the Latin conveys this better than any translation:

> loripedem rectus derideat, Aethiopem albus;
> quis tulerit Gracchos de seditione querentes?
> quis caelum terris·non misceat et mare caelo,
> si fur displiceat Verri, homicida Miloni,
> Clodius accuset moechos, Catilina Cethegum . . .

The effect of wit is derived from the contrast between the anti-
theses of the first line *(loripedem rectus . . . Aethiopem albus)* and
the synonyms of the remaining lines. 'Straight-legged' and 'club-
footed' are genuinely antithetical, a fact which justifies the straight-
legged man's laughter, while 'Verres', 'Milo' and 'Clodius' are all
synonymous with 'thief', 'murderer' and 'adulterer', a fact which
points up the absurdity of their moral posturing.

One is inclined to accept H. A. Mason's assessment[32] of Juvenal's
ethical temperament. In his view, the tenth satire is inferior to
Dr Johnson's imitation, which possesses 'an incomparably finer

moral interest'. The absence of moral interest in Juvenal is 'horrifying', and yet 'his success as a master of wit' depends on the absence of reference to inner moral life. Mason shows that Juvenal's satiric tone is one of deflationary wit, involving a 'harsh belittling sarcasm or contemptuous *animus* which Juvenal directs against his figures', a wit which is essentially devoid of central moral concerns and dependent for its appreciation upon a taste for the conventions of the obscene (in the manner of Martial) and of the horrific. One might not wish to endorse Mason's application of Leavisian moral criteria to Juvenal's satire and the accompanying denial of 'classic' status to the satirist, but his analysis of Juvenal's moral *stance* is convincing.

Juvenal's ethical tone is narrowed still further by his bitter class-feeling, his violent chauvinism and his acute xenophobia. One does not need to look for biographical or cultural reasons for these attitudes, although they might easily be found. Even though hostility to Greek immigrants and other foreigners was prevalent in contemporary Rome,[33] such attitudes are general and even characteristic of Juvenalian satire in all cultural climates. Classical conservative idealism turns against both the corruption of the nobility and the general worthlessness of the working classes. In Satire IV the emperor Domitian, after receiving a gift of a huge turbot, summons his inner cabinet and in absurd solemnity debates how the fish should be treated. Juvenal concludes the satire by declaring that these follies are harmless compared to Domitian's wicked destruction of the finest nobility *(claras . . . illustresque animas)* of Rome. This potentially tragic remark is transformed into bitter class animus when he adds: 'He could steep himself in the blood of the Lamiae [ancient nobility]; but when once he became a terror to the lowest classes *[cerdonibus]* he met his doom.' The remark is quite gratuitous, and calculated to give the satire a bitterly witty conclusion. The tirade against the Greek inhabitants of Rome in Satire III is a perfect vehicle for Juvenal's *indignatio*: 'I cannot abide, Quirites, a Rome of Greeks; and yet what proportion of our dregs comes from Greece?' But abuse soon gives place to scornful wit, for example in a passage reminiscent of Dryden:

> Say, what do you think that fellow there to be? He has brought with him any character you please; grammarian, orator, geometrician; painter, trainer, or rope-dancer; augur, doctor or astrologer – the fasting Greekling knows every art; bid him to Hell and he will go. (75–8)

Compare Dryden's portrait of Zimri:

In the first rank of these did Zimri stand:
A man so various, that he seem'd to be
Not one, but all Mankind's epitome.
Stiff in opinions, always in the wrong;
Was everything by starts, and nothing long:
But, in the course of one revolving moon,
Was chymist, fiddler, states-man, and buffoon.
(*Absalom and Achitophel,* I, 544–50)

Dryden believed that his portrait of Zimri represented a more
Horatian kind of satire, in which abuse is avoided in favour of
a delicate jesting (a 'fine raillery'). Nevertheless, in respect of
verbal wit, the passage quoted above is closer to Juvenal, even if
Juvenal is more abusive.

In the past a good deal has been made of the fact that Juvenal
wrote in an age of 'rhetoric'. His habit of 'declamation', of
addressing the reader as if he were haranguing a jury or a political
meeting, has led to a number of damaging judgements. Many, like
René Rapin, have found the rhetoric unconvincing: 'He scarce
persuades at all; because he is always in a *choler,* and never speaks
in cold blood.'[34] Juvenal doesn't have the 'natural' touch of
Horace. On the other hand, the romantic critics (notably D.
Nisard) found the rhetoric frigid and symptomatic of Juvenal's
artificiality and insincerity. It is easy to see how the whole
issue could be made to turn upon this question of sincerity. To
come to Juvenal's defence is to accede to the romantic terms of
reference. It is necessary to remove the question of rhetoric from
the problematics of biography and psychology, and to ask instead
what literary gains, if any, result from Juvenal's use of the re-
sources of declamation. It is not enough to argue that he could
not escape the current language of declamation, and that his
literary stature depends upon the extent to which he has succeeded
in transcending the limitations of these resources. The declamatory
commonplaces are not a vicious taint which is miraculously
transfigured, but the very currency of expression. Donne did not
transcend scholastic logic (as the spirit transcends the flesh), but
appropriated it as an expository medium and renewed its poten-
tialities. Consider a passage describing the diseases of old age, which
Mason, who considers that 'Juvenal's art is at its best in hyperbole',
regards as gratuitously obscene:

. . . circumsilit agmine facto
morborum omne genus, quorum si nomina quaeras,
promptius expediam quot amaverit Oppia moechos,
quot Themison aegros autumno occiderit uno,
quot Basilus socios, quot circumscripserit Hirrus

> pupillos; quot longa viros exorbeat uno
> Maura die, quot discipulos inclinet Hamillus;
> percurram citius quot villas possideat nunc
> quo tondente gravis iuveni mihi barba sonabat.
>
> (X, 218–26)

(. . . diseases of every kind dance around him in a troop; if you
ask of me their names, I could more readily tell you the number of
Oppia's lovers, how many patients Themison killed in one autumn,
how many partners were defrauded by Basilus, or wards by Hirrus,
how many pupils were perverted by Hamillus, and how many men
big Maura drains in one day; I could sooner run over the number of
villas now belonging to the barber under whose razor my stiff
youthful beard used to grate.)

The literary quality of the passage cannot be determined effectively
in accordance with a standard of moral perception, no matter how
refined the critic's own sensibility. Nor should it be seen as a
mere rhetorical exercise. It might be more accurate to say that
it is a finely rendered *parody* of the declamatory devices of hyper-
bole and anaphora (repetition). Anaphora marks the subtle varia-
tion in length of clause and metrical unit:

```
– – – – – – quot – – – – – – –'
quot – – – – – – – – – – – – – –
quot – – – – 'quot – – – – – – –
– – 'quot – – – – – – – – – – –
– – 'quot – – – – – – – – – – –'
– – – – – – quot – – – – – –
– – – – – – – – – – – – – – –'
```

The initial *quot* is preceded by *promptius expediam*; the terminal
anaphora is preceded by an echo and inversion *(percurram citius)*.
Wit derives from a combination of rhetorical articulation and the
use of a literary formula ('there is no way of numbering . . .').[35]
The irony lies in the vigorousness of the examples, which contrast,
sometimes pointedly, with the sapped impotence of the old man
who is attacked by the army of diseases. The exuberance of the
passage is marked: the vitality of the rhetorical pattern, the
hyperbolic accumulation, the very excess of the corruption de-
picted, all create an impression of rampant vigour which con-
trasts with the surrounding context ('now his blood runs cold in
his body . . . that man is crippled in his shoulder . . . this one in
his loins . . . this one in his hip'). The contrast is heightened by
the allusion to Juvenal's youth. The passage is a sort of objective
correlative of the world that is lost to the old.

Juvenal makes substantial and continuous use of the devices of rhetoric, especially 'theses' (for example, 'whether one ought to marry', 'whether noble birth has any intrinisc value'), 'examples', 'comparisons' (especially the past and the present), aphorisms, colourful syntax (dialogue, apostrophe, exclamation, question, antithesis and hyperbole), and figures of speech (particularly anaphora and apanalepsis).[36]

Juvenal's aphorisms are an important source of his reputation as serious moralist. They are pithy and quotable: 'No one becomes profoundly wicked all at once' *(nemo repente fuit turpissimus)*; 'Nowhere is it easier to ditch a client [than in Rome]' *(nusquam minor est iactura clientis)*; 'a man's credit extends as far as the money he keeps in his cash-box' *(quantum quisque sua nummorum servat in arca,/tantum habet et fidei);* 'eloquence is rarely found beneath a shabby coat' *(rara in tenui facundia panno).* As in his use of 'comparisons', Juvenal is usually interested not in the noble morality of a particular aphorism (we have become too accustomed to the English moral maxim), but rather in its satiric possibilities. He is particularly fond of the harsh effect of a hyperbolic aphorism:

There is nothing that a woman will not permit herself to do, nothing that she deems shameful, when she encircles her neck with green emeralds, and fastens huge pearls to her elongated ears: there is nothing more intolerable than a wealthy woman.

(VI, 457–60)

Exaggeration is Juvenal's stock in trade. Once this is recognized we cease to look for or expect an accurate reflection of Roman society in the satires. Evidently the satirist 'refers' to a historical Rome, but to regard his satires as social documents would be quite misleading. Juvenal's claim, characteristic of the Lucilian plain-style tradition, that he treats the ordinary life of men *(quidquid agunt homines)*, has been viewed by some, not as a claim built into the satiric mode distinguishing it from other literary modes of a more elevated (heroic, tragic) reference, but as a statement of documentary intention.

Although Juvenal claims to speak of ordinary life, he speaks in language which is far from ordinary. That elegant spoken idiom *(sermo)* which is fundamental to Horace's satiric style is largely absent from Juvenal's. While Horace's style is essentially plain (conversational, 'rational', dialectical), Juvenal's is essentially mixed. The predominant idioms are heroic (Virgilian) and vulgar. Satiric effects are derived from the clash of styles and from the resulting incongruity. He enjoys the stylistic incongruity which

results from the juxtaposition of an idiom of high-style epic decla-
mation and a demeaning naturalism or harsh and vulgar material-
ism. Sejanus' fame (in Satire X) is set against chamberpots, Cicero's
genius against third-rate verse, the glories of war against the cheek-
strap of a broken helmet, Hannibal's ambition against a little ring.
Mason is right in saying that Juvenal's primary satiric device is
'the belittling remark in the style of epic grandeur'.

We find in the satires both the absurd inflation of the vulgar
by the incongruous use of epic language and the scornful diminu-
tion of the grand by the use of bathetic language. These effects
appear in succession in Satire IV, in which Juvenal ridicules the
catching of the gigantic turbot:

> What time the last of the Flavii was flaying the half-dying
> world, and Rome was enslaved to a bald-headed Nero, there
> fell into a net in the sea of Hadria, in front of the shrine of
> Venus reared high on Dorian Ancona, a turbot of wondrous
> size, filling up all its meshes, – a fish no less huge than those
> which lake Maeotis conceals beneath the ice till it is broken up
> by the sun, and then sends forth, torpid through sloth and
> fattened by long cold, to the mouths of the roaring Pontus.
> (37–44)

The editor of the seventeenth-century Delphin text of the satires
comments on the opening lines: *Magnificum exordium quasi grandia
narraturi* ('an elevated introduction worded as if the narrator were
about to tell of heroic events'). But the grand temporal clause is
deflated by the bathetic 'bald-headed Nero', an unflattering cir-
cumlocution for 'Domitian'. The remaining lines are pure epic
with their sonorous proper nouns *(Hadriaci, Veneris, Dorica, Ancon,
Maeotica, Ponti)* and romantic descriptions. But their application
to a 'turbot' *(rhombus)* is an absurd inflation of a totally unheroic
fish; the effect is mock-heroic.

Juvenal is particularly fond of the savage deflation of the pre-
tentions of overweening ambition. His scornful narration of
Hannibal's rise and fall in the Italian campaign gains its effect largely
by the well-contrived use of bathos: the rising rhythm of the heroic
lines is punctured three times by vulgar words *(aceto, Subura,
luscum)* placed in terminal positions in the line:

> This is the man for whom Africa was all too small . . . Spain
> is added to his dominions: he overleaps the Pyrenees; Nature
> throws in his way Alps and snow: he splits the rocks asunder,
> and breaks up the mountain-side with *vinegar!* And now Italy
> is in his grasp, but still he presses on: 'Nothing is accom-

plished,' he cries, 'until the Punic host breaks down the city gates, and I plant my standard in the midst of *Soho!*' O what a sight that was! What a picture it would make, the Gaetulian beast [elephant] carrying a general *with one eye!* (148, 151–8)

John Dennis's contrast between the 'tragick Eloquence' of Juvenal and Horace's 'Comick' humour raises the question of Juvenal's conception of the stylistic level and poetic status of the genre satire. As we have seen, Horace regarded satire as a 'non-poetic' genre which employs a style nearer to ordinary speech: a line of Ennius even quoted out of context has the aura of 'poetry' about it which is missing from satire. Juvenal, in his first satire, appears to adopt an attitude towards epic writing which is in the tradition of the plain style: he will avoid the artificial subject-matter of epic and concentrate on the everyday life of Rome. The satire opens with a stinging attack on the windy reciters of mythology and epic, whose rantings have no bearing on life as it is lived. But, in Satire VI, when the satirist is in full cry, flaying vicious women who murder their own children, we learn that it is not the *style* of tragedy which Juvenal rejects, but only the fictitious subject-matter.

> This is all fiction, no doubt, and satire is adopting the tragic buskin. Do you think I have overstepped the limits and the laws of my predecessors, and am now mouthing in Sophoclean tones a grand theme unknown to the . . . skies of Latium? I wish it *were* all false! But Pontia shouts 'Yes! I did it, I confess, I poisoned my own children.' (634–8)

Juvenal is saying: 'It might appear that in adopting the tragic style of Sophocles I am abandoning the traditions of satire in writing of the violent passions of Clytemnestras and Procnes who belong to a remote time and place. But in fact our women are just like those of Greek tragedy, only worse.' The high style is appropriate to the everyday life of contemporary Rome, where people are as vicious as the worst sinners of Greek mythology. Unlike the tragedian, however, Juvenal does not weep the tears of Heraclitus, but prefers to pour scorn upon vice in the manner of Democritus. Juvenal's commitment to the style of epic as the principal vehicle of his satire is nowhere more clearly indicated than in Satire XI, where he contrasts the extravagant entertainments of modern Rome with his own ascetic tastes. At *his* feasts the *Iliad* will be recited and the 'lays of high-sounding Maro [Virgil]'. In contrast, Horace longs to return to a country life filled with days of idleness and reading, crowned by intimate supper-parties when friends chat about questions of ethical philosophy (II, vi, 60–76). Juvenal's vision is grand and self-righteous; Horace's is plain, modest and playful.

The contrasting features of Horatian and Juvenalian satire may now be summarised:

(1) Horace prefers a tone of jesting *(ridiculum)* which is moderate and 'rational' in its approach to the reforming role of satire. Juvenal's tone is indignant and 'irrational'.

(2) Horace expresses a concern for formal correctness and artistic labour. Juvenal affects a careless contempt for literary artifice for its own sake, a stance which is consistent with the unrestrained 'spontaneity' of the satirist's *ira*.

(3) Horace's ethical 'philosophy' is relativistic and permits a 'rational' discrimination between degrees of wrongdoing. Juvenal's moral stance is Stoic and absolutist, in that it does not permit such discrimination: affectation in dress is castigated as vehemently as infanticide. On the other hand, the moral stance in Juvenal is usually complicated by irony and is often entirely lacking.

(4) In respect of social and political attitudes, Horace is a well-integrated and quiescent conformist, while Juvenal is a disaffected and reactionary Jeremiah. Horace is a commonsensical and 'moderate' elitist, while Juvenal is a dogmatic reactionary whose idealism has gone sour.

(5) Horace's satire is based upon the plain-style values of *sermo*: it is essentially conversational and familiar. The adoption of a plain-style basis enables Horace to satirise by means of irony and the deployment of delicate *nuances* of style. Juvenal's satire is rhetorical and declamatory, and his effects are often derived from violent juxtaposition of high and low styles. He is especially fond of witty incongruity produced by the scornful application of epic style to the victims of satire.

THE REPUTATION OF THE ROMAN SATIRISTS DURING THE RENAISSANCE

Before we examine the Elizabethan satirists, we shall set the scene by concluding this chapter with a short account of the traditions of interpretation of Roman satire as they were established in the European Renaissance. Most discussions of the satirists in this period take the form of an opposition between the satire of Horace and the satire of Juvenal (Persius was usually aligned with Juvenal.) On the whole Renaissance scholars between Julius Caesar Scaliger and Daniel Heinsius were agreed upon their broad *descriptions of the satirists,* but the incompatibility of their *definitions of true satire* led them to disagree about the *status* of the satirists.

Scaliger was the first to elaborate the case for the superiority of Juvenal based upon an acceptance of the traditional association of tragedy and satire. His general description of the satirists would not have been controversial: 'As we have said elsewhere, there are two kinds of satiric style. One is more gentle like the Horatian kind, and closer to *sermo*. The other, preferred by Juvenal and Persius, is more spirited.'[37] He defends Juvenal against his detractors, who believe that satire is essentially elegant and gentle and that the rough boldness of Juvenal had spoilt the beauty of satire. The accusation that Juvenal is merely a declaimer *(non satyrum, sed declamatorem)* provokes Scaliger to remind the reader incorrectly that satire is a derivative of the ancient Greek 'satyr' plays.[38] He argues that like the 'satyr' play, Juvenal's satire is to be regarded as a tempering *(diluendam)* of the vehemence of tragedy and not as a blot *(labem)* upon the placid surface of the Horatian satiric tradition.

Scaliger regards the stylistic elegance of Horace, and his 'improvement' of the crudities of Lucilius, as no more than a necessary stage in the process of cultural refinement. Scaliger's ideal of stylistic and metrical fluency is Virgilian (and Ciceronian); his model of 'grandeur' *(maiestas)* is Virgil. Juvenal is an improvement on Horace not only in vituperative power *(acrimonia reprehensionis)* and in the rhetorical powers of invention, organisation and richness of thought, but even in wit and urbanity.

Following Isaac Casaubon's demolition of the theory of satire's derivation from tragedy,[39] Heinsius and Vossius adopted a definition of satire which is unabashedly Horatian. Heinsius's famous definition, which Dryden characteristically fused with Scaliger's, attempts the kind of comprehensiveness of definition which Horace had attempted in his programme satires: satire combines playful jest with vehement attack, but is essentially a plain and familiar genre.[40] In a passage based on Horace's discussion of the *poeta* in *Satires,* I, iv, Heinsius argues that, just as orators elevate their speech by suggesting the cadences of poetry without writing poetry, so, conversely, the poets of the plain style, whose subject-matter is devoid of grandeur, modify their verse in the direction of prose without lapsing into prose. He concludes: 'Those who love full and sonorous verse and who play the orator in their argument when their subject-matter is mundane and prosaic, are the most troublesome fools.' No argument could be more carefully designed to place Juvenal below Horace. For Juvenal, the daily life of Rome is not a mundane subject-matter but a subject suitable for the tragic style and the voice of the public orator.

The opposition between Juvenal and Horace in terms of style is put concisely by Heinsius's fellow Dutch critic Vossius: 'The end of satire is to correct [*emendare*] moral behaviour; so it takes the form of *jest* . . . the open jest is in the style of speech partly vehement and satirical, partly delicate and urbane. The former gave greater pleasure to Juvenal, the latter to Horace.'[41] Casaubon's Horatian definition of satire is here brought to bear on the practice of the satirists: the resultant description does not differ in content from Scaliger's, but differs in implied stylistic allegiance. Scaliger had regarded *acrimonia reprehensionis* as essential to the ultimate intention (*finis*) of satire, while Heinsius and Vossius consider the intention to be essentially corrective (*emendare*). From these distinctions derive the recurrent arguments in later theorising about 'vices' and 'follies', about 'railing' and 'raillery', and in general about the best models of satire.

Chapter 2

The Elizabethan
Satyr-Satirist

Although the Elizabethan satirists were the first English writers
to produce formal verse satires in the manner of Horace and
Juvenal, there lay behind them a long tradition of native satire of
considerable richness and vitality. Unlike their successors in the
later seventeenth century, the Elizabethan satirists did not aspire to
a classical 'correctness', any more than Shakespeare did when he
imitated the comic plots of Plautus. The medieval tradition
asserted itself strongly, especially in the more serious side of the
satirist's persona; the representation in allegorical form of the
seven deadly sins remained a common motif in Elizabethan verse
satire, and occupied a central position in the early Jacobean satire
of melancholy humour. Langland's allegorical *The Vision of Piers
the Plowman,* with its attacks on religious corruption, gave
rise to a long satiric tradition of religious satire presented from
the point of view of the common man.

During the reigns of Henry VII and Henry VIII, the forms of
satire were extended in the poetry of Skelton and Wyatt. The
former developed a poetry of personal insult ('flyting') in satires
like *Against the Scottes, Colyn Clout,* and *Why come Ye not to
Court?* The latter poem, an attack on Cardinal Wolsey, includes
what is probably the first allusion to Juvenal's best-known line:

> I am forcebly constrained
> At Juuinals request
> To wryght of this glorious gest
> Of this vaine glorious beast . . .
> *Quia difficile est
> Satiram non scribere.*[1]

Wyatt, in three remarkable poems written in the early 1540s,
introduced Horatian satire into England. The poems are reflective
and non-vituperative; they possess Horace's delicate irony and
moral balance, filtered through the Italian satires of Alamanni. Ben

Jonson was the only major poet to follow in Wyatt's steps before the reign of Charles I.[2] Elizabethan verse satire before the 1590s remained in the mould of the medieval 'Complaint'. Robert Crowley's *One and thyrtye Epigrammes* (1550), Edward Hake's *Newes out of Powles Churchyarde* (1579) and George Gascoigne's *The Steele Glas* (1576) all shared a traditional preoccupation with religious abuses and the corruption prevalent in public affairs.

The religious themes of Elizabethan verse satire were, in the best work, saved from didactic tediousness by a racy realism derived partly from earlier Elizabethan prose writings, especially from Thomas Nashe's *Pierce Penilesse* (1592), which was a satiric homily on the seven deadly sins in the manner of Langland. The style was vigorous, garrulous, daring and extravagant. Nashe developed a taste for personal invective and literary controversy, notably in his somewhat obscure 'quarrel' with Gabriel Harvey. A few years later, Marston, Hall and Jonson indulged in similar 'quarrels', which in many ways anticipate the Augustan 'Battle of the Books' and the warfare between the satirists and the Dunces of Grub Street.

The four most interesting satirists of the 1590s were Thomas Lodge, John Donne, Joseph Hall and John Marston. Lodge had the distinction of being the first in print *(A Fig for Momus,* 1595), although some of Donne's satires were circulating in manuscript before that date. Hall issued his *Virgidemiarum Sixe Bookes (Six Books of Rods)* in two parts (1597–8), the first consisting of 'three Bookes of Tooth-lesse Satyrs', the second of 'three Bookes of byting Satyres'. John Marston's satires appeared pseudonymously in 1598 in two volumes, *The Metamorphosis of Pigmalions Image and Certaine Satyres,* and *The Scourge of Villanie.*

The satiric wits of the 1590s, Donne, Sir John Davies, Hall, Marston, Weever and Guilpin, shared a common social and cultural milieu which had an important conditioning effect on their satiric writings. They formed a set of young men who came from the universities in the 1590s to the Inns of Court to study law and seek preferment at court. Their outlook was cynical and elitist.[3] Their classical reading was extensive, but did not finally determine their conception of the form and content of literary genres: they drew upon Horace and Juvenal for themes, for structural devices and for a sense of the satirist's persona, but the deeper level of their thinking, the level of their world-view, was still dominated by a medieval Christian idea of moral struggle.

Not until the time of Dryden did it become usual to describe the choice of style and tone available to the verse satirist as a choice between Horace and Juvenal. With the emergence of native formal satire in the sixteenth century, the choice was often expressed as one between profane laughter and Christian tears. Thomas Drant's *A Medicinable Morall* (1566), which combines in one volume a translation of Horace's satires and the Lamentations of Jeremiah, presents the alternative attitudes to sin in this way:

> Therefore as it is meete for a man of god rather to wepe than to iest: and not indecent for a prophane writer to be iestyng, and merie spoken: I have brought to passe that the plaintiue Prophete *Ieremie* shoulde wepe at synne: and the pleasant poet *Horace* shoulde laugh at synne. Not one kynde of musike delitheth all passions: nor one salue for all greuances. ('To the Reader')

The distinction clearly owes something to Juvenal's contrast between Democritus the laughing philosopher and Heraclitus the weeping philosopher. Heraclitus' tears were beyond Juvenal's comprehension, but were more congenial to the Christian moralist. Donne makes a similar distinction in his third satire:

> Kinde pitty chokes my spleene; brave scorn forbids
> Those teares to issue which swell my eye-lids;
> I must not laugh, nor weepe sinnes, and be wise,
> Can railing then cure these worne maladies?
>
> (1-4)

For Donne, the alternatives cancel one another out. Many of the bizarre and self-contradictory features of Elizabethan satire stem from attempts to combine the roles of Christian prophet and pagan social critic. The cynical Juvenalian invective of the pagan satirist conflicted with the sober Christian values which formed the ethical substance of the satires. Before considering the Elizabethan transformation of the Juvenalian voice, we must examine the native strain in satire, which was to reappear so often in Elizabethan verse satire.

THE SURVIVAL OF 'COMPLAINT'

Until the middle of the fourteenth century, a 'goliardic' and Anglo-Norman satire of roguish wit and gaiety predominated in England. During the later fourteenth century, a period of increasing social and economic crisis, there emerged a native satire of solemnity and pessimism, usually called 'Complaint'.[4] The characteristics of Complaint are, in several respects, antithetical to those of classical satire. While the latter has a concrete, and particularised 'scene' and a personalised satirist, Complaint

is conceptual, allegorical and impersonal. While satire is varied
in tone from urbane and witty to vituperative and libellous, Com-
plaint is primarily moral and corrective.[5] Complaint itself is a new
form composed from an amalgam of various traditions: diatribes,
lamentations, verse homilies, moral poems and fables, and *timor
mortis* poems. The essential tone is homiletic: general and specific
abuses of the time in society at large are attacked with Hebraic
bitterness. The present is placed against a backcloth of a noble
and ideal past and against a foreground of death, judgement
and retribution. The style of Complaint is usually racy, vivid
and colloquial and is addressed to a popular audience. It has two
dominant forms: invectives on behalf of the common people
against their oppressors, and religious protest against wantonness
and luxury.

Complaint survived into the middle and later years of the
sixteenth century and was revived in the early seventeenth century
before the rising neoclassicism finally banished this quaint medieval
relic. Robert Crowley, a controversial puritan divine of the mid-
sixteenth century, was a late exponent of the tradition. His satiric
epigrams were written at a time of social crisis and transition after
the dissolution of the monasteries and during the emergence of
the commercial middle class and the accompanying decline of
feudal ties. In 'Of the Colier of Croydon', Crowley laments the
new commercial aspirations of the gentry, which had upset the old
order:

> For when none but pore Colyars
>   dyd wyth coles mell,
> At a reasonable price,
>   they dyd theyr coles sell;
> But sence oure Knyght Colyars
>   haue had the fyrste sale,
> We haue payed much money
>   and had fewe sackes to tale.[6]

The style and perspective of the passage are far removed from the
conservative rhetoric of Juvenal or the elitist gentility of Horace.
Like the upstart parvenus who are the stock villains of the com-
plainant's sermon, the 'Knyght Colyars' disturb the ordered
hierarchy of duties which goes with a well-ordered realm. But
unlike the attacks on *novi homines* in Juvenal's satires, Crowley's
criticism of the 'Knights' is presented from a perspective much
lower down the social scale: the complainant speaks with the voice
of the common man, whose life was seriously affected by the price
inflation of the times. The Hebraic seriousness of Crowley's
puritan exhortations reminds us of how remote the Judaeo-

Christian tradition was from the classical. Hallett Smith gives us a useful characterisation of the tradition of social satire which descended from *Piers Plowman* and to which Crowley belongs:

> [This] tradition . . . emphasised the unity of religious and social concerns, strengthened and kept alive the medieval manner of considering society as a group of the various 'estates' and trades which made it up, and gave prestige to a style that was uncouth, rough, or plain, devoid of rhetoric, and trying for simple truth and rugged honesty rather than for polished wit.[7]

An interesting and incongruous synthesis of the Judaeo-Christian Complaint and the classical satire is to be found in Thomas Drant's *A Medicinable Morall* (1566), a translation of Horace's satires. As we have seen, Horace is the jester who laughs at sin, while Jeremiah is the 'plaintive Prophete' who weeps at sin. Thus the medieval complainant and the humble satirist each have their say. But an altered Horace emerges in the process. As the title suggests, Horace is imperceptibly improved: 'I have wyped awaye all his vanitie and superfluitie of matter.' In the true spirit of the Complaint, Horace's 'private carpyngs' are 'drawn . . . to a general moral'. An original poem,[8] substituted for Horace's fifth satire, shows that Drant was conscious of the obsolesence of the Complaint. He 'wots not what to wryte' since neither prophets nor 'silly Satyrists' have the power to amend incorrigible men. (sig. C5^r)

Horace had already emerged in fresh Renaissance garb in the satires of Sir Thomas Wyatt, which appeared posthumously in *Tottel's Miscellany* in 1557. These satires banish completely the sober seriousness and medieval impersonality of the Complaint. We hear an educated man talking in private to a friend rather than a man of the people delivering a sermon in public. Despite their Chaucerian diction, the satires present for the first time the civilised conversation and intimate self-revelation which was to become the underlying note of neoclassical satire in the seventeenth century, but which does not appear in the satires of the 1590s.

While the Complaint ceased to be the dominant form of satire during the sixteenth century, its voice may still be heard in the formal satire of the latter part of the century. Indeed, there are grounds for believing that the conventions of the Complaint reinforced the Elizabethan preference for the Juvenalian manner. The declamatory style of Juvenal has much greater affinities with the homiletic tone of Complaint than with the autobiographical persona of Horace with its self-indulgent playfulness and nuanced wit. The Complaint's social attitudes, though presented from a different perspective, have a general structural likeness to those of Juvenal, whose attacks on women, on parvenus and on the follies of the rich, and whose role of *laudator temporis acti*, were easily blended with similar features in the Complaint. On the other hand, Juvenal's note of personal animus (and not Horace's autobiographical candour) displaces the impersonal sobriety of the complainant.

The most significant and yet most imperceptible formative influence of the Complaint arises from its Judaeo-Christian refusal of the separation of styles, which we noted in Crowley. The 'realism' of Juvenal is quite unlike that of the satire of the Christian era in its treatment of the commonplace and the mundane. The proletariat of Rome, the cosmopolitan rabble, the degraded clients, the despised poor and even the homeless Codrus are part of an irretrievably low-style world, which can never be transfigured by a vertical dimension of transcendental meaning or purpose. But the humble style of the Complaint has the seriousness of a tragic vision of life. When the late Elizabethan satirists adopt the persona of the savage and indignant satirist of Rome, they inevitably transfuse the Christian 'mixed style' into the satirist's presentation of human life, sometimes synthesising the declamatory and the homiletic, sometimes transforming the Juvenalian stylistic incongruity into a Christian 'mixed style'.

Despite the survival of Complaint in works such as Edward Hake's *Newes out of Powles Churchyarde* (1579), and George Gascoigne's *The Steele Glas* (1576), John Peter's assessment of the general development is clearly correct: 'The whole tendency of the age was away from the broad anonymity of Complaint, and it was more at a sort of scandalous gossip than at generalized moral judgements that the poets began to aim' (p. 121). Nevertheless, Complaint remains an element in tradition which alters the possibilities of writings for the post-classical satirist.

THE 'SOUR AND CRABBED FACE' OF JUVENAL

The victims of Elizabethan satire were presented almost invariably as knaves, often incorrigible in their folly. In the depraved world of John Marston's satires, the struggle against vice is abandoned in a rhetorical gesture of despair:

> Now Satyre cease to rub our gauled skinnes,
> And to vnmaske the worlds detested sinnes.
> Thou shalt as soone draw *Nilus* riuer dry,
> As clense the world from foule impietie.[9]
>
> (*Certain Satires*, II, 157-60)

The hyperbolic gesture comes at the end of a long Juvenalian tirade against fair-seeming rogues, and marks the high point of a blistering castigation of the Elizabethan Sodom. The combination of Hebraic lamentation and pagan acrimony is characteristic of Elizabethan verse satire in general, but within that combination a considerable variety of tones, stances and style is possible. The resources of Juvenalian satire were deployed in entirely different ways by the major satirists, Donne, Marston and Hall.

The broadly Juvenalian cast of Elizabethan satire was recognised in the second part of *The Return from Parnassus* (*c.* 1601), in which Ingenioso (probably Nashe) enters reading Juvenal:

> *Difficile est, Satyram non scribere, nam quis iniquae*
> *Tam patiens urbis, tam ferreus ut teneat se?*
> I, Juuenal: thy ierking hand is good,
> Not gently laying on, but fetching bloud:
> So, surgean-like, thou dost with cutting heale,
> Where nought but lanching can the wound auayle ...
> Thy purer soule could not endure to see
> Euen smallest sport of base impurity,
> Nor could small faults escape thy cleaner hands.[10]

Ingenioso is a parodied stereotype of the Elizabethan satirist, a violently idealistic and vehement moralist. The general features of Elizabethan satire are clearly indicated: first, a deliberate harshness of style and tone; and secondly, a self-righteous moral stance.

The image of the Roman Lucilius lacerating knaves with drawn sword prevails over the sly witty Horace. In his punning Latin poem 'De suis Satyris', Joseph Hall sports with a playful etymology of *satira* (sat-irae)[11] on the basis of the idea that *Ira facit Satyram* (compare Juvenal's *facit indignatio versum*). Although Hall regards his own style ('my quiet style') as lacking in vehemence, he affirmed that

> The *Satyre* should be like the *Porcupine*,
> That shoots sharpe quils out in each angry line.
> (*Virgidemiae*, V, iii, 1–2)

A preference for asperity of tone links the Elizabethans with Juvenal (and Persius) rather than with Horace, and in this preference they were following the Renaissance critics (especially Scaliger and Minturno). As we have seen, it was not until after Isaac Casaubon's book on satire (1605) that the European critics (notably Heinsius and Vossius) established Horace as a preferred model. After the bishops' banning of satire in 1599, a brief reaction against Juvenalian satire set in. John Weever, in his curious *Faunus and Melliflora* (1600), boldly criticises the Elizabethan style:

> But I was borne to hate your censuring vaine
> Your enuious biting in your crabbed straine.[12]

Violence of tone and moral purpose are linked in the fashionable imagery of medical purgation and corporal punishment: satire is a scourge, a whip, a surgeon's scalpel, a cauterising iron, a strong cathartic. A selection of titles indicates the prevalence of this conception of satire: *Virgidemiae* (rods), *The Scourge of Villanie*, *The Whipping of the Satyre*, *The Letting of Humours Blood*, *The Scourge of Folly*, *Abuses Stript and Whipt*, *A Strappado for the Diuell*. Much of this violent scourging of vice is quite devoid of moral seriousness: there is a good deal of whipping for whipping's sake.[13] The satirists themselves are often honest in their recognition of a sadistic[14] element in their role as scourge:

> But as for me, my vexed thoughtfull soule,
> Takes pleasure, in displeasing sharp controule.
> (Marston, *Poems*, p. 102)

The association of satire with the planet Saturn[15] reinforced the idea of the satirist's malignant and baleful disposition, and linked him with the general type of the malcontent and the melancholy humorist. The satirist purged his melancholy by giving vent to splenetic laughter. Marston in particular cultivated a melancholy humour, floundering in 'wits darke gloomie straine'. His satiric persona, a fictional development of the Elizabethan theory of the humours, was to be elaborated in *As You Like It* (in Jaques), in *Hamlet* and in *The Anatomy of Melancholy*.[16]

The Elizabethan satirists extended the idea of roughness of tone to that of roughness of metre. The metrical irregularity of Donne's satires[17] seems to have been suggested by the versification of Persius, which was asymmetrical and closer to speech rhythms than Horace's. The association of satire and irregular prosody should be seen in the general context of the late sixteenth-century movement which affected prose as much as verse, and which emphasised the importance of ideas, 'invention' and vigorous speech, against ornament, refinement and smooth harmonious expression. The Anti-Ciceronians (like the Anti-Petrarchans) scorned melodious rhythms and 'effeminate' smoothness in favour of 'masculine' vigour and intellectual toughness. In his couplets, Donne avoids regular parallelism by the use of enjambement, unequal rhythmic phrases and irregular rhyming (masculine with feminine). He favours abrupt rhythms and thoughts, which he achieves by introducing stress shifts, elisions, extra syllables and weak stresses. Donne's satires were probably known to writers like Marston, Hall and Guilpin during the five years before the publication of their satires.[18] While a packed and rugged 'strong line' became the norm for satire (and for other verse forms), it is interesting to note that Hall did not regard metrical roughness as a characteristic of Roman satire but only of English satire, since the latter could find no other way of expressing the vigorousness of the Roman satires. The conflict of rhyme and caesural pause creates an effect of 'dissonance'. Metrical roughness then, according to Hall, is necessary for a 'true and naturall Satyre' only in so far as English prosody can supply no other effect in emulating Latin satire. Ben Jonson later rejected the idea that the imitation of Latin caesural irregularity necessarily resulted in roughness, and goes on to attack the kind of negligent composition he found in the Elizabethan satirists:

> *Others,* that in composition are nothing, but what is rough, and broken . . . And if it would come gently, they trouble it of purpose. They would not have it run without rubs, as if that stile were more strong and manly, that stroke the eare with a kind of unevenesse.[19]

Closely associated with the practice of 'manly' versification was the general late Elizabethan vogue for a 'strong-lined' verse which is marked by abstruseness and intellectual depth. The assumption that the Roman satirists veiled their attacks on contemporaries by adopting a 'difficult' and oracular style made the strong-lined manner seem particularly appropriate. It was thought that the first satire of Persius affected obscurity in order to veil an attack on Nero. Even though this idea was erroneous,[20] there remain a number of features of Persius' style common in first-century rhetoric which seem to justify the notion of satire's obscurity and intellectual abstruseness. Suppressed transitions, intense brevity, rapidly shifting dialogue with undesignated speakers and veiled ambiguous expressions[21] were to become the regular characteristics of Elizabethan verse satire.

There is an elitist spirit in the satirists' cult of obscurity. One might compare their straining after learned allusions and abstruse wit with the sophistication of the founders of modern jazz (Charlie Parker and Dizzy Gillespie), who sought to complicate and intellectualise the rhythmic and harmonic structure of jazz in order to exclude the plagiarists and *hoi polloi*. Chapman's exclusiveness is perhaps the most strident among the Elizabethans:

'The prophane multitude I hate, & onlie consecrate my strange Poems to those serching spirits, whom learning hath made noble and nobilities sacred.'[22] One can trace a similar 'aristocratic' superiority of tone in the satires of the young university scholars and inns-of-court men, who aimed to dissociate themselves from the rising tide of popular and semi-popular literature which addressed itself to the new middle-class readership at the end of the century. John Weever once again provides a contemporary comment which hits the mark:

> Say you that I am obscure?
> Why this is yong mens Rhetoricke . . .[23]

A characteristic contradiction in Elizabethan satire is between the cultivation of a cryptic and opaque style and the claim that the satirist is an honest fellow who calls a spade a spade. As in Roman satire, the plain-style subject-matter *(quidquid agunt homines)* demands a candid and down-to-earth satirist. All three Roman satirists ascribed clear stylistic boundaries to the genre satire, and emphasised its antipodean relationship to tragedy and epic. Both Persius and Juvenal indulge in sarcasm and invective at the expense of the bombastic bard and the mouthing tragedian. Both insist on the 'realism' and the contemporary relevance of satire, its concern for a truthful depiction of the urban nightmare which presented itself to the senses of the satirist. Persius' interlocutor *(adversarius)* praises the satirist's manner in explicitly plain-style terms:

> Let those who meditate lofty themes gather vapours on Mount Helicon . . . But you are not one that . . . croaks to himself some solemn nonsense with hoarse mutterings like a crow . . . No; your language is that of everyday life [*verba togae*]; skilled in clever phrasing, rounded but not full-mouthed, you know well how to castigate the pale debauchee, how to hit off men's foibles with well-mannered pleasantry. (V, 7, 10, 11–12, 14–16)

The stylistic values expressed here are essentially Horatian: satire is a plain-style genre *(sermo pedestris),* which avoids both the lofty themes and grand style of epic, but which is acceptably elegant and cultivated. However, in Persius, and especially in Juvenal, the plain-style claim delimits only subject-matter and not language or stance. The principle of decorum in its 'ideal' form requires a complete homology between the components of a particular level of style. Thus, in satire, the 'ideal type' stylistically would include a plain (mundane) subject-matter, plain (though elegant) diction and a 'rational' authorial stance, while in tragedy, subject, diction and stance would be uniformly high. But, in practice, the principle is continually undermined by the conflicting requirements of invective and moral indignation. Where the ideal of Horatian 'well-mannered pleasantry' *(ingenuus ludus)* is subverted, allegiance to the plain style is strained or even contradicted. Joseph Hall's pronouncements on this subject are fraught with contradictions. He recognises his own tendency to a plain style ('my quiet stile'), but regards true classical satire as obscure, riddle-like and sublimely violent in style. He hopes that he may be succeeded by 'some raging rough *Lucile*' (Lucilius) who might write with the grandeur of an Aeschylus. Conversely, John Marston, the most difficult and tortuous stylist among the Elizabethan satirists, voices a rejection of obscurity which contradicts his own practice at every point:

> Know I hate to affect too much obscuritie, & harshness, because they profit no sence . . . I will not deny there is a seemely decorum to be obserued, and a peculiar kinde of speech for a Satyres lips, . . . yet let me haue the substance rough, not the shadow. I cannot, nay I will not delude your sight with mists; yet I dare defend my plainnes gainst the veriuyce face, of the crabbed'st Satyrist that euer stuttered. (*Poems,* pp. 100–1)

The obscurity of Persius and Juvenal, argues Marston, is an accident of time which has made even Chaucer 'harde . . . to our understandings'. Harshness of content ('substance') should not be allowed to obscure the rational coherence of the style. But in practice the violent indignation of Marston's 'satyr' is quite incompatible with an Horatian plainness and rationality. Like Juvenal, the Elizabethan satirists enjoy the clash of styles, which threatens to overthrow all sense of decorum. The Elizabethans inevitably go beyond Juvenal in undermining the classical separation of styles[24] itself, according to which a sublime style cannot coexist with the mundane and the lowly without destroying the sublimity of the style and turning it into burlesque or bombast. Marston's satires offer the most extreme example of stylistic conflict: the grand style of tragic declamation and religious exhortation is conflated with a gamut of non-poetic styles ranging from the colloquial to the obscene and the grotesque. The effect is of an unprecedented mixture of incongruous elements jostling in an unstable and restless state of interaction.

Many of the characteristic features of the Elizabethan satires examined so far – the preference for Juvenal, the acerbity of tone, the roughness of metre, the obscurity and restless complexity of style – may be related to the widely accepted characterisation of the satirist as woodland 'satyr' and to the traditional association of satires and satyr plays. According to the fourth-century grammarian Aelius Donatus, in his history of tragedy and comedy prefixed to his edition of Terence, satire was the utterance of 'satyrs' and, like these dirty and lascivious woodland deities, was harsh and savage in its attacks on vice.[25] The Elizabethan satirists usually adopt the mask of a semi-bestial satyr 'so that they might wiselye, vnder the abuse of that name, discouer the follies of many theyr folish fellow citesens'.[26] The frontispieces of volumes of satires of this period are commonly illustrated with a picture of a shaggy aggressive satyr. George Wither's characterisation is typical:

> Though in shape I seeme a Man;
> Yet a Satyr wilde I am;
>   Bred in Woods and Desert places,
>   Where men seldome shew their faces;
> Rough and hayrie like a Goate,
> Clothed with Dame Natures Coate.[27]

According to Donatus, the satire, which was descended from Old Comedy, was succeeded in turn by the satyr play, in which the savage attacks on individuals reappeared. The extant Greek satyr plays do not confirm the theory, but the close association of the satyr plays and the tragic drama[28] seems to have encouraged a most un-Horatian view of the stylistic affinities of satire. Despite Isaac Casaubon's refutation of the false etymology *(satyrica >
satira)* in his carefully titled *De Satyrica Graecorum poesi &
Romanorum Satira Libri duo* (1605), Milton based his castigation of Hall's satirist upon the old association:

> For a Satyr, as it was borne out of a *Tragedy,* so ought to re-
> semble his parentage, to strike high, and adventure dangerously
> at the most eminent vices among the greatest persons, and not
> to creepe into every blinde Taphouse, that fears a Constable
> more then a Satyr.[29]

An addiction to the traditional theory endorsed a Juvenalian view of satire as sublime indignation, while Casaubon's refutation of the theory led him to regard Horace as the true model of urbane and polite satire. Evidently Milton's ideal is of a truly heroic satire of the kind to be found forty years later in Dryden's *Absalom and Achitophel.* The tragic posture of Marston may have found greater favour with Milton, but the odour of the taphouse would doubtless have offended him. The indignation of Marston, Guilpin and Rankin is no more sublime than that of Juvenal: the declamatory grandeur is fused with a low-style naturalism which robs grandeur of heroic perception. Both the image of the satyr-satirist and the association with tragedy reinforced the Juvenalian cast of Elizabethan satire. For Juvenal's satirist, both impotent rage and the high-stepping shoes of tragedy *(altus cothurnus)* are justified in the face of contemporary depravity. The mad Hieronimo himself, in *The Spanish Tragedy,* uses a *tragoedia cothurnata,* which contains 'matter, and not common things', in order to unmask Horatio's murderers. (IV, i)

FORMAL SATIRE OF THE 1590s

The satires of Hall and Marston, which appeared in the last years of the decade, are usually regarded as the most characteristic of the period. It is true that *Virgidemiae* and *The Scourge of Villanie* established the pattern of formal verse satire which was to remain current for two centuries. But it is also true that earlier in the decade both Thomas Lodge and John Donne wrote satires which not only make distinctive contributions to the tradition, but also differ significantly from the Juvenalian type established by their successors.

Thomas Lodge's *A Fig for Momus* (1595) still preserves something of the impersonality of Complaint. He makes the conventional disclaimer that his satires are aimed at the correction of vices in general and not at particular men, but, unlike the later satirists, his practice conforms to his claim. However, his general theory of satire does not conform to his practice. In his *Defence of Poetry* (1579) Lodge accepts the traditional derivation of satires from 'satyrs', 'those monsters' who 'were then as our parasites are now adayes: suche as with pleasure reprehended abuse'.[30] But he does not adopt the frenzied rhetoric of a Hall or a Marston. While Lodge contributes to the development of a formal verse satire pattern by introducing numerous themes and topics from Juvenal, his style lies somewhere between the unsophisticated native plainness of the Complaint and the conversational style of Horace.

In 'Satyr 4', Lodge takes Juvenal's grim sermon on the horrors and disappointments of old age (X, 188–288) and transforms it into an address to a friend in the Horatian manner:

> I heare of late (but hould it verie strange)
> (That such vaine newes is common in the change)
> How being old, and drawing to the graue,
> Thou waxest greedie, and desir'st to saue:

> As if thy life of sorrowes had no store,
> But thou in policie shouldst purchase more?[31]

The tone is rationally controlled, the rhythms are balanced and quite without the affected turbulence of Marston.

'Satyr 5' opens with an explicit version of Juvenal's tenth satire:

> In euery [sc. land] from *Gades* to *Ganges* flood
> Too few they be that thinke vpon their good:
> Too few that by discretion can discerne
> What profite rightly doth themselues concerne.
>
> (p. 48)

Juvenal's famous closing lines of (mock-)Stoic comfort are preserved in a form which is remarkably secular:

> What then in right for good may we elect? . . .
> An humble cote entapissed with mosse,
> A lowlie life that feares no sodaine losse:
> A mind that dreads no fal, nor craues no crowne,
> But makes his true-content, his best renowne.
>
> (p. 51)

Instead of the Christianised conclusions which we find later in the versions of Ben Jonson, Henry Vaughan and Dr Johnson, Lodge gives us a re-creation of Juvenal in the image of a native Horace. The humble aspirations of Horace's sixth satire of Book Two ('Hoc erat in votis') are superimposed on Juvenal's astringent and deformed Stoicism. But Lodge's balanced couplets, sober epistolary style, smooth integration of Juvenalian and Horatian elements and native social themes did not become the characteristic type of Elizabethan satire. Hallett Smith is right in arguing that Lodge's satires lacked the satiric vigour and realism of the prose pamphlets of the time, notably the Martin Marprelate tracts, Greene's cony-catching pamphlets, the lampoons of Nashe and Harvey, and Lodge's own prose pamphlets against usury and contemporary evils. Horatian satire of the plain style in balanced heroic couplets was, of course, a thing of the future: yet one can hear the Augustan voice very clearly in Lodge's couplets:

> For nature, ioyned with custome, neuer failes
> But by her selfe, and in her helpes preuailes:
> And why? because what children apprehend
> The same they like, they follow and commend.
>
> (p. 35)

Lodge's 'Horatian' experiment did not exhaust the possible transformations of the classical model. But, before Ben Jonson's revival of Horace, Juvenal and Persius were to have their say. Donne's satires, written probably between 1593 and 1597, owe no servile debt to any classical models: their re-creation of traditional materials is too innovative to be categorised as 'Horatian' or 'Juvenalian'. If he is to be categorised at all, then 'Persian' is perhaps more appropriate. Indeed, a contemporary epigrammatist declared of Donne's satires: "I prithee, Persius, write another book.'[32] Certain superficial analogies which have been drawn more recently between Persius and Donne have a deeper appropriateness than has been realised.[33] As satirists, they share a distaste for extravagantly expressed and unqualified idealism (Persius' opposition to Alexandrian refinement and Silver Latin romanticism is paralleled by Donne's rejection of Petrarchan mellifluousness), and the styles of both combine colloquial plainness (Persius' *plebeia prandia*) and philosophical or religious elevation. The methods used by the New Critics to illuminate Donne's poetic language have now been applied by classical scholars to the study of Persius' metaphorical complexities.[34] Persius' condensation, elliptical grammar, abrupt transitions, mixed diction and figurative density are all features which Donne shares with Marston and Hall, but which in the later satirists are combined with Juvenal's aggressive declamation and subjective *animus*. It would appear that the metrical roughness, which became the norm for verse satire, was first introduced by Donne partly in imitation of Persius, whose versification is certainly the most 'negligent' among the Roman satirists. The most important poetic affinity between Donne and Persius relates to their 'mixed style'. Persius is remarkable for his deepening of the moral and perceptual ambience of satire to an extent that almost exceeds the limits of classical decorum. Towards the end of his second satire, Persius' satirist delivers a proto-Christian lament on the weakness of the flesh:

O Souls bowed down to earth, and devoid of heavenly thoughts! What good can it do to introduce our moral ideas into the temples, and to deduce from this sinful flesh of ours [*haec scelerata pulpa*] what is pleasing to the gods? (II, 61–3)

The eulogies of this passage by Christian commentators[35] can be seen as a response to the stylistic composition of the passage. 'Sinful flesh' corresponds exactly to the Christian 'mixed style', in which the lowest aspect of human life ('flesh') is given the most serious and problematic significance (it is 'sinful'). The familiar term *pulpa* is combined with the serious word *scelerata* to form a phrase which has scarcely any classical precedent.[36] In Juvenal, the 'mixed style' usually involves parody, which does not evade the principle of decorum because its effects derive from *incongruity*. Satire of all periods has exploited the possibilities of stylistic incongruity for effects of ridicule, raillery, sarcasm, bathos and irony, but Donne's 'mixed style' is remarkable for its intensity of perception and feeling and its total subversion of classical decorum. Donne's poetry is marked by an 'incarnational conviction',[37] a sense of the interpenetration of the spiritual and the sensual, the sublime and the carnal. Opposites do not exclude but include one another. In the satires, the serious and the ridiculous are similarly felt to overlap.

The satires against the fashionable world (Satire I), against lawyers (Satires II and V), and against the tedious gossip (Satire IV) are traditional enough in subject-matter but new in poetic language and perception. The first satire opens in a manner which resembles Pope's 'Epistle to Dr Arbuthnot':

> Away thou fondling motley humorist,
> Leave mee, and in this standing woodden chest,
> Consorted with these few bookes, let me lye
> In prison, and here be coffin'd, when I dye;
> Here are Gods conduits, grave Divines; and here
> Natures Secretary, the Philosopher;
> And jolly Statesmen, which teach how to tie
> The sinewes of a cities mistique bodie;
> Here gathering Chroniclers, and by them stand
> Giddie fantastique Poëts of each land.
> Shall I leave all this constant company,
> And follow headlong, wild uncertaine thee?
>
> (1–12)

The satirist sits in his narrow chamber in Lincoln's Inn (if we read autobiographically), preferring imprisonment among his books to the foolish company of a gallant who tries to tempt the satirist out of doors to view the town. Like Horace's satirist, Donne's is not without some self-irony; his scholarly confinement is not presented as an idealised retreat invaded by an impetuous wastrel, but is itself wittily portrayed. But unlike Horace's, the satirist's wit has a complexity of tone[38] which implies a 'unified sensibility', in which thought and feeling are undissociated (although T. S. Eliot's concept requires a non-psychological application in terms of stylistic production). The witty transformation of the scholar's closet to the imprisoning coffin has a serious connotation which we are reminded of at the end of the poem when the gallant abandons the satirist for his mistress:

> At last his Love he in a windowe spies,
> And like light dew exhal'd, he flings from mee
> Violently ravish'd to his lechery.
>   (106–8)

The carnal force of the last line (unleashed in the savage thrusts
of the three stresses) is intensified by the expansive and mocking
lyricism of the previous line: the gallant's mortal weakness is
both absurd and tragic and yet neither absolutely. Similarly, the
scholar's books are pretentious and ridiculous ('jolly Statesmen'
and 'Giddie fantastique Poets'), and at the same time sublime ('Here
are Gods conduits, grave Divines'). The 'jolly' (i.e. arrogant)
politicians are seen in both ways, for their pretensions are im-
plicitly also noble aspirations, for they 'teach how to tie/The
sinewes of a cities mistique bodie'. Of course, Donne's Christian
and Neoplatonic touches ('Gods conduits', 'Natures Secretary',
'mistique body') can be called to rational account and reduced to
mock-seriousness and self-deflation, but this is to miss entirely that
undissociated quality which Eliot found in the love poetry, and
which is present everywhere in Donne's work.

C. S. Lewis, whose strong antipathy for Elizabethan satire is
apparent throughout his account, pointedly regrets the absence
of a Horatian balance in Donne's satires:

> There is a complete absence of that cheerful normality which
> in Horace relieves the monotony of vituperation. In Donne if
> any smile or allusion leads us away from the main theme, it
> leads us only to other objects of contempt and disgust – to
> coffins, 'itchie lust', catamites, death, pestilence, . . . excrement,
> botches, pox, 'carted whores'. Instead of a norm against which
> the immediate object of satire stands out, we have vistas open-
> ing into corruption in every direction.[39]

The explicit statement and the continually implied presence of
a norm is probably the most characteristic feature of classical and
neoclassical satire. But satire of the Auerbachian 'mixed style' is
continually shifting its perspective from human animosity to divine
contemplation with the result that we have no settled sense of a
normative perspective. The instability of this type of Elizabethan
satire may be a result of what John Peter calls 'the immiscibility
of *Satura* and Christianity'.[40] However, Donne solves the dilemma
by translating the classical satire of incongruity into the Christian
satire of the 'mixed style'. When the scholar-satirist finally
succumbs to the gallant's invitation to view the town, he expresses
his guilty state of mind as follows:

But since thou like a contrite penitent,
Charitably warn'd of thy sinnes, dost repent
These vanities, and giddinesses, loe
I shut my chamber doore, and 'Come, lets go'.
But sooner may a cheape whore, that hath beene
Worne by as many severall men in sinne,
As are black feathers, or musk-colour hose,
Name her childs right true father, 'mongst all those:
Sooner may one guesse, who shall beare away
Th' Infant of London, Heire to 'an India:
And sooner may a gulling weather-Spie
By drawing forth heavens Scheame tell certainly
What fashion'd hats, or ruffes, or suits next yeare
Our subtile-witted antique youths will weare;
Then thou, when thou depart'st from me, canst show
Whither, why, when, or with whom thou wouldst go.
But how shall I be pardon'd my offence
That thus have sinn'd against my conscience?

(49–66)

The paragraph is framed by religious metaphors which have the characteristic serio-comic ambivalence referred to above. Within the frame is a large empty space, functionless as argument or narrative, in which is situated a string of the devices which Milgate calls 'ironic or illustrative allusion to things not strictly relevant to the main subject of satire' (p. xix). The two framing sentences and the long inner sentence each begin with 'But'. Within the frame are three illustrative analogies each beginning with 'sooner'. Embedded in the first analogy is a simile ('As are black feathers'). The analogies are richly interlinked. The first analogy is structured in three elements: analogy's subject + simile + analogy's predicate. The first element ('cheape whore') is linked by contrast to the second analogy ('Heire to 'an India', i.e. to great wealth); the second element ('feathers' and 'hose') is linked by association with the third analogy ('hats', 'ruffes', 'suits'); the third element (bastard with no father) is linked by contrast to the second analogy ('Infant of London').[41] There is, finally, a fourth linkage – between the first element ('Worne . . . in sinne') and both parts of the frame ('warn'd of thy sinnes' and 'That thus have sinn'd'). The interweaving of the paragraph's imagery is not merely a piece of rococo artistry but a baroque mixing of styles. The allusion to the vanity of fashionable dress is deepened as satire by the surrounding context. The potentially mock-serious framing metaphors are driven half-way back to a literal meaning by the remarkable first analogy. The 'cheape whore' starts a movement away from the scholar's chamber into the low-style world of the city, but the double linkage with the frame and the horrifying

metaphor ('worne by as many severall men in sinne') restore the
satiric landscape to the full dimensions of the Christian universe
in which even a cheap whore is problematic and fraught with
creatural significance. It is illuminating to compare this passage
with Juvenal's analogies between the diseases of old age and the
number of Oppia's paramours, the victims of Dr Themision, etc.
As we saw in Chapter I (p. 38), the passage aims at an exploitation
of the literary possibilities of rhetoric and is without the deeper
significance attaching to Donne's use of the illustrative device.
The 'irrelevance' of the illustrations in Donne's practice is energised
at a deeper level.

Donne's nearest approach to a classical model is the fourth
satire which is loosely related to Horace's satire on the bore, a
distant cousin of the gallant of Donne's first satire. The satire opens
in most un-Horatian manner with a sustained mock-religious con-
fession:

> Well; I may now receive, and die; My sinne
> Indeed is great, but I have beene in
> A Purgatorie, such as fear'd hell is
> A recreation to, 'and scant map of this.
> My minde, neither with prides itch, nor yet hath been
> Poyson'd with love to see, or to bee seene,
> I had no suit there, nor new suit to show,
> Yet went to Court.
> (1–8)

Donne may have been attracted to Horace's satire by the presence
there of a few mock-heroic touches which give the hint for Donne's
extended mock-religious opening. Ben Jonson's adaptation of
Horace's satire in *Poetaster* (III, i) captures precisely Horace's
playful self-mockery when, despairing of release, 'Horace' declares
in mock-portentous manner:

> I now remember me, sir, of a sad fate [*fatum triste*]
> A cunning woman, one Sabella, sung,
> When in her urn she cast my destiny . . .

But Donne's purgatory has none of the self-mockery of Horace's
plight. We are reminded of Donne's Christian inheritance when, at
line 155, having escaped the clutches of the bore, he shifts his point
of view from a Horatian one to that of the medieval dream-vision
with an allusion to Dante's *Inferno*:

> At home in wholesome solitarinesse
> My precious soule began, the wretchednesse

> Of suiters at court to mourne, and a trance
> Like his, who dreamt he saw hell, did advance
> It selfe on mee . . .

Like the scholar-satirist of the first poem, Donne's satirist becomes embroiled in sin merely by being in the vicinity of the Elizabethan Vanity Fair and is reduced thereby to the level of the objects of his satire:

> So'it pleas'd my destinie
> (Guilty 'of my sin of going,) to thinke me
> As prone to'all ill, and of good as forget-
> full, as proud, as lustfull, and as much in debt,
> As vaine, as witlesse, and as false as they
> Which dwell at Court, for once going that way.
>   (11–16)

The sheer force of self-recrimination and the accumulation of self-debasement compel the reader to transmute the mock-serious into the problematic and the melancholic. The bore himself has none of the glib vapidity of Horace's bore. Donne gives us a Bosch-like pictorial presentation of a grotesque 'thing', 'A thing more strange, then on Niles slime, the Sunne E'r bred'. The satirist's persona is one of profound subjective intensity, far removed from the urbane and detached viewpoint of the Horatian persona. Far from controlling the situation through the imposition of a normative and rational perspective, Donne's satirist becomes the spiritual victim of the bore's babel-like speech and poisonous vision:

> I more amas'd then Circes prisoners, when
> They felt themselves turne beasts, felt my selfe then
> Becomming Traytor, and mee thought I saw
> One of our Giant Statutes ope his jaw
> To sucke me in; for hearing him, I found
> That as burnt venom'd Leachers doe grow sound
> By giving others their soares, I might grow
> Guilty, and he free: Therefore I did shew
> All signes of loathing; But since I am in,
> I must pay mine, and my forefathers sinne
> To the last farthing . . .
>   (129–39)

The rapid displacement of images and metaphors by one another serves to enhance the impression of the satirist's overwhelming mental torment. There is wit, but it is the wit which we find in Donne's most sin-conscious 'Holy Sonnets' or in the soliloquies of Hamlet. It is a wit which is the very antithesis of that Horatian

neoclassical wit so perfectly embodied in the satiric poetry of
Ben Jonson. When John Peter, referring to a passage in the second
satire, speaks of Donne's 'almost light-hearted tolerance of Sin',
he overstates the satiric detachment of such passages. Peter
correctly stresses 'the yawning gap between his [Donne's] own
attitude and those of Complaint',[42] but misses the active presence
in the satires of that Hebraic bitterness which distinguishes Com-
plaint from *Satura*. Donne's satires combine the 'mixed style' of
Complaint, a searing post-Reformation individualistic vision, and
the sophisticated dramatic compression of classical satire.

The Horatian experiments of Lodge and of Donne's more idio-
syncratic (and therefore inimitable) satires made available a number
of conventions which contributed to the formation of a native
pattern of formal verse satire. But the uncongenial flatness and
sobriety of Lodge and the relative inaccessibility of Donne's manu-
scripts left the field open for further attempts to fix the native
form. A fresh note of Juvenalian rhetoric has already been intro-
duced in the prose of Thomas Nashe, most forcibly in *Pierce
Penilesse* (1592). Joseph Hall's claim to have been the first English
satirist was justified in so far as he was the first to produce a
printed collection of formal satires in heroic couplets closely
modelled on the Roman *Satura*.

Joseph Hall presents us with the interesting phenomenon of
the Horatian satirist manqué. His satires were not fully ap-
preciated until the eighteenth century when the Horatian elegance
of his couplets was remarked by Thomas Warton, who saw how
Hall had modified the Juvenalian wild man:

> Hall's acknowledged patterns are Juvenal and Persius, not
> without some touches of the urbanity of Horace. His parodies
> of these poets, or rather his adaptations of ancient to modern
> manners, a mode of imitation not unhappily practised by
> Oldham, Rochester and Pope, discover great facility and
> dexterity of invention. The moral gravity and censorial de-
> clamation of Juvenal he frequently enlivens with a train of more
> refined reflection . . . [43]

Warton's eighteenth-century reflections are summed up well in the
sentence, 'The indignation of the satirist is always the result of
good sense' (p. 367).

As a theorist, Hall was perfectly orthodox:

> The *Satyre* should be like the *Porcupine*,
> That shoots sharpe quils out in each angry line . . .
>
> (p. 83)

He regrets that he cannot emulate the 'bolder stile' of the ancients in his own work, but hopes to pass on the torch to a more vigorous successor:

> But from the ashes of my quiet stile
> Henceforth may rise some raging rough *Lucile* . . .

The arrangement of *Virgidemiae* (1598) in two groups of satires, three books of 'tooth-lesse Satyrs' and three books of 'byting satyres', seems to have been an attempt, following J. C. Scaliger's classification of satire, to write both comic and tragic (or Horatian and Juvenalian) types of satire. The dividing-line between the groups is not always clear, but Hall himself considered that the first book of biting satires 'doth somewhat resemble the soure and crabbed face of *Iuuvenals*' (p. 99). It is noticeable that in the third book of the toothless satires Hall makes positive use of Horace's plots and themes,[44] but without Horace's tone of irony and detachment. Hall is decidedly eclectic, but his overt model is certainly Juvenal.[45] His adaptations are by no means slavish and require close reading for full appreciation.

The sixth satire of Book IV resembles Lodge's 'Satyre 5' in its use of the opening and closing lines of Juvenal's tenth satire. The theme of the 'Vanity of Human Wishes' is announced as follows:

> I wote not how the world's degenerate,
> That men or know, or like not their estate:
> Out from the Gades vp to the Easterne morne,
> Not one but holds his natiue state forlorne.
>
>   (1–4)

The material from Juvenal is neatly interwoven with echoes of Horace's first satire, and is expressed in a native diction, close to Complaint, but refined by a classical economy and poise. Hall's account of the restless affectations of contemporary dress has all the lively naturalism of Elizabethan prose.[46] Hall differs from Juvenal in his attitude towards the Stoic life of retreat and scholarship. Where Juvenal presents a horrifying picture of the fate of those who abandon physical work for the schools of rhetoric, Hall advocates a pure Stoic withdrawal from the active life:

> 'Mongst all these sturs of discontented strife
> Oh let me lead an Academicke life, . . .
> Enuye ye Monarchs with your proud excesse
> At our low Sayle, and our hye Happinesse.
>
>   (82–3, 88–9)

In the Prologue to Book I, Hall expresses the same confident sense
of normative values in stylistic terms:

> Goe daring Muse on with thy thanklesse taske,
> And do the ugly face of vice unmaske:
> And if thou canst not thine high flight remit,
> So as it mought a lowly Satyre fit,
> Let lowly Satyres rise aloft to thee
> Truth be thy speed, and Truth thy Patron bee.
>
> (19–24)

Satire may be a humble genre, but its moral status is high. Unlike
Marston's, Hall's satirist expresses the confidence of positive
values, which is typical of Horatian satire. But Hall's positive
values do not possess Horace's pragmatic eclecticism, but stem
from a commitment to Stoicism. The explicit statement of this
commitment is frequent outside the satires:

> The divines of the old heathens were their moral philos-
> ophers . . . These were the overseers of manners, correctors of
> vices, directors of lives, doctors of virtue . . .[47]

Stoic 'right reason' accommodated to Christianity forms the basis
of Hall's rational stance in the satires. From this secure stand-
point, Hall attacks the wilful evil of men, who are the victims of
their passions and who threaten the providentially sustained har-
mony of the world. Clearly such men are knaves, but their
knavery does not unhinge the satirist's brain or destroy his value
system. While Juvenal's glimpses of a Golden Age of rustic sim-
plicity ('the acorn-belching spouse') are jaundiced and ironic,
Hall's extended vision anticipates the expression of Horatian
ideals as re-created by Ben Jonson in poems like 'To Penshurst':

> Time was, that whiles the Autumne fall did last,
> Our hungry sires gap't for the falling mast of the *Dodonian* okes . . .
> Their royall plate was clay, or wood, or stone:
> The vulgar, saue his hand, else had he none.
> Their onely seller was the neighbour brooke:
> None did for better care, for better looke.
>
> (III, i, 5–6, 22–5)

Hall's distinction as an Elizabethan satirist lies in his successful
balancing of Stoic 'right reason' and the role of the Juvenalian
satyr-satirist. Later attempts to conflate these roles by William
Rankins, T. M. and Everard Guilpin result in an unstable and self-
contradictory moral stance, which few satirists of the Juvenalian

type have successfully avoided. The calm philosopher easily slips into the role of sadist, the corrector of vices becomes the prurient gloater, and the idealist is transformed into the cynic.

The Stoic note is more prominent in the toothless satires, which are also less overtly Juvenalian in tone. The biting satires introduce not only a more savage and more obscure style, but also a less 'literary' subject-matter. While the first three books had concentrated on literary satire in the classical manner, the biting satires return to the social themes of Complaint. Hall attacks the new business class (IV, v), the landlords (V, i), social discontent (IV, vi), the decline of 'housekeeping' and charity (V, ii), the enclosure of the common lands (V, iii), and the plundering of the New World (V, i). Hallett Smith invites us to believe that a knowledge of social and economic context will illuminate satires of this type. It is evident that satires 'reflect' society in some sense, but the literary critic is in a position to resist the over-deterministic assimilation of literature to its social context. Not only is literature itself a part of the social world, but its own relatively autonomous development will sometimes 'determine' the nature of its 'reflection' of society. For example, when Hall describes the decline of hospitality, we need not only a knowledge of the rise of capitalism and the alterations which arose in social (class) relations, but also a knowledge of the fictional remaking of these extra-literary historical levels of social reality. When Hall laments the passing of traditional hospitality in the country houses, he is echoing the complaints of his contemporaries and at the same time presenting the social world through literary forms and conventions. The metonymic association of hospitality and chimney smoke produces the conceit which reappears frequently in the satire of the following decade:[48]

> Nor halfe that smoke from all his chymneies goes
> Which one Tabacco-pipe driues through his nose.
> (V, ii, 73–4)

The general social theme really fits the classical theme of the decline of patronage, enabling Hall to present the Elizabethan scene in terms of an imitation of Juvenal's fifth satire. The last forty-five lines of the satire rehearse in Elizabethan terms the sufferings of the client at the hands of Virro: the client's inferior bread and wine, the indignities at the hands of servants, and the patron's ostentatious luxury. Thus social 'realism' is heavily conditioned by the forms, themes, conventions, topics and stylistic possibilities of the fictional world. The Roman theme of legacy-hunting (in Horace's fifth satire of Book II, for example) is similarly superimposed on the popular Elizabethan theme of 'cony-catching'.[49]

If Hall's satirist is the reluctant satyr-satirist, the Horatian Stoic manqué, then Marston's is the apotheosis of the Elizabethan ideal type, the wild man of the woods. Marston's satirist has a persona so full of contradictions that the critics have been quite unable to agree on an interpretation of its meaning and value. Like the work of a number of his contemporaries (Samuel Rowlands, Joseph Hall, Everard Guilpin), Marston's early work is an energetic and explosive rejection of the romantic and idealistic fashions in Elizabethan literature. Marston's earlier poem, *The Metamorphosis of Pigmalions Image* (1598), has been regarded as both a salacious development of the fashionable neo-Ovidian erotic 'epyllia' *(Hero and Leander, Venus and Adonis)* and as a *parody* of the fashion. Marston himself invites the second interpretation, but many modern critics[50] have been unwilling to accept his claim, which they regard as rationalisation after the event. The absence of an explicit or a consistent point of view is characteristic of Marston's satires, especially *The Scourge of Villanie* (1598), which followed closely on the heels of Hall's *Virgidemiae*.

Marston's claim to be regarded as the Elizabethan Juvenal has some justification. More than Hall he develops the mixing of styles by which Juvenal gains his effects of incongruity (especially bathos) and demeaning sarcasm. The low-style world which Marston views from his assumed sublime perspective, infects his 'poetic' style and transforms it into a grotesque and unstable medium:

> O what dry braine melts not sharp mustard rime
> To purge the snottery of our slimie time?
> (p. 108)

> But if you hange an arse, like *Tubered* . . .
> (p. 128)

> Yon's one hath yean'd a fearfull prodigie,
> Some monstrous mishapen Balladry,
> His guts are in his braines, huge Iobbernoule,
> Right Gurnets-head, the rest without all soule.
> (p. 136)

In *The Poetaster,* Ben Jonson successfully parodies Marston's outlandish and concocted style in the rants of Crispinus:

> Rampe up, my genius: be not retrograde:
> But boldly nominate a spade, a spade.

> What, shall thy lubricall and glibberie *Muse*
> Live, as shee were defunct, like punke in stewes?
> . . . teach thy *incubus* to poetize:
> And throw abroad thy spurious snotteries.[51]

Thomas Warton responded with an Augustan distaste to the contradictions of Marston's style: 'This stream of poetry, if sometimes bright and unpolluted, always betrays a muddy bottom.'[52]

In 'Reactio' (*Certain Satires, IV*) Marston puts on the poet's robes in an attack on Hall's 'vile detraction':

> What Satyre! sucke the soule from Poesie
> And leaue him spritles? o impiety!
>   (p. 84)

Marston declares that Hall's style is without the elevation of true poetry, and that as a result his censure is mere malice. But Marston's self-righteous and pseudo-religious pose is unconvincing even as rhetoric. The only real distinction between his own 'Grim-fac'd Reproofe' and Hall's 'vile detraction' is a stylistic one. Hall admits that his satiric 'manner' has fallen below his Roman models in 'too much stouping to the lowe reach of the vulgar' (p. 98). Marston's stance is the very antithesis of this:

> O how on tiptoes proudly mounts my Muse,
> Stalking a loftier gate then Satyres vse.[53]
>   (p. 158)

The high-style stance underlies several features of the satirist and his language: the mask of Hamlet-like melancholy, the Tamburlaine-like self-assertiveness, the high-flown poetic idiom with its fantastic compound words, neologisms, mythological music and abstruse allusions, and above all the Juvenalian declamatory violence. Morse Allen calls Marston's style 'Senecan rhodomontade',[54] linking it with the ranting style of Senecan tragedy, which the Elizabethans imitated with such exuberance. The second satire in the *Scourge* takes Juvenal's *difficile est satyram non scribere* as its motto and proceeds to out-Juvenal Juvenal in indignant rant:

> I cannot hold, I cannot I indure
> To view a big womb'd foggie clowde immure
> The radiant tresses of the quickning sunne.
> Let Custards quake, my rage must freely runne.
> Preach not the Stoickes patience to me,
> I hate no man, but mens impietie.
> My soule is vext, what power will'th desist?

> Or dares to stop a sharpe fangd Satyrist?
> Who'le coole my rage? Who'le stay my itching fist
> But I will plague and torture whom I list?
>
> (1–10)

Never has the satirist's persona declared itself so boldly as a fictional product, a reworking and development of a literary type. There is a sense of energies being derived from within the fictional world. Such a voice could never possess the controlling rational perspective of the Horatian satirist which gives the reader a sense of a 'real' personality and a coherent psychological ordering. Marston's cultivation of a moody, changeable persona leads to some very odd effects, for example, in Satire XI ('Humours') when he appears to flirt with a more genial and Horatian voice, invoking 'my iocond Muse'. But the experiment (which probably influenced Milton's *L'Allegro* and *Il Penseroso*) appears to fail, and the satirist declares:

> Fie, whether's fledde my sprights alacritie?
> How dull I vent this humorous poesie.
> In fayth I am sad, I am possest with ruth
> To see the vainenes of fayre *Albions* youth.
>
> (184–7)

Marston ends the satire with an oddly contradictory declaration:

> Here ends my rage, though angry brow was bent,
> Yet I haue sung in sporting merriment.
>
> (239–40)

The satirist, like Feliche the satirist-commentator in Marston's *Antonio and Mellida* (1599), combines the excoriating fury of Juvenal with the Stoic role of 'happy man' whose soul is above the vile spirit of the malignant detractor.[55] This contradiction may be viewed as a symptom of Marston's artistic failure and of his psychotic vision. Alternatively, we may choose to regard the voice of the Stoic teacher-philosopher as Marston's 'real' voice as opposed to the 'rhetorical' voice of the indignant satirist. However, the polysemous quality of the text does not permit such easy reduction.[56] The presence of neo-Stoic rhetoric ('Synderesis', 'Opinion', the metaphor of the fountain and the flower) does not displace the conflicting fury of the sharp-fanged satirist or of the inexorable pessimism of the gloomy Calvinist. Davenport is right to regard Marston's Calvinistic pose as hardly compatible with moral satire (p. 21). In denying the efficacy of good works and the power of human will, and in affirming the failure and corruption of human reason ('alas our *Cognisance* is gone'), Marston cancels the satirist's corrective role, leaving him with an unqualified licence to bite. The concepts and terminology of neo-Stoicism and Calvinism become, as it were, free-floating stances without normative significance, which are deployed at will as satiric counters and are caught up in a self-generating literary process of astonishing exuberance. However, a kind of coherence is perceptible in the alternations of perspective: the Calvinistic stance reinforces the dominant Juvenalian voice, while the neo-Stoic stance reinforces the subordinate Horatian voice. Occasionally the stances come together and jostle incongruously:

> Here ends my rage, though angry brow was bent,
> Yet I haue sung in sporting merriment.

The domination of the melancholy pessimist's voice produced a combination of elements of style and perception which were to be redeployed in the great tragedies of the Jacobean period in the poetic language of Hamlet, Othello, Thersites and Bosola. A corrupt and diseased world is described in a language which is densely metaphoric, gross (even salacious), declamatory and subjectively intense.

The torrent of formal satires which appeared in 1598 and 1599 (including work by Middleton, Everard Guilpin and William Rankins) was briefly redirected into new channels in June 1599 by the Bishops' prohibition and burning of satiric and erotic writings of the kind associated with Marston. Immediately, the biting satirist found his way into the comic and tragic satire of Jonson, Marston and Shakespeare. Formal satire continued in a less vehement form in the low-life vernacular narratives of Samuel Rowlands and the satires of Nicholas Breton, who revives the gravity and sobriety of the Complaint and declares, 'Let vs then leaue our biting kinde of verse', and let 'each . . . Christianharted brother . . . be vnwilling to offend another'.[57] The verse satire of the Jacobean period is dominated by a fusion of Complaint and Juvenalian bitterness made popular by George Wither's *Abuses Stript and Whipt* (1613). The Bishops' prohibition deflected the intellectual and neoclassical satire away from the formal type and left the field open for the more pious middle-class satirists, who were reviving the main native tradition in satire which had run from *Piers Plowman* to Crowley and Hake in the mid-sixteenth century. At the same time, they, for the most part, advocated a more rational tone and an almost Horatian ethical stance, but failed to develop a new satiric style.[58] Horace awaited a more classical revival.

Chapter 3

Commonwealth and Restoration Satire

In this chapter we shall examine the development of verse satire between the onset of the Civil War (1642) and the end of the seventeenth century. The most striking difference between the satires of this period and those of the Elizabethan and Jacobean periods lies in the shift from the attack on general human types to the castigation of particular people in contemporary historical situations. While Donne, Hall and Marston concerned themselves with the courtier, the lawyer, the cony-catcher, the pedant and the lecher, Cleveland attacks the political and religious enemies of Charles I, Marvell satirises the Duke of York for his part in the Dutch war of 1665, Rochester attacks his fellow poets, and Dryden satirises Shadwell, Shaftsbury, Buckingham, Monmouth and the King himself. Restoration satire is topical and personal to a degree without precedent in literary history. The gradually established ascendancy of 'Augustan' or neoclassical literary values in no way diminished the variety and individuality of verse satire, but it established a stricter sense of stylistic decorum than had been current in the late sixteenth century. The sense of stylistic decorum went with a strong sense of normative values of rationality and social order. It is significant that the leading satirists of the Restoration period (Butler, Rochester, Oldham and Dryden) all ridicule deviations from a strongly held rational norm in the spheres of philosophy, religion, politics or literature. It is true that the sceptical Butler and the Hobbesian Rochester themselves depart from that Augustan norm of rationality which was to be expressed definitively by Locke in the final decade of the century. Nevertheless, they acted as the front-line troops in the Augustan negative criticism of the 'irrational' beliefs and 'dangerous' dogmas of the past:

> When *civil* Fury first grew high,
> And men fell out they knew not why.
> (*Hudibras*, I, i, 1–2)

The brief revival of republican and puritan satire[1] against the monarchy, which followed the first ten years of Charles II's reign, was soon eclipsed by the potent conservative 'moderation' of Dryden's *Absalom and Achitophel* and generally by the domination of the literary and cultural life by the Court wits and their clients (who included Dryden). The major feature of Augustan satire was its development of a satiric rhetoric which reflected its total cultural domination and its successful exclusion of the emerging bourgeoisie from elite status. Those writers (Settle, Shadwell, Behn) who were important voices in the new middle-class culture became the 'dunces' of Augustan satire.

During this period, Roman satire was widely read, translated and imitated. The developing Augustan values of 'common sense', 'moderation', 'clarity' and 'naturalness' would seem to favour the Horatian model. In fact, Juvenal was at least equally in vogue. Two complete translations of Horace appeared in the seventeenth century, one edited by Alexander Brome (1666) and the other written by Thomas Creech (1684). Juvenal's complete satires were translated by Sir Robert Stapylton (1647), Barten Holyday (1673), Dryden and others (1693).[2] If one ignores Brome's collection (in which the imitations by Cowley and Sprat appeared), only the flat and insipid translation of Horace by 'painful' Creech appeared in the Restoration period. Horace awaited the attentions of Swift and Pope in the eighteenth century when the ideology of 'common sense' was fully absorbed into the culture.

HERACLITUS' TEARS

The Renaissance image of Juvenal as an enraged declaimer was seriously challenged at the beginning of the seventeenth century by Ben Jonson, whose criticisms of Marston have been discussed in Chapter 2. While Jonson's scholarly classicism and admiration for Bacon's rationalism disposed him to adopt Horace's literary values in general, in his more personal satiric verses he adopts something of Juvenal's astringent tone but eschews the impotent rage of the Elizabethan Juvenal. His conception of Juvenal emerges vividly in his adaptations, which are serious and even Christian in tone.

'To Sir Robert Wroth' belongs with 'To Penhurst' in the category of the rural ode in celebration of good 'housekeeping' and owes a great deal to Horace (see Jonson's translation of 'Epode II'). After an idealising description of Wroth's estate, Jonson passes to a semi-satirical account of the vain efforts of envious men, and concludes with a celebration of Wroth's spiritual and moral health:

Thy peace is made: and, when man's state is well,
    'Tis better, if he there can dwell.
God wisheth, none should wracke on a strange shelfe:
    To him, man's dearer, then to' himselfe.
And, howsoeuer we may thinke things sweet,
    He alwayes giues what he knowes meet;
Which who can vse is happy: Such be thou.
    Thy morning's, and thy euening's vow
Be thankes to him, and earnest prayer, to finde
    A body sound, with sounder minde;
To doe thy countrey seruice, thy selfe right;
    That neither want doe thee affright,
Nor death; but when thy latest sand is spent,
    Thou maist thinke life, a thing but lent.
                  (93–106)

The closing lines of Juvenal's tenth satire are here closely imitated and totally transformed. Jonson, whose commitment to the plain style has been well demonstrated by Wesley Trimpi,[3] tempers the extremes of Juvenal's mock-Stoic conclusion by careful omission. Juvenal's elevated philosophical pessimism and his deflating particularity (the little white pork sausages) disappear in a controlled and dignified plain style. The changes suit the requirements of the rural ode, but also reflect the 'Augustan' and Baconian tendency in Jonson's work which generally favours the plain style. Juvenal's Stoicism is at least partially ironic, while Jonson's is deeply Christian. The stylistic variety and exuberance of Jonson's plays should not mislead us into ignoring the firm commitment to a controlling plain style. His human ideal is the man of balanced disposition – 'a creature of a most perfect and diuine temper . . . in whom the humours and elements are peacably met, without emulation of precedencie.'[4] His stylistic ideal is always expressed in terms of balanced plainness and the avoidance of pedantry and extremes.[5]

The chastened and Christianised Juvenal, who appears briefly in Jonson's poem, reappears in Henry Vaughan's under-read translation of Juvenal's tenth satire, which is the first total re-creation of the Latin poem in English. Vaughan's version represents a step towards the Augustan mode of translation, although he does not anticipate the radical path of Cowley. The translation exalts and refines his model: gross details are purified or suppressed, and the ethical tone is intensified in a manner which anticipates Dr Johnson in *The Vanity of Human Wishes*. The prefatory remarks emphasise that the pagan Juvenal is being seen through the eyes of the Christian Stoic:

The *Satyre* . . . is one of his, whose *Roman* Pen had as much true

Passion, for the infirmities of that state, as we should have *Pitty,* to the distractions of our owne.[6]

Vaughan boldly alters Juvenal's jest at the expense of the weeping philosopher to a more emotive statement:

> Smiles are an easie purchase, but to weep
> Is a hard act, for teares are fetch'd more deep.
> > (p. 19)

The grotesque indignities to which Sejanus' statue is subjected are made less ridiculous and more pathetic. The degrading details which the Restoration versions exploit fully are omitted. Vaughan inserts in Juvenal's character of Hannibal a parenthesis which introduces a sublime and eschatological dimension totally absent in the original:

> . . . (Ye gods! that give to men
> Such boundles appetites, why state you them
> So short a time? either the one deny,
> Or give their acts, and them Eternitie) . . .
> > (p. 23)

Later, in a passage where Juvenal, with no apparent irony for once, gives some warrant for such a tone, Vaughan enlarges brief hints into a tragic but Christian vision:

> But grant age lack'd these plagues; yet must they see
> As great, as many: Fraile Mortalitie
> In such a length of yeares, hath many falls,
> And deads a life with frequent funerals.
> The nimblest houre in all the span, can steale
> A friend, or brother from 's; there's no Repeale
> In death, or time; this day a wife we mourne,
> To morrowes teares a sonne, and the next Urne
> A Sister fills; Long-livers have assign'd
> These curses still: That with a restles mind,
> An age of fresh renewing cares they buye,
> And in a tide of teares grow old and dye.
> > (p. 27)

The combination of a dignified homiletic note and a measured plain style place Vaughan clearly in the line of Jonson (via George Herbert). The couplet form, with its combination of Roman enjambed lines and carefully modulated caesura, is very close to Jonson's ideal.[7] The nature of Vaughan's transformation of Juvenal may be glimpsed in a comparison of his version of a Juvenalian apothegm with those of Holyday and Stapylton:[8]

> ... 'Tis made known,
> What Dwarfs our Bodies are, by Death alone.
> (Holyday, p. 188)

> Death doth alone deal plainly, and declare
> What things of nothing humane bodies are.
> (Stapylton, p. 340)

> The Highest thoughts, and actions under Heaven,
> Death only with the lowest dust layes even.
> (Vaughan, p. 25)

Because Vaughan belongs to the line of Jonson and Herbert, the tendency to heighten is controlled by a standard of strength, smoothness and transparency. In this too he resembles Dr Johnson, who stands to Dryden and Pope as Vaughan stands to Ben Jonson. Vaughan was writing at a time when the 'jerking hand' of the Elizabethan Juvenal was revived in Cleveland's 'keen Iambicks'. Vaughan and Cleveland were both royalist, and both 'metaphysicals', but their conceptions of the nature of satire were antithetical. Dr Johnson and Charles Churchill are the eighteenth-century heirs of their experiments.

THE NEOCLASSICAL HORACE

During the second half of the Jacobean period the emergence of a neoclassical standard of plainness in verse coincided with a revival of interest in Horace's poetry. Ben Jonson's utilitarian classicism, like Bacon's and Horace's, insisted on the priority of matter *(res)* over words *(verba)*, and established a rapidly growing neoclassical tradition which rejected the hyperboles and 'hard' conceits of the metaphysicals in favour of a new, noble but austere plain style. Royalist writers such as Dudley North,[9] John Ashmore[10] and Sir John Beaumont[11] advocated a poetic of smoothness, weight, perspicuity and elegance which anticipated the neoclassicism of the 1630s and 1640s (Falkland, Cartwright, Berkenhead, Katherine Phillips, Waller and Cowley).

Sir John Beaumont's 'To his late Maiesty, concerning the true forme of English Poetry' is one of the earliest statements in England of neoclassical literary principles (probably influenced by Ben Jonson's *Discoveries*). He advocates:

> Pure phrase, fit Epithets, a sober care
> Of Metaphors, descriptions cleare, yet rare,
> Similitudes contracted smooth and round,
> Not vext by learning, but with Nature crown'd.[12]

Like John Ashmore, Beaumont anticipates the vogue of the Horatian poetry of 'The Happy Man' *(beatus ille)*. Cowley's famous collection of the poems of this type is partly fore-shadowed in Beaumont's posthumously published work, which includes versions of Horace's 'Epode II', *Satires,* II, vi, *Odes,* III, xxix, Martial's forty-seventh epigram, and Claudian's much-translated epigram on the old man from Verona.[13] The combined Stoic and Epicurean rhetoric of 'simple fare', modest retreat *(parva rura)* and moderate pleasures had attractions for the aristocratic proponents of the plain style long before the Civil War added its reinforcing pressures. Beaumont's translations of Persius' second satire, Juvenal's tenth and Horace's sixth (of Book II) challenge the pre-vailing Jacobean satiric fashion for a baptised Marstonian harsh-ness. The stylistic incongruities and vehement tone of Persius[14] and Juvenal are subdued to a calm and elegant Jonsonian manner.

Horace's second epode and sixth satire (of Book II), two of the most influential poems in the 'happy man' tradition, are compli-cated, in the Latin, by an ironic and deflationary content which is smoothed away by Beaumont and by later neoclassical imi-tators. The slightest hint of indelicacy or unaristocratic rusticity is elegantly corrected. When Horace's satirist pipe-dreams about the lazy enjoyments and the simple fare of country living, Beaumont refines the passage (omitting 'and cabbage dressed with a little bacon fat') with a neoclassical decorum far stricter than Horace's:

> When shall my sight
> Againe bee happy in beholding thee,
> My countrey farme? Or when shall I be free
> To reade in bookes what ancient writers speake,
> To rest in sleepe, which others may not breake,
> To taste (in houres secure from courtly strife)
> The soft obliuion of a carefull life?
> O when shall beanes vpon my boord appeare,
> Which wise *Pythagoras* esteem'd so deare?
> (p. 40)

Beaumont imposes a regular rhythm and a balanced rhetoric ('To reade . . . /To rest . . . /To taste . . .'). Horace's *inertibus horis* ('lazy hours') is expanded to 'in hours secure from courtly strife', an early example of the characteristic neoclassical formalisation of the Epicurean *topos* of rural retirement. The *topos,* derived from what is no more than an occasional theme in Horace, becomes so inseparable from Horace in the neoclassical mind, that Horace is made to conform to it. These interpolations cumulatively modify Horace in the direction of the Cavalier image of the modest *beatus.*

The cavalier image of Horace came into its own during and

immediately after the Civil War, especially in the later work of Abraham Cowley, who, having attempted the metaphysical style in *The Mistress* (1647) and a neoclassical epic in the *Davideis* (1668), turned finally to the poetry of retreat. The cavalier exiles (especially Denham and Cowley) developed modern theories of translation and imitation[15] (probably under the influence of d'Ablancourt) which mark the beginning of the Augustan mode of direct assimilation of classical literature. Casual modernisation of a foreign text can be found long before: Chaucer modernised Boccaccio, Wyatt changed Alamanni's 'Provence' to 'Kent', and Ben Jonson alters Catullus' 'Libyan sands' to 'Chelsea Fields'. John Denham developed the theory of consistent modernisation,[16] but it was Cowley who established the *practice* in his imitations of Horace *(Odes,* I, v, 'Epode II', and *Satires,* II, vi). With their imitation of Horace's 'The Town Mouse and the Country Mouse', Abraham Cowley and his biographer Bishop Sprat inaugurate the Augustan tradition of formal 'imitation' by introducing consistent modernisation and paraphrase of the classical model. The imitation is also important for its elaboration of the 'happy man' topic which had been emphasised by Beaumont.

The commonplaces of the Epicurean wish for retirement are fused with and revitalised by the aristocratic stance of disillusion and the spirit of retrenchment which pervades Cowley's *Essays* and informs the tone of Sprat's *Life of Cowley*. His account of Cowley's retirement is coloured by the Horatian *topos* in the description of Cowley's delight in 'temperate Pleasures . . . solitary Studies' and 'Some few Friends and Books'. Here life and fiction are inextricably mixed.

The opening of Cowley's imitation of the fable is not as ironic as it appears:

> At the large foot of a fair hollow tree,
> Close to plow'd ground, seated commodiously,
> His antient and Hereditary House,
> There dwelt a good substantial Country-Mouse.[17]

A playful wit arises from the incongruous weight of 'commodiously', 'antient and Hereditary', and 'substantial' (none of which appear in Horace), but the *Essays* make it clear that Cowley's ideal landscape was not very different from this: 'And I never then proposed to my self any other advantage from His Majesties Happy Restoration, but the getting into some moderately convenient Retreat in the Country' (p. 220); 'I never had any other desire so strong, and so like to Covetousness as that one which I have had always, that I might be master at last of a small house and large garden, with very moderate conveniences ioyned to them' (p. 168). The Augustan poetry of retirement is often unconvincing to modern ears because its cultivation of humble self-sufficiency is so evidently a literary veneer adorning a genteel and far from humble existence. The epithets 'small' and 'little' become Cowley's short-hand obeisance to the Horatian happy man. They often perform the function of modifying and tempering an otherwise affluent description: 'I confess, I love Littleness almost in all things. A little convenient Estate, a little chearful House . . . a very little Feast . . .' (p. 179).

While Sprat's imitation of the first part of the poem is consistently plain and even Baconian in spirit,[18] Cowley introduces a neoclassical mixed style which owes something to Butler's *Hudibras* and which points the way towards the mock-heroic style of Dryden. Horace's playful mock-epic descriptions in the fable are transformed by Cowley into a bolder style. The formulaic 'Night had reached the mid-point of her journey across the heavens' becomes pure burlesque:

> It was the time, when witty Poets tell,
> That *Phoebus* into *Thetis* bosom fell:
> She blusht at first, and then put out the light,
> And drew the modest Curtains of the night.
> Plainly, the troth to tell, the Sun was set.
>
> (p. 162)

Compare Butler:

> We should, as learned Poets use,
> Invoke th'assistance of some *Muse.*
>
> (I, i, 631–2)

> The Sun had long since in the Lap
> Of *Thetis,* taken out his *Nap.*[19]
>
> (II, ii, 29–30)

Sometimes Cowley modulates into a more decorous neoclassical heroic style (in the manner of his own *Davideis*), still, of course, with comic intention:

> About the hour that *Cynthia's* Silver light,
> Had touch'd the pale Meridies of the night.
>
> (p. 162)

In the paraphrase of Horace, the impulse to refine and modernise the classical epic is finely balanced against a burlesque intention. Cowley intensifies the mock-heroic elements in the satire and extends the comic disparity of style and subject. Horace's description of the country mouse's modest fare is expanded by Cowley, who describes the food as:

> The precious Reliques, which at Harvest, he
> Had gather'd from the Reapers luxurie.
> (p. 161)

The Guest's pompous distaste for the rustic dwelling becomes a piece of satiric inflation in the manner of Restoration heroic drama:

> Why should a Soul, so virtuous and so great,
> Lose it self thus in an Obscure retreat?
> Let savage Beasts lodg in a Country Den.
> (p. 161)

Here we have satire on the kind of fustian rhetoric which was debunked in Buckingham's *The Rehearsal*. Sprat's and Cowley's imitation of Horace is important as the first formal 'imitation' of a Roman satire, as an aristocratic appropriation of the Horatian happy man and as an exploration of the resources of the neoclassical burlesque and mock-heroic.

CLEVELAND AND OLDHAM: EXTREMISTS VS EXTREMISTS

The balanced and decorous neoclassicism cultivated by Denham, Waller and Cowley during and after the Civil War was not the sole literary mode employed by the royalists in their resistance to the Puritans and the republicans. Two sides of Donne's poetic persona were developed into two quite different cavalier styles: the cynical plain style of Carew and Suckling, and the burlesque metaphysical style of Cleveland. It is of great historical significance that all three royalist poetic styles, the neoclassical, the libertine and the late metaphysical, drew upon the resources of materialistic or rationalistic philosophy.[20] The neoclassical voice ultimately established its hegemony, but in the process assimilated something from the other two.

When the tide began to turn against the royalists in the mid-1640s, John Cleveland revived the savagery of Elizabethan satire and deployed it against his immediate political enemies. In 1644, the invasion of England by the Scottish army stung Cleveland into Marstonian fury:

> Ring the bells backward; I am all on fire,
> Not all the buckets in a Countrey Quire

> Shall quench my rage . . .
> And where's the Stoick can his wrath appease
> To see his Countrey sicke of *Pym's* disease.[21]

The 'extremism' of the Parliamentary and Presbyterian mal-
contents is answered by a satiric extremism through which the
traditional Juvenalian stance (in the alternative mask of Archi-
lochus the Greek satirist) is almost burlesqued:

> Come keen *Iambicks,* with your Badgers feet,
> And Badger-like, bite till your teeth do meet.
> Help ye tart Satyrists, to imp my rage,
> With all the Scorpions that should whip this age.
> *Scots* are like Witches; do but whet your pen,
> Scratch til the blood come; they'l not hurt you then.

(p. 29)

The introduction of an Elizabethan satiric sadism seems more in-
congruously artificial in a contemporary political pamphlet than
in the coterie academic satires of a Marston or a Guilpin. But
Cleveland's adherence to the Elizabethan theory of satiric rough-
ness[22] should not blind us to his real qualities as a poet.

Cleveland's development of the Donnean conceit has often
been regarded as decadent and uncontrolled. But the polemical
purpose of Cleveland's conceits required a new method. He
ridicules the Westminster Assembly and the Scottish army by
setting in motion trains of incongruous metaphors and similes
which reduce the satiric victim to the level of the grotesque
and the monstrous. The 'Mixt Assembly' of clergy and laity is
presented in imagery of *disorder* and *incongruity*. A train of animal
images runs through the poem ('Fleabitten Synod', 'Woolpack
Clergie', 'strange *Grottesco*', 'pye-bald crew', 'ring-streaked
lambs', 'Miscellany Satyr') and is interwoven with imagery of
cosmological and theological disorder ('Rude Chaos', 'they'l not
own/Their fellowes at the Resurrection', 'they'l passe in Story/
For sinners half refin'd in Purgatory'). The theme of incongruity
implicit in the title is further developed in a series of scornful
parallel terms: 'Clerks and Elders *ana*', 'Lay-men . . . Clergie',
'Church and States', 'Lay-thiefe . . . Clergie', 'Burgesse . . . Vicar'.
Finally a series of images relate to disordered generation: 'Dis-
colour'd Mates', 'borne a dappl'd son', 'brought forth speckled
and ring-streaked lambs', 'all th'Adulteries of twisted nature',
'Make a couple', 'saddle', 'get a clap', 'twill not be/A Child-birth,
but a Goale-Deliverie', 'Mules . . . generate'. The last lines of the
poem serves to recapitulate a number of these image rows:

Thus *Moses* Law is violated now,
The Ox and Asse go yok'd in the same plough.
Resign thy Coach-box *Twisse; Brook's* Preacher, he
Would sort the beasts with more conformity.
Water & earth make but one Globe, a Roundhead
Is Clergy-Lay *Party-per-pale* compounded.

(p. 28)

The mixing of sublime and low imagery (the cosmic and the bestial) was to be developed in Augustan satire by Oldham, Dryden and particularly by Pope, whose *Dunciad* diminishes the Grub Street hacks to the level of insects, maggots and vermin, and degrades their work in the imagery of disordered births and cosmic parody. A similar aristocratic presumption of shared traditional values informs Pope's poem, and enables the satirist to present images of disorder without himself lapsing into disorder. Pope's satire differs in so far as he allowed the neoclassical tradition of Cowley and Dryden and the satiric delicacy of Horace to control the violent fulminations of the imagery. Cleveland's assumption of the Marstonian persona gives an impression of impotent rage which is further intensified by the grotesque ingenuity of the conceits. The Scot's hunger is described in a series of associated images:

No; the *Scots-Errant* fight, and fight to eat;
Their Estrich-stomacks make their swords their meat:
Nature with Scots as Tooth-drawers hath dealt,
Who use to hang their Teeth upon their Belt.
Yet wonder not at this their happy choice;
The Serpent's fatall still to *Paradise.*
Sure *England* hath the Hemerods, and these
On the North Posterne of the patient seize,
Like Leeches: thus they physically thirst
After our blood, but in the cure shall burst.

(p. 31)

Fuller in his life of Cleveland[23] described his metaphors as 'carrying in them a *difficult plainness, difficult* at the *hearing,* plain at the *considering* thereof'. The remark captures well the combination of harsh metaphysical wit and Augustan rational toughness and economy of expression. The progression of metaphors is perverse yet logical: the Scots become successively ostriches, dentists, serpents, haemorrhoids (both 'piles' and 'serpents') and leeches. The display of useless fangs does not make the Scots incapable of doing harm in England ('Paradise'); they are, on the contrary, serpents ('Hemerods') whose bite was thought to cause unstanchable bleeding. Cleveland's intellectual wit, his tone of arrogant

superiority and his doctrinaire royalism, produced satire of un-
precedented pungency and virulence in support of traditional
law and order against the threat of anarchy posed by the Puritans
and Roundhead parliamentarians.

Cleveland's scurrilous wit influenced the royalist poetry of the
early 1660s. Robert Wild, in his popular royalist panegyric 'Iter
Boreale'1660), remembers the satirist's frustration in the days of
the Commonwealth:

> I that enraged at the times and Rump,
> Had gnaw'd my goose-quill to the very stump,
> And flung that in the fire, no more to write,
> But to sit down poor Britain's Heraclite . . .[24]

Christopher Wase, in *Divination* (1666), a reply to an anti-loyalist
poem, revives the Elizabethan satiric vein in a more crabbed and
obscure form than Cleveland's. But these are exceptions. The new
generation of court wits, nurtured by the elegant couplets of
Denham, Waller and Cowley, found Cleveland's 'strong lines'
distasteful and overstrained.

The only major Restoration satirist who successfully revived
the older conception of Juvenalian satire was John Oldham, who
died at the age of thirty in 1683. Dryden's famous Elegy praises
Oldham with reservations which remind us of Oldham's un-
Augustan qualities:

> O early ripe! to thy abundant store
> What could advancing Age have added more?
> It might (what Nature never gives the young)
> Have taught the numbers of thy native Tongue.
> But Satyr needs not those, and Wit will shine
> Through the harsh cadence of a rugged line.
> A noble Error, and but seldom made,
> When Poets are by too much force betray'd.[25]

Dryden grapples delicately with a characteristic neoclassical
dilemma: stylistic decorum suggests that a 'harsh cadence' and a
forceful style are appropriate to satire (a low-style genre), but the
overriding value of 'correctness' and 'urbanity' dictate a smooth-
ness of 'numbers' and a rational poise quite absent from Oldham's
satires. William Soames reprimands 'school-Master' Oldham (he
was private tutor to Sir Edward Thurland's grandson) without
any of Dryden's elegiac equivocation:

> From the Boys hands, take Horace into Thine,
> And thy rude Satyrs, by his Rules, refine.[26]

This criticism applies particularly to Oldham's earlier phase which culminated in the violently Juvenalian *Satyrs upon the Jesuits* (1681). In the 'Advertisement' to *Some New Pieces* (1681), Oldham revives the Elizabethan theory of verse satire as a vituperative and rugged genre:

> I did not so much mind the Cadence, as the Sense and Expressiveness of my Words . . . And certainly no one that pretends to distinguish the several Colours of Poetry, would expect that *Juvenal*, when he is lashing of Vice, and Villany, should flow so smoothly as *Ovid*, or *Tibullus*, when they are describing Amours and Gallantries, and have nothing to disturb and ruffle the Evenness of their Stile.[27]

Oldham's commitment to 'roughness' in satire and to the ancient conception of satire as a curse is usually regarded as retrograde in the context of the age of Dryden. However, it should be remembered that the Augustan norm of elegant correctness was never without rival aesthetics. Translators of Juvenal during the succeeding decade followed Oldham's theory of prosodic decorum and not Dryden's. Thomas Shadwell, for example, echoes Oldham in requiring a turbulent style in satire:

> . . . I do not think great smoothness is required in a *Satyr*, which ought to have a *severe* kind of *roughness* as most fit for *reprehension*, and not that gentle *smoothness* which is necessary to *insinuation*.[28]

The most eloquent defence of Oldham's Juvenalian vehemence came from the satirist Robert Gould, who in his elegy defends Oldham against the aspersions of the polite wits:

> How wide shoot they, that strive to blast thy Fame,
> By saying, that thy Verse was rough and lame;
> They would have Satyr their Compassion move,
> And writ so plyant, nicely, and so smooth,
> As if the Muse were in a Flux of Love:
> But who of Knaves, and Fops, and Fools would sing,
> Must Force, and Fire, and Indignation bring
> For 'tis no Satyr if it has no Sting:
> In short, who in that Field would Famous be,
> Must think, and write like *Juvenal* and Thee.
> (Oldham, *Works*, IV, sig. B5^v)

Paul Korshin sees Oldham as a leading exponent of the poetics of 'dissent' in contrast to the poetics of 'concord' propagated by Dryden, Mulgrave and others.[29] The political and ideological significance of this stylistic struggle is considerable. The use of an Elizabethan satiric rhetoric of 'extremism' in contemporary political and religious controversies served to exacerbate the polemical atmosphere and to heighten the social contradictions. Dryden's eclectic satiric theory, blending the sharpness of satire with the 'majesty' of the heroic style, corresponds to the rhetoric of 'moderation' which emerged triumphant at the political level in the constitutional settlements of 1688, at the level of thought in the philosophy of Locke, and at the level of literary history in the crystallisation of the neoclassical tradition associated with Walsh, Temple and Congreve, whose call for 'correctness' was answered by the young Alexander Pope.

Oldham's importance as a satirist lies in his extension of the resources of the Juvenalian voice. A characteristic device is his inversion of the satiric persona first used in the Pindarique 'Satyr against Vertue', in which a profane abuser of virtue speaks with the voice of magniloquent authority and righteous indignation. The effect of the poem is partly one of ironic ridicule (of Rochester's libertinism) and partly one of witty play. The abuse of virtue is couched in the language of courtly refinement:

> Vertue! thou solemn grave impertinence,
>   Abhor'd by all the Men of Wit and Sense.
> Thou damn'd Fatigue! that clogst lifes journey here
>   Though thou no weight of wealth or profit bear;
>
>   (*Works*, I, 93–4)

Oldham sometimes anticipates the ironic heroic style of Dryden's *Absalom and Achitophel*:

> If Human Kind to thee e'er Worship paid;
>   They were by Ignorance misled,
> That only them devout, and thee a Goddess made.
>   Known haply in the Worlds rude untaught infancy,
> Before it had out grown its childish innocence,
>   Before it had arriv'd at sense,
> Or reach'd the Manhood, and discretion of Debauchery.
>
>   (p. 95)

The stylistic effect here should be clearly distinguished from mock-heroic. In the latter, knaves and fools are lashed or ridiculed by the satiric speaker, who attributes to them an incongruously heroic role which is deflated by the introduction of occasional bathetic details. In Oldham's poem, the knave is the speaker and virtue is lashed in an ironical heroic style. In mock-heroic, the heroic is normative; in the ironic heroic, the libertine perspective ('Debauchery') is presented as if it were normative. Oldham's later recantation of his abuse of virtue (in 'Counterpart to the Satyr against Vertue') reminds us that irony in the presentation of a dramatised persona was an unstable ingredient, whose effects could not be safely predicted. The materialism of Hobbes and the libertinism of Rochester were persuasive enough to put in doubt the readers' response to such indirect attacks upon their ethics.

Oldham's use of the knavish persona in *Satyrs upon the Jesuits* is unambiguous. 'Loyala's Will', the third satire, is a Juvenalian rant in the voice of Ignatius Loyola, the founder of the Jesuit mission. Ambiguity is prevented by the use of a narrative frame, which briefly directs the Juvenalian indignation to its proper object:

> Like Delphic Hag of old, by Fiend possest,
> He swells, wild Frenzy heaves his panting Breast,
> His bristling Hairs stick up, his Eye-balls glow,
> And from his Mouth long strakes of Drivel flow:
> Thrice with due Rev'rence he himself doth cross,
> Then thus his Hellish Oracles disclose.
>
> (p. 40)

Loyala incites his followers in the grandiloquent tones of a Tamburlaine:

> Plot, enterprize, contrive, endeavour, spare
> No Toil, nor Pains, no Death, nor Danger fear:
> Restless your Aims pursue: let no defeat
> Your sprightly Courage, and Attempts rebate,
> But urge to fresh, and bolder, ne'er to end
> Till the whole World to our great *Caliph* bend.
>
> (pp. 41–2)

The first satire, 'Garnet's Ghost addressing to the Jesuits', is a pure soliloquy. The absence of 'the satirist' required an overtly satanic speaker, who urges the Jesuits to plot against James I and to harden their hearts against religion and virtue:

> Let no such Toys mislead you from the Road
> Of Glory, nor infect your Souls with Good:
> Let never bold incroaching Virtue dare
> With her grim holy Face to enter there,
> No, not in very *Dream* . . .
> Let true substantial wickedness take place, ⎫
> Usurp and Reign; let it the very trace   ⎬
> (If any yet be left) of good deface.   ⎭
>
> (p. 11)

In the second satire, the satirist speaks in *propria persona,* castigating the Jesuits in the savage manner of Marston and the Jacobean satirists:

> Monsters avaunt! May some kind Whirlwind sweep
> Our Land, and drown these *Locusts* in the deep:
> Hence ye loath'd Objects of our Scorn, and Hate
> With all the Curses of an injur'd *State:*
> Go, foul *Impostors,* to some duller Soil.
>
> (p. 37)

It is perhaps significant that Oldham indulged in the Elizabethan style of direct abuse in only one of the satires; the association of the 'satirist' with a 'squint-eyed' diseased vision was unacceptable to the developing neoclassical taste and could only prove effective when the cankered muse spoke through the persona of the victim of reprehension. To this extent the Juvenalian vehemence of the *Satyrs* is accommodated to the requirements of Augustan 'good taste'. Mere scurrility is transformed by irony and indirection into complex literary art. In this respect we are right to feel that the Elizabethan and Juvenalian gestures made in the 'Prologue' to the Satyrs are not a reliable guide to Oldham's practice. His use of the 'Indignation' *topos* leads us to expect direct invective:

> 'Tis pointed *Satyr,* and the *shafts* of Wit
> For such a *Prize* are th' only Weapons fit:
> Nor needs there Art, or *Genius* here to use,
> Where *Indignation* can create a Muse:
> Should Parts, and Nature fail, yet very spite
> Would make the arrant'st *Wild,* or *Withers* write.

His 'rank envenom'd spleen' will whet his 'stabbing Pen' and his ink will 'gnaw' like '*Aquafortis*'. These traditional teeth-barings do not lead us to expect the renewal of traditional methods achieved in the satires which ensue. In the final satire, following a hint from Horace's *Satires,* I, viii, Oldham introduces an extreme displacement of perspective by making the speaker an object (the wooden image of St Ignatius). The device enables Oldham to subject the Jesuit to gratuitous indignities:

> Now on my Head the Birds their Relicks leave,
> And Spiders in my mouth their Arras weave:
> And persecuted Rats oft find in me
> A refuge, and Religious Sanctuary.
>
> (p. 74)

Here we are far removed from the abusive rhetoric of Marston and Cleveland; the stylistic sophistication announces the mock-heroic idiom of Dryden and Pope. The sublime and the ridiculous are mixed in an Augustan brew with a strong infusion of rational poise and elegant wit.

After the *Satyrs upon the Jesuits,* Oldham fell under the neo-classical influence of Boileau and Dryden, and in his translations and imitations of the Latin satirists he began to favour a tempered satiric voice, abandoning the native strain of 'extremist' polemic for the assimilative classicism of Cowley and Dryden. Following Dryden's liberal theory as expressed in the Preface to Ovid's *Epistles* (1680), Oldham directed his energies to a re-creation and modernisation of classical culture. Rachel Trickett rightly notes that 'the topical vigour characteristic of contemporary satire was held in check by continual allusion to another poet's work, of which the general moral reflections were allowed to remain unchanged'.[30] The practice of imitation was based on the assumption that nature is universal and unchanging and that the classics embodied the essential features of general nature: 'Nature and Homer were . . . the same.' Such a view, which became dominant in the first half of the eighteenth century, favoured a range of satiric voices which remained on the Horatian side of Juvenal and which preserved the satirist's persona from the moral ambiguities and factitious irrationality of the scourge of villany. Oldham was the last major satirist to cultivate successfully the cankered muse.

BUTLER AND ROCHESTER: LOW-STYLE SATIRE

Having defined 'Horatian' satire as that mode of satire which conforms to a plain-style norm, we have been able to reserve the category of low-style satire for that historical moment when a true low-style transformation of the satiric persona was conceivable. Only in the seventeenth century were the conditions appropriate for the genesis of a satiric style which was based upon a *low view of man.* The Greek atomists (Epicurus, Democritus and Leucippus) produced no 'materialist' culture; the Roman Lucretius, in *De Rerum Natura,* transforms Epicurus' philosophy into a divine vision in the high style. In contrast, the rationalism, materialism and scepticism of Hobbes, Bacon and Glanvill are paralleled or reflected in the work of the major poets of the century. Samuel Butler's *Hudibras* and Rochester's satires cannot be fully understood outside the context of seventeenth-century scientific and materialist thought. The absence of classical precedent for low-style verse satire highlights the innovative nature of the

English writers' work, which makes a remarkably fresh use of the classical tradition.

The overt object of satire in Butler's *Hudibras* is the moral, social, political and intellectual character of the defeated enemies of the restored monarchy. Hudibras himself is a Presbyterian knight whose faith is blind and hypocritical, and whose scholastic learning is useless and obscure. Ralph, his squire, is a mystical enthusiast (probably based on Thomas Vaughan) who belongs to the camp of the Independents. The mock-heroes of the narrative incongruously inhabit the world of chivalric romance, which provides the poem's allegorical[31] framework of adventure, armed combat and gallantry. Butler's anti-heroic stance is central to his satiric manner, and is more thoroughgoing than even Juvenal's. The rationalist critique of epic poetry conducted by Cowley, Davenant and Hobbes in the 1650s corresponds closely to Butler's attitudes. Hobbes's anti-romantic theories were well-known:

> There are some that are not pleased with fiction, unless it be bold, not onely to exceed the *work,* but also the *possibility* of nature: they would have impenetrable Armors, Inchanted Castles, invulnerable bodies, Iron Men, flying Horses, and a thousand other such things . . . Against such I defend you . . . In old time amongst the Heathen such strange fictions and Metamorphoses were not so remote from the Articles of their Faith as they are now from ours.[32]

While Davenant and Cowley wrote neoclassical epics which conformed to rationalist articles of faith, Butler performed a complementary task in castigating the irrationality of the Puritan and republican articles of faith. His choice of allegorical vehicle enabled him to associate the tenets of Puritanism with the outmoded machinery of the romance epic. The satire is thus double-edged. The knight's horse Rosinante is ridiculous in comparison with the romance ideal, but, at the same time, the romance ideal itself is deflated. Bucephalus is compared *unfavourably* with Rosinante:

> That *Caesar's* Horse, who, as fame goes,
> Had Corns upon his feet and toes,
> Was not by half so tender-hooft,
> Nor trod upon the ground so soft.
>
> (I, i, 427–30)

W. O. S. Sutherland rightly emphasises that 'the anti-heroic is basic to the poet's conception, not just a technique'.[33] The absence of positive ideals in Butler's satire gives the anti-heroism its bleak and pervasive quality. All theological speculation, whether Puritan or Catholic, is unprofitable. All heroic ethics are suspect. In *Hudibras,* Part I, canto iii, Butler parodies the Stoic distinction between active and passive valour by arguing that Hudibras's heroism is enhanced by his defeat. The knightly connotations of valour and honour are degraded by the introduction of imagery drawn from the Puritan commercial world of the urban bourgeoisie. Butler offers no alternative heroism, explicitly or implicitly. In satirising the utilitarian aspects of Puritanism, Butler projects a conception of heroism which is the antithesis of the Puritan vision of Christ's passive heroism as expressed in the ninth book of *Paradise Lost:*

> He that is valiant, and dares fight,
> Though drubb'd can lose no honour by't.
> Honours' a *lease for lives to come,*
> And cannot be *extended* from
> The legal Tenant: 'tis a Chattel,
> Not to be forfeited in battel.
> (1041–6)

Even scientific investigation is inclined to indulge in wild fancy and useless speculation. The wizard Sidrophel represents both the medieval and the modern abuses of learning: early in Part II he is an astrologer, but is later transformed into a Royal Society experimeter. This absolute scepticism anticipates Swift's in the voyage to Laputa. Robert Hooke's observations made with the microscope are satirised in demeaning fashion:

> He [Sidrophel] knew whats'ever's to be known,
> But much more then he knew, would own . . .
> How many scores a *Flea* will jump,
> Of his own length, from head to rump; . . .
> Whether his *Snout* a perfect *Nose* is,
> And not an Elephants *Proboscis,*
> How many different *Specieses*
> Of Maggots breed in Rotten Cheese,
> And which are next of kin to those,
> Engendered in a *Chaundler's* nose.
> Or those not seen, but understood,
> That live in *Vinegar* and *Wood.*
> (II, iii, 297–8, 311–12, 315–22)

Butler is linked to the neoclassical tradition primarily by his linguistic values. The bizarre linguistic surface of *Hudibras* (doggerel rhythms, deformed rhymes, cant idioms, indecorous diction) testifies to the values of lucid speech which are *implied* throughout. Like Jonson, Butler believes that a man is expressed in his language; the distortions of language which prevail in *Hudibras* are an expression of man's distortion of reason. Butler's Baconian empiricism, his rejection of useless learning and metaphysical speculation, were to be fully assimilated into the main Augustan tradition and re-expressed by Swift, Pope and the Scriblerians in the early eighteenth century, notably in *Gulliver's Travels, The Memoirs of Scriblerus* and *The Dunciad.* However, Butler's scepticism is quite unrelenting, and his vision of man is certainly the lowest of the major Augustan satirists. While Bacon's account of the 'idols' (false ways of seeing) presupposes a potentially healthy functioning of the human mind, Butler's pessimism is unrelieved in satires such as 'Satyr upon the Royal Society', 'The Elephant in the Moon', 'Satyr upon the Weakness and Misery of Man', and 'Satyr upon Marriage', in which an airy and unrealisable image of 'Reason' fades before the reality of man's incorrigible irrationality. In the 'Satyr upon the Licentious Age of Charles II', Butler expresses a deeply depressing view of man's failure to respond to the appeals of the new Age of Reason:

> So simple were those Times, when a grave *Sage*
> Could with an Oldwive's-Tale instruct the Age;
> Teach Virtue, more fantastick Ways and nice,
> Than ours will now endure t'improve in vice,
> Make a dull Sentence, and a moral Fable
> Do more, than all our Holdings-forth are able;
> A forc'd obscure Mythology convince,
> Beyond our worst Inflictions upon Sins . . .
> What Fops had these been, had they liv'd with us,
> Where the best Reason's made ridiculous;
> And all the plain and sober Things we say,
> By Raillery are put beside their Play?[34]

Butler sees no virtue in the primitive times when men's minds were clouded with superstition and fancy. There is no nostalgia for a simple pagan morality, but only bitterness at the perversity of Restoration society, which, having overcome the Puritan régime and its irrational 'enthusiasm', undermines reason in an orgy of sophisticated libertinism. It is significant that it required the editorial engineering of Zachary Grey (1744) to establish the Tory orthodoxy of *Hudibras.*[35] The Augustan positives which were widely assumed by the conservative literary establishment of the mid-eighteenth century were no doubt supplied mentally by the reader of Butler's entirely negative satires.[36]

The Earl of Rochester is the most controversial of the Restoration satirists; the critical reactions to his work are confusingly

various. Pinto regards him as a 'spiritual explorer';[37] Dale
Underwood sees him as an unintelligent nihilist;[38] D. M. Vieth
claims that he is a traditional Augustan;[39] and D. H. Griffin thinks
he is a 'perplexed rather than a dogmatic doubter'.[40] Evidently
exclusive choices cannot be fruitfully made, but of Rochester's
remarkably vigorous materialism there can be little doubt. As a
court wit and as an amateur in poetry, he inevitably failed to
think through his philosophical ideas in a consecutive and dis-
cursive form. Yet, embedded in the poems, there is a warmly
realised materialism which is far removed from mere libertinism.
Gilbert Burnet's persuasive and humanely liberal account of his
conversations with the ailing Rochester[41] give one a vivid im-
pression of Rochester's scrupulous consistency in his rejection of
metaphysical or transcendental ideas. While he confesses that he
believes the soul is a separable entity, Rochester concludes that
with the destruction of the brain and its memory cells the soul
must 'begin a new Course'. Similarly, while Rochester acknow-
ledges a vitalistic conception of God as a 'vast power' scarcely
discernible from Nature, his views on 'Revealed Religion' were
advanced:

> God's communicating his Mind to one Man, was the putting it
> in his power to cheat the World: for Prophecies and Miracles,
> the World had been always full of strange Stories; for the
> boldness and cunning of Contrivers meeting with the Simplicity
> and Credulity of the People, things were easily received ... And
> the first three Chapters of *Genesis* he thought could not be
> true, unless they were Parables ... The believing Mysteries, he
> said, made way for all the Jugglings of Priests; for they getting
> the people under them in that Point, set out to them what they
> pleased; and giving it a hard Name, and calling it a *Mystery*
> the People were tamed ... *(Some Passages,* pp. 65–6, 72)

Rochester's views, which have something of William Blake's
antinomial pungency, are related by a master of Christian apolo-
getics, who adds a full measure of confutation. The death-bed
conversion, which followed, according to Burnet, a year after
these conversations, is perhaps not surprising in a man of such
strong convictions. In Burnet's words, 'none of all our Libertines
understood better than he, the secret Mysteries of Sin'.
    Kenneth Murdock once wrote 'there must have been some sense
of values that transcended those that his professed materialism
allowed',[42] which I would reword as 'his materialism assumed
values which transcended its professed meaning'. Rochester's late
conversion resembles the passage from one side of a mirror to the

other: the apparent contradiction of his materialism is really its restatement in a form which involves no more than a graceful (if painful) inversion of its propositions. Much of Rochester's finest poetry takes the form of inverted religion.

The satires of Rochester are produced from three main materials: first, the tradition of in-group scandal and topical lampoon; secondly, the classical formal satire (especially as modernised by Boileau); and thirdly, the philosophy of Thomas Hobbes and contemporary Epicureanism. Rochester tempers the abusive directness of lampoon with the elegance of a court wit without diluting its obscenity and racy naturalism. He developed the subjective dimension of the satiric persona which had hitherto evolved only in the Horatian tradition of Jonson and Cowley or in the restricted declamatory voice of Marston's satyr-satirist. The normal 'satirist' in Rochester's work is a bibulous rake of an unorthodox materialist persuasion. Anthony à Wood, a contemporary, observed that 'The Court . . . not only debauched him; but made him a perfect Hobbist.'[43] The term 'Hobbist' was loosely used to denote 'free-thinker', but we are justified in treating the epithet in its strict sense when considering the ethical and epistemological attitudes associated with Rochester's satiric persona.[44]

In the opening pages of *Leviathan* (1651), Hobbes lays down the foundations of his ethical and political views in terms of a rigorously argued sensationalist psychology, according to which man is a self-motivating machine, whose mind is governed by the same laws of mechanical motion which govern the physical world. Man's moral values and political principles are an extension of his physiology: whatever sustains bodily 'motion' is good and whatever interferes with it (ultimately death) is bad. In 'A Satyr against Reason and Mankind', Rochester compares the 'instinct' of animals favourably with the 'Reason' of man. By 'Reason', Rochester means the 'Right Reason' of the Neoplatonists and the Puritan enthusiasts, who pursue metaphysical dreams and 'leaving light of nature, sense, behind' try to swim 'with bladders of philosophy' (that is, metaphysics). Rochester later introduces an *adversarius* in the character of a Puritan divine (with 'formal [Geneva] band') who praises that 'Reason, by whose aspiring influence/We take a flight beyond material sense'. Rochester's satirist replies in orthodox Hobbesian terms:

> But thoughts are given for action's government;
> Where action ceases, thought's impertinent.
> Our sphere of action is life's happiness,
> And he who thinks beyond, thinks like an ass.
> Thus, whilst against false reasoning I inveigh,

> I own right reason, which I would obey:
> That reason which distinguishes by sense
> And gives us rules of good and ill from thence . . .
>
>   (94–101)[45]

Christian Neoplatonic 'Right Reason' is ousted by Hobbesian 'right reason'. Ethical values are derived from 'sense'. Rochester proceeds with a Hobbesian analysis of man's moral motivation, which, it is argued, is 'all from fear, to make himself secure'. But he departs from Hobbes in regarding the slavish concern for security as an ignoble trait which contrasts with the honest instinct of the animal. Indeed, Rochester's humanistic and courtly values drive him to the point of suspending his materialist convictions:

> But a meek, humble man of honest sense,
> Who, preaching peace, does practice continence;
> Whose pious life's a proof he does believe
> Mysterious truths, which no man can conceive,
> If upon earth there dwell such God-like men,
> I'll here recant my paradox to them,
> Adore those shrines of virtue, homage pay,
> And, with the rabble world, their laws obey.
>
>   (p. 101)

This was the chink in Rochester's philosophical armour which Burnet probed. Rochester's 'low' view of man is not an ignoble view. The unqualified cynicism of the early 'Tunbridge Wells' ('What a Thing is Man') is untypical. His disgust at the base irrationality of man is expressed with an intensity of feeling which heightens the most naked obscenity of language. In 'A Ramble in St James's Park', Rochester castigates his mistress Corinna's coldly calculating sexual promiscuity with bitter intensity:

> There's something generous in mere lust.
> But to turn damned abandoned jade
> When neither head nor tail persuade;
> To be a whore in understanding,
> A passive pot for fools to spend in!
>
>   (p. 43)

Like D. H. Lawrence, Rochester gives the life of the senses a kind of moral dignity. A 'low' view is given an intensity of realisation which makes it normative. On the other hand, Rochester's world is one of disillusion and disappointment[46] and not of messianic hope.

As a low-style satirist, Rochester differs from Butler in stance and in satiric tone. Butler tempers a Baconian rationalism with a scepticism bordering on cynicism, while Rochester intensifies and deepens a Hobbesian naturalism. Butler's hudibrastic style was usually regarded as having affinities with the 'low and familiar way' of Horace. Dryden, who preferred a more majestic style, found Butler's undignified manner unsuccessful: 'for it turns earnest too much to jest, and gives us a boyish kind of pleasure'.[47] While Rochester's satires do not conform to Dryden's conception of Juvenal's majestic and 'sounding' reprehension, he has strong affinities with the native Elizabethan *vir iratus*. Rochester often employs Juvenalian rhetoric to legitimise his use of the popular lampoon, which Dryden regarded as a poor way of making a man 'appear a fool, a blockhead, or a Knave'.[48] One of the points of controversy which emerges in Rochester's 'quarrels' with John Dryden, the Earl of Mulgrave and Sir Carr Scroope is a disagreement about the satirist's proper role. Mulgrave's Horatian credentials are boldly displayed in the *Essay on Poetry* (1682):

> Rage you must hide, and prejudice lay down;
> A Satyr's Smile is sharper than his Frown.[49]

Carr Scroope's replies to Rochester's attacks rest on the claim that the attacks are malicious and written in the spirit of 'ill-natured jest'. The Earl's reposte in 'On Poet Ninny' opens with an attack on Scroope's 'harmless malice':

> Crushed by that just contempt his follies bring
> On his crazed head, the vermin fain would sting:
> But never satyr did so softly bite,
> Or Gentle George [Etheridge] himself more gently write.
>
> (p. 141)

Here, unadorned by poetic ornament, is the contemptuous *animus* of Pope's portrait of Lord Harvey (Sporus).[50] While the Augustan satirist often undermines his victim by declaring him creatively inert and impotent, Rochester's brand of 'biting' satire has something of the sadism of primitive satire. When Burnet questioned Rochester's spiteful and vengeful attitude to satire, the earl replied:

> A man could not write with life unless he were heated by Revenge; For to make a *Satyre* without Resentments, upon the cold Notions of *Phylosophy,* was as if a man would in cold blood, cut men's throats who had never offended him. (*Some Passages,* p. 54)

Rochester is adding a new dimension to the Juvenalian emphasis on subjective *animus*. The subjectivity of Juvenal is a depersonalised declamatory voice which lacks the autobiographical 'honesty' of Horace's persona. Rochester adopts the expressive first-person apologetics of the Horatian speaker, but makes the traditional 'Honest Muse' speak with a starker and more sensuous immediacy. The half-witty, half-penitential 'To the Postboy' is a low-style equivalent of Horace's confessional satires, in which he honestly acknowledges his own moral shortcomings, thus enhancing the autobiographical authenticity of the satires.

In other respects, too, Rochester entered into a creative engagement with the Horatian tradition in satire. His most important contribution to the Augustan tradition is perhaps his influential 'An Allusion to Horace, the Tenth Satire of the First Book' which is the first fully-fledged English Augustan 'Imitation'.[51] However, Rochester is by no means an orthodox transmitter of Horatian ideas. Horace's easy assumption of shared 'rational' cultural values unerringly guides the reader's interpretation of his irony and mock-devices. Rochester's relationship with the reader is less unquestioningly congruent. On the one hand, his aristocratic rank and milieu inevitably strengthened a taste for refinement and wit; on the other hand, his naturalistic philosophical attitudes inclined him to the racy idiom of the town and the honest obscenity of the rake. In 'Timon', an imitation of Boileau's third satire, loosely related to Horace's satire on the bore, Timon tries to shake off the bore's attentions by belittling his own poetic talents in a most un-Augustan manner:

> I vowed I was no more a wit than he:
> Unpracticed and unblessed in poetry.
> A song to Phyllis I perhaps might make
> But never rhymed but for my pintle's [penis's] sake.
>
> (p. 66)

The ironic self-abasement of the first couplet is balanced by the brazen confession of the second couplet.

In 'An Allusion', Rochester's Augustan orthodoxy is no less in doubt. Leaving aside the unflattering implications of the substitution of Dryden for the primitive Lucilius, the reader is torn between a recognisably Augustan poetic doctrine (which recommends decorum, elegance and good-humoured satire) and an un-Augustan admiration for the artless 'Nature' embodied in the plays of Thomas Shadwell. His admiration is qualified, but is quite at odds with Dryden's judgement in *Mac Flecknoe*. Rochester's sympathy with the 'bourgeois' dramatist's unsophisticated and naturalistic style is reinforced by his distaste for the

affected sophistication of Dryden's early style. But such is his dis-
like of the upstart Dryden that he is not above turning the courtly
neoclassical values against him:

> And may not I have leave unpartially
> To search and censure Dryden's works, and try
> If those gross faults his choice pen does commit
> Proceed from want of judgement, or of wit;
> Or if his lumpish fancy does refuse
> Spirit and grace to his loose, slattern muse?
>
> (p. 125)

Rochester appears to adopt contradictory literary values. What is
admired in 'hasty Shadwell' is censured in Dryden. But it makes
more sense to regard Rochester's apparent inconsistency as a sign
of an ambitiously extended perspective; neoclassical values are
augmented by the 'bourgeois' values of individuality and spon-
taneity, which were later to inform the work of Addison and
Steele thirty years or more after Rochester's death.

Rochester develops Horatian satire's use of personae, and
especially the use of the *adversarius* or interlocutor. He goes
beyond Horace in the counterposing of 'points of view', and his
unorthodox ethical stance allowed him to explore the varieties of
'rationality' in a manner anticipated only by Ben Jonson.[52] The
dominant aristocratic libertine persona of 'Timon', 'Tunbridge
Wells', 'A Satyr on Charles II' and 'The Imperfect Enjoyment' is
given unqualified endorsement, but, in several of the later poems,
Rochester introduces a complicating interplay of personae or an
ambiguous dramatisation. In the 'Satyr against Reason and Man-
kind', the interplay of personae is unambiguous: the qualified
Hobbesian voice eclipses entirely the Puritan 'formal band and
beard', who is no more than a dramatised antagonist.

In 'A Letter from Artemisia in the Town to Chloe in the
Country' a double satiric perspective is developed. Artemisia is a
politer, more Augustan voice than Rochester's normal libertine
persona, but there remains a strong naturalistic note; the bitter
arguments against heartless lust which heighten the rollicking wit
of 'A Ramble . . .' reappear in a more elegant form:

> They [women] call whatever is not common nice,
> And deaf to nature's rule, or love's advice,
> Forsake the pleasure to pursue the vice.
>
> (p. 106)

Artemisia relates the arrival in town of a foppish and loquacious
'fine lady' whose dramatic monologue dominates the rest of the

poem. Her affectations and endless chatter are satirised by Artemisia, but not without a qualifying admiration. The lady is 'this mixed thing . . . So very wise, yet so impertinent'. The lady's account of the predatory Corinna, who seduces, robs and murders a booby heir, has all the honest disgust of the satirist in 'A Satyr against Reason . . .', but the disgust is mediated by a voice which is itself the object of Artemisia's more orthodox satiric eye. The interplay between Artemisia and the fine lady is absorbingly complex. Rochester's 'delicate' presentation of the fine lady succeeds in questioning the certainties and conventions of Augustan rationality; the affected domineering woman is not treated with a simple, witty dismissiveness. Rochester is here anticipating Pope's *Rape of the Lock* and the 'Moral Essays' on women. Harold Love, in his valuable essay on Rochester, stresses the transitional nature of the poem: 'The day of the irresponsible censor, the malevolent atom, was passing: the satirist must learn to be an educator as well.'[53]

Rochester wrote two very different dramatic epistles in the voice of John Sheffield, Earl of Mulgrave. In 'A Very Heroical Epistle in Answer to Ephelia', Mulgrave is ridiculed as a pompous and self-centred Ovidian rake who uses the idiom of the heroic drama to justify his libertine attitudes to love. In 'An Epistolary Essay from M. G. to O. B. upon Their Mutual Poems', the same self-centred character is presented in a much 'lower' form. Mulgrave is made to imply literary values which are ridiculous from the point of view of neoclassical aesthetics. He writes only to please himself in despite of the critics. He proceeds to develop an analogy in the best Rochesterian manner in defence of his bad writing:

> Perhaps ill verses ought to be confined
> In mere good breeding, like unsavory wind.
> Were reading forced, I should be apt to think
> Men might no more write scurvily than stink.
> But 'tis your choice whether you'll read or no;
> If likewise your smelling it were so,
> I'd fart, just as I write, for my own ease,
> Nor should you be concerned unless you please.
>
> (p. 145)

The low analogy debases the perspective and confirms its unacceptability. Mulgrave claims an individuality and originality which is subversive of Augustan assumptions about shared cultural values:

> In all I write, should sense and wit and rhyme
> Fail me at once, yet something so sublime

> Shall stamp my poem, that the world may see
> It could have been produced by none but me.
> And that's my end, for man can wish no more
> Than so to write, as none e'er writ before.
>
> (pp. 145–6)

It is significant that Rochester acknowledges neoclassical values in this implicit fashion. His *literary* values were rarely in harmony with his moral and philosophical ideas. In his later work, he allowed his use of the native tradition of lampoon to be softened by his commitment to the recently developed neoclassicism of Boileau, but his qualified Hobbist stance did not permit the adoption of an unequivocal and orthodox Augustan poise. Rochester was England's most subversive Horatian satirist.

DRYDEN: MOCK-HEROIC, HEROIC AND FINE RAILLERY

The rationalistic and sceptical temper of Restoration satire produced a remarkable range of 'parodic' styles, developed from the incongruous imitation of epic. A typology of 'burlesque' styles, however tentative, assists us to make necessary critical discriminations. The following table is a modified version of one proposed by R. P. Bond in 1932:[54]

(1) *Travesty:* parody of a particular heroic work, using a low style and a high subject-matter. Examples: Cotton's *Scarronides* (1664–5) and James Scudamore's *Homer à la Mode* (1664).
(2) *Low burlesque:* a general parody of the heroic, using a low style and a low subject in a heroic guise. Example: Butler's *Hudibras.*
(3) *High Burlesque or Mock-heroic:* a parody (particular or general) of the heroic, using a high style and a low subject-matter. Examples: Dryden's *Mac Flecknoe,* Garth's *Dispensary,* John Philips's *Splendid Shilling* and Pope's *The Rape of the Lock.*
(4) *Heroic Satire:* a general parody of the heroic, using a high style and a high subject-matter. Examples: Dryden's *Absalom and Achitophel* and Marvell's *Last Instructions to a Painter.*

Evidently the model requires qualification in so far as individual burlesques are not consistently of one type. *Mac Flecknoe* includes low-style diction; the characters in *The Rape of the Lock* are unheroic but not 'low'; in *Absalom and Achitophel* not all the characters are equally 'high'. In this section we shall examine those satires which fall into the third and fourth categories, that is, those which possess a more serious relationship with the heroic.

It has often been noticed that, in the early Augustan period, heroic and panegyric verse shared a very long and unstable boundary with burlesque and mock-heroic verse. The Renaissance' artist's conception of monarchs and heroes was part of a larger integrated world-view which saw heroic action as divinely sanctioned and as part of an ordered cosmos. The secularised theories of kingship, which arose in the first part of the seventeenth century in a context of violent constitutional struggle, reflected rapidly shifting economic forces and the final waning of a surviving medieval world-view. The panegyrics on Cromwell by Dryden, Waller, Marvell and others, emphasised the Protector's *secular* greatness and not merely his providential instrumentality. The conception of a hero as a man who possesses individual *virtù* and exercises it in a specific historical situation begins to emerge. Marvell's Cromwell is the most explicitly modern historical actor:

> So much one man can do
> Who does both act and know.
> ('The Horatian Ode')

After the Restoration, the force of anti-puritan scepticism and the emerging empirical outlook of the Royal Society (established in 1662) did not permit the revival of traditional heroic and panegyric forms. Instead, the old conventions were re-expressed in secular form. Wylie Sypher has described the heroic styles of this period as 'baroque', where 'baroque' signifies the 'secularisation of the transcendental'. Hieratic symbols and religious imagery are displaced by sensuous splendour and grandiose cosmic imagery. Emphasis is placed on a hero's physical splendour, on his martial exploits, and on the grandeur of the feelings evoked by his heroism.[55] There is an accompanying tendency to heighten and inflate the mundane and the prosaic. A demystified world-view is endowed with a spurious sublimity. One might say that the secular is transcendentalised. The earliest expression of this tendency is to be found in Cowley's *Pindaric Odes* in which the secular world of science and philosophy is celebrated in the sublime language of Neoplatonism.

The development of a neoclassical heroic style required the formation of a poetic diction and a versification which would permit sublimity without the loss of rational poise and control. An 'aureate' diction was formed during the first half of the seventeenth century mainly through the assimilation of the conciseness, decorum, rhetorical formality and pathos of Silver Latin poetry. Geoffrey Tillotson demonstrated the germinal influence of Sylvester's *Du Bartas* (1605), Sandy's *Ovid* (1626), Thomas May's *Lucan* (1626) and Ogilby's *Aeneid* (1649) in the development of the characteristic form of Augustan diction.[56] The perfection of the heroic couplet took place during the same period and was accomplished by Waller, Denham and Cowley.

During the early years of the Restoration, there was a spate of panegyric verse culminating in Waller's grandiose celebration of the Duke of York's victory over the Dutch at Lowestoft in June 1665. By adopting (from the Italian poet Busenello) the device of the poet instructing the painter on the heroic scene to be painted, Waller was able to emphasise the pictorial impressiveness of the events, and the secular splendour of the heroism. The *Instructions to a Painter* (1665) crystallises a number of features of Restoration baroque which gave rise to a devastating satiric response. Consider the description of the Duke of York:

> Where burning ships the banish'd sun supply,
> And no light shines but that by which men die,
> There York appears, so prodigal is he
> Of royal blood as ancient as the sea,
> Which down to him, so many ages told,
> Has through the veins of mighty monarchs roll'd!
> The great Achilles march'd not to the field
> Till Vulcan that impenetrable shield
> And arms had wrought, yet there no bullets flew,
> But shafts and darts which the weak Phrygians threw.
> Our bolder hero on the deck does stand
> Expos'd, the bulwark of his native land:
> Defensive arms laid by as useless here
> Where massy balls the neighboring rocks do tear
> Some power unseen those princes does protect,
> Who for their country thus themselves neglect.[57]
>
> (121–37)

Cosmic imagery (sun and sea) magnifies the heroic stature of the duke without endowing his actions with divine significance. York's willingness to sacrifice his blood might easily have taken on Christomimetic meaning, but instead Waller stresses the *scale* and *extent* of his lineage. The imagery is entirely secular, aiming at pageant-like splendour rather than at symbolic or figural meaning. The heroic analogy is not with Christ Victorious or Samson, but with the pagan Achilles. York's superior courage remains courage of the same order as that of Achilles; he excels in those 'acts of prowess eminent/And great exploits' which Milton found devoid of true *virtù*. The description emphasises sheer physical power and grandeur. The suggestion of divine protection is left without an explicit Christian reference ('Some power unseen'), and could as easily be interpreted as the intervention of a Homeric deity.

The secularised nature of the heroic extends to the epic similes introduced in the poem. Waller cultivates, in a concise and 'prosaic' form, the Homeric animal simile, but the poem's epigrammatic and rationally proportioned comparisons lack the pagan simplicity of Homer's, and have an inherent tendency to bathos:

> His [York's] winged vessel like an eagle shows,
> When through the clouds to truss a swan she goes.
> (175–6)

> Like falcons these [the English], those [the Dutch] like
> a num'rous flock
> Of fowl which scatter to avoid the shock.
> (57–8)

The fleet was visited at Harwich in May by the Duchess of York and her 'glorious train'. The patently amorous purpose of the visit is lightly varnished over with elegant heroics:

> But who can always on the billows lie?
> The wat'ry wilderness yields no supply:
> Spreading our sails, to Harwich we resort,
> And meet the beauties of the British court.
> (77–80)

The propitious attitude of pagan deities ('gazing sea-gods', 'Neptune's court') is celebrated, and the duchess is likened to 'Thetis with her nymphs'. The mythological and Petrarchan allusions are purely decorative, and the absence of moral or religious depth tends to draw attention to the incongruously prosaic occasion. The analogy between the navy's victualling activities and the invigorating effects of the ladies' presence serves only to emphasise the lowest meaning of the latter:

> The soldier here his wasted store supplies
> And takes new valor from the ladies' eyes.
> (89–90)

The slightest gleam of irony would transform this into satire. Marvell, the probable author of several mock 'Painter' satires, found it easy to satirise the Harwich affair without radically altering Waller's heroic manner:

> See where the Duchess, with triumphant tail
> Of num'rous coaches, Harwich does assail!
> So the land crabs, at Nature's kindly call,
> Down to engender at the sea do crawl.
> (*Second Advice*, 1666, lines 55–8)

The low aspect of the visit is made explicit by the satiric deployment of the animal simile. Marvell similarly demeans the vulnerable cosmic imagery of Waller's poem, for example by debasing the metaphor of the imperial sun:

> What boots it that thy light does gild our days
> And we lie basking in thy milder rays,
> While swarms of insects, from thy warmth begun,
> Our land devour and intercept our sun?
> (347–50)

Marvell's *Last Instructions to a Painter* (1667), probably the most impressive of the long series of 'Painter' poems, is remarkable for its experimental exploration of the satiric modes which had proliferated since the beginning of the Commonwealth period. In addition, it is the most specific and comprehensive treatment of public affairs in English satire. The satiric styles range from the Hudibrastic and Clevelandesque to the high heroic. Marvell here anticipates Dryden's blending of the Horatian and Juvenalian traditions: urbane raillery and majestic invective are in balanced tension.[58] More significant for the mock-heroic is Marvell's discovery of a new form of heroic satire which no longer relies upon the innate fragility of the baroque heroic style for its effects. Parallel to the baroque style (and sometimes in the work of the same writers) there was a developing Virgilian style, which possessed that weight, dignity and Roman pathos which was to be perfected in Dryden's marmoreal couplets. The satiric deployment of such a style required a much greater rational poise and an ironic play of mind which is far removed from the explicitness of the tradition of Butler and Cleveland. Marvell uses this style when he describes Charles musing 'on th' uneasy throne' in the manner of Macbeth or Richard III. A vision of an allegorical naked virgin presents itself to the king at night:

> Paint last the King and a dead shade of night,
> Only dispers'd by a weak taper's light,
> And those bright gleams that dart along and glare
> From his clear eyes (yet these too dark with care).
> There, as in th' calm horror all alone
> He wakes and muses of th' uneasy throne,
> Raise up a sudden shape with virgin's face . . .
> (885–91)

There is a complete absence of declamation and indignant intonation; the diction is chaste and Virgilian in its controlled pathos ('dead shade', 'dark with care', 'calm horror'). The modulation into satire is managed without the introduction of Juvenalian bathos or Hudibrastic infusions:

> The object strange in him no terror mov'd:
> He wonder'd first, then piti'd, then he lov'd
> And with kind hand does the coy vision press
> (Whose beauty greater seem'd by her distress),
> But soon shrunk back, chill'd with her touch so cold,
> And th' airy picture vanish'd from his hold.
>
> (899–904)

Here Marvell anticipates what Reuben Brower referred to in Dryden as 'a Virgilian refinement of "raillery"' and in Pope as 'the tone of Roman cultivation'.[59] The satiric ridicule is expressed in the language of epic pathos recalling the Virgilian style of the second and sixth books of the *Aeneid*.

As we have seen, two distinct types of mock-heroic emerged during the 1660s: the deflated baroque heroic and the ironised Virgilian heroic. The former usually reinforced a Juvenalian manner; the latter required a more neoclassical rational poise. Dryden became the master of both forms.

Dryden's *Discourse concerning the Original and Progress of Satire* (1693) is the chief critical discussion of verse satire in the Augustan period. The characteristics of Juvenalian and Horatian satire (and to a lesser extent the satire of Persius) are examined from several points of view. The direction of the discussion is erratic and at times apparently contradictory. But the form of Dryden's comparison is also an expression of what might be called his negative capability, which includes opposites without negating the essential features of the alternatives. The absence of dogmatism links Dryden with Horace, whose refusal to follow one master was adopted in the motto of the Royal Society *(nullius in verba)*, of which Dryden was a member. In this respect, Augustan classicism and Baconian science speak with one voice against the vanity of dogmatising.[60] The dedication to the Earl of Dorset enables Dryden to establish at once the required neoclassical tone. Dorset possesses that 'good nature' which consists in a generous attitude towards men's failings and a rejection of the ill-natured ethic which condemns a man without discrimination of degree. Having given this clear hint, Dryden proceeds to confirm his general preference for Horace, who is superior even to Virgil 'in the delicacy of his turns, his choice of words, and perhaps the purity of his Latin.'[61] With an eye, no doubt, to Rochester's satires,

Dryden notes that Horace abandoned the libellous scurrility of his *Epodes* when he came to write satires. Satire against an individual is justified only when 'he is become a public nuisance' (II, 126). The lampoons are incapable of exacting admonitory revenge because they are undiscriminating and lacking in 'good sense':

> No decency is considered, no fulsomness omitted; no venom is wanting, as far as dullness can supply it. For there is a perpetual dearth of wit; a barrenness of good sense and entertainment . . . There can be no pleasantry where there is no wit. (II, 127)

Having established the genteel and urbane credentials of the true satirist, Dryden confesses that 'good manners' are not enough:

> His [Horace's] urbanity, that is, his good manners, are to be commended, but his wit is faint; and his salt . . . almost insipid. Juvenal is of a more vigorous and masculine wit . . . he treats his subject home; his spleen is raised, and he raises mine. (II, 130)

Dryden concludes that Juvenal 'was the greater poet, I mean in satire. His thoughts are sharper; his indignation against vice is more vehement' (II, 131–2). It emerges that Dryden's ideal is represented in Boileau's heroic satire, in which 'the majesty of the heroic' is 'finely mixed with the venom' of satire (II, 149). Dryden is here returning by another route to his cherished gentility.[62] Boileau's and Dryden's conception of satire as a 'species' of heroic poetry places an emphasis on the good breeding and delicacy of the writer in its *noblest* and *sublimest* form. One is reminded of Neander's arguments in *Of Dramatic Poesy* (1668) on the naturalness of rhyming couplets, which are considered 'nearest nature, as being the noblest kind of modern verse' (I, 87). This stress upon *noble* good-breeding as opposed to merely urbane good-breeding inclines the balance further in Juvenal's favour:

> His expressions are sonorous and more noble; his verse more numerous, and his words are suitable to his thoughts, sublime and lofty . . . The low style of Horace is according to his subject that is, generally grovelling. (II, 130)

While he admits the decorum of Horace's *sermo pedestris* as being appropriate to his subject ('blind sides and follies'), Dryden gives the preference to the sublime style, but fails to clarify the extent to which Juvenal's 'spleen' is accommodated to the requirement of 'good manners' by his noble style. This imprecision opens the door once again to Horace:

I cannot give . . . up the manner of Horace in low satire so easily. Let the chastisements of Juvenal be never so necessary for his new kind of satire; let him declaim as wittily and sharply as he pleases: yet still the nicest and most delicate touches of satire consist in fine raillery. (II, 136)

Once again we return to the Horatian ideal of genteel and inoffensive ridicule. Dryden claims that his characterisation of Zimri in *Absalom and Achitophel* is in this manner, avoiding 'the mention of great crimes', and representing only 'blindsides, and little extravagancies' (II, 137). He concludes, 'This manner of Horace is indeed the best' (II, 138). Dryden appears to recognise Horace's superiority in *ethical stance,* and Juvenal's in *style* ('performance'). The latter preference reappears later as yet another apparent change of mind:

How come lowness of style, and the familiarity of words, to be so much the propriety of satire . . . Is the . . . sublimity of Juvenal, to be circumscribed with the meanness of words and vulgarity of expression? (II, 143–4)

'The majestic way' of Juvenal is an improvement, a refinement, just as Virgil's was in relation to Homer. The adulation of Boileau adds the final synthesising touch to the undogmatic comparative analysis. One draws the conclusion that the ethical good sense of Horace is to be combined with the stylistic good sense of Juvenal, that the 'venom' of satire is to be tempered by the nobility of epic verse, that good manners require the savour of 'masculine wit' and noble 'spleen'. The series of accommodations and qualifications is never explicitly codified: the alternatives are left in benign and unforced coexistence.

Whether or not one agrees with Edwin Morgan's view that Dryden ultimately preferred the majesty of declamatory satire to the more delicate rallying manner, there is little doubt that Dryden always upheld Virgil's style as normative. Like Pope, he associates the low style with meanness of culture: the sordid landscape of *Mac Flecknoe* is the objective correlative of the vulgarity of Shadwell's writing. On the other hand, the Augustan taste for the 'majestic way' is controlled by a wider taste for 'correctness', elegance, and smoothness. The requirements of rationality and urbanity keep the epic style within the ambit of a genteel plain style. According to Dryden, Virgil 'maintains majesty in the midst of plainness'.[63]

Dryden's conservative electicism gave him the best possible stock of stylistic resources with which to assimilate Juvenal to a neo-classical aesthetic. The heroic drama gave him an early opportunity to experiment with the satiric possibilities of the heroic style. Bruce King has argued that Dryden's heroes defend their actions by allusion to Hobbes's psychological and political determinism; the materialistic imagery which expresses these ideas 'subverts the character's idealised explanations of his moods . . . Dryden's characters may speak in an heroic manner, but his imagery warns us that they are appetitive matter in search of satisfaction.'[64] While King may have exaggerated the *satiric* effects of the rhetorical posturing of characters such as Maximin (in *Tyrannick Love,* 1670). Almanzor (in *Conquest of Granada,* 1672) and Morat (in *Aurengzebe,* 1676), there is no doubt that by inflating the amoral ethics of his pagan heroes Dryden strongly suggests the absurdity of their attitudes. D. W. Jefferson defines more convincingly Dryden's 'capacity to achieve occasionally an unequivocal seriousness without actually throwing off the imaginative equipment that is elsewhere chiefly active in the modifying or subversion of seriousness'.[65] Juvenal's portraits of Sejanus, Alexander and Xerxes in the tenth satire involve a similar method: the 'low' ambition of an heroic figure is ridiculed by an incongruous epic style and by the infusion of bathetic detail.

In his translations of Juvenal, Dryden frequently exaggerates the stylistic disparities in the Latin to produce a Restoration mock-heroic which has strong affinities with the heroic drama.[66] An examination of the Restoration versions of Juvenal's tenth satire[67] reveals that only Dryden attempted to reproduce the heroic idiom upon which Juvenal bases his satiric style. Dryden was conscious of his originality in this respect; he wrote: 'We have actually made him more sounding, and more elegant, than he was before in English.'[68] A comparison of the versions by Dryden and by Thomas Shadwell reveals an interesting facet of famous rivalry.[69] While Shadwell favoured a style ranging from the plain to the low, in which he emulated Jonson's *Bartholomew Fair,* Dryden strove to combine the languages of epic and satire. Their versions of the description of Hannibal's military progress demonstrate their methods:

> *Spain* first he won, the *Pyrenaeans* past,
> And steepy *Alps,* the Mounds that Nature cast:
> And with Corroding Juices, as he went,
> A passage through the living Rocks he rent.
> Then, like a Torrent, rowling from on high,
> He pours his head-long Rage on *Italy*;
> In three Victorious Battels overrun;
> Yet still uneasie, Cries there's nothing done:
> Till, level with the Ground, their Gates are laid;
> And *Punick* Flags, on *Roman* Tow'rs displaid.

> Ask what a Face belong'd to this high Fame;
> His Picture scarcely would deserve a Frame:
> A Sign-Post Dawber wou'd disdain to paint
> The one Ey'd Heroe on his Elephant.
> (Dryden)[70]

> *Spain* must be joyn'd: the *Pyrenaeans* now
> Be passed; Nature opposes th' *Alpes* and Snow.
> Rocks he devided, and the Mountains he ⎫
> With Vinegar broke, making his passage free; ⎬
> And takes possession then of *Italy*. ⎭
> Yet after all, says he; still pressing on,
> My *Carthaginian* Troops have nothing done,
> Till we the Gates of *Rome* have overthrown,
> And fix'd our Banners in th' Heart of all the Town.
> Rare Visage, what a Picture 'twould appear,
> When the *Gaetulian* Beast does th' one Ey'd *General* bear!
> (Shadwell)[71]

The original operates a simple but effective technique of mock-heroic bathos: the heroic diction and imagery are deflated by three words in terminal positions *(aceto, Suburra* and *luscum).*[72] In Shadwell's version, these effects are dissipated by the flatness and uniform plainness of the diction. Dryden unifies and strengthens the satiric force of the passage by removing the bathetic *aceto* (which becomes 'Corroding Juices', a decorous circumlocution) and *Suburra,* by inflating the heroic diction and intensifying the final bathos. His initial additions to Juvenal's description of Hannibal's irresistible career are reminiscent of his heroic drama[73] or of his translation of the *Aeneid:*

> Then, like a Torrent, rowling from on high,
> He pours his head-long Rage on *Italy;*
> In three Victorious Battels overrun . . .

Parallels are not hard to find in Dryden's rather baroque rendering of the *Aeneid:*

> Or as two neighb'ring Torrents fall from high . . .
> They rowl to Sea with unresisted Force . . .
> As when a Fragment, from a Mountain torn
> By raging Tempests, or by Torrents born . . .
> Rowling from Crag to Crag . . .
> So *Turnus,* hasting headlong to the Town . . .
> (XII, 764, 766, 991, 995, 999)[74]

Juvenal's final couplet in the passage is subtly manipulated by Dryden: he takes *tabella* (picture) as his hint for an extension of the low-style bathos; 'this high Fame' (not in the Latin) is deflated by 'Frame' and 'Sign-Post Dawber', culminating in the 'one-Ey'd Heroe on his Elephant'.

Dryden's counterpointing of epic dignity and demeaning particularity is an effect made possible by his mastery of the neoclassical plain style. While he disagreed with Horace on the question of the proper style for satire, nevertheless the values of *sermo pedestris* underlie and control his mock-heroic exuberance. In a similar way, a delicate Horatian irony controls the use of the high style in the opening lines of *Mac Flecknoe*:

> All humane things are subject to decay,
> And, when Fate summons, Monarchs must obey:
> This *Flecknoe* found, who, like *Augustus,* young
> Was call'd to Empire, and had govern'd long.
>
> (1–4)

The stately rhythms of the funeral elegy are perfectly achieved without burlesque distortion or exaggeration. The satire gradually emerges from an ironic inversion of terms ('Realms of Non-sense', 'wage immortal War with *Wit*'). The delicacy of the satire lies in its sophisticated distortion of an otherwise perfectly achieved neoclassical high style. The satiric deflections are often slight: 'But Shadwell never deviates into sense' (we expect 'from sense'). These effects are knowingly achieved from a refined sense of the correct and conventional forms of elegant 'conversation' *(sermo)*. More than any other major Augustan poet, Dryden exploits the full range of styles from the grandiloquent to the vulgar and obscene without abandoning the 'prose'[75] values of the plain style.

If Dryden modified Juvenal by introducing the Horatian ethos of 'fine raillery', then we cannot doubt that if he had attempted translations of Horace he would have heightened the Roman's 'grovelling' style. Some idea of a Drydenian Horace is conveyed by Matthew Prior who, in *The Hind and the Panther Transversed* (1687), satirised Dryden's Catholic apology by retelling the allegory in terms of Horace's fable from *Satires*, II, vi, using the dramatic machinery of *The Rehearsal*. Bayes's (Dryden's) remarks on his heightened rendering of Horace's fable are, of course, meant to carry all the satiric sting of *The Rehearsal*, but they also may be seen as a not inaccurate delineation of Dryden's views on the true style of satire:

> You remember in him [Horace] the *Story* of the *Country-Mouse,* and the *City-Mouse;* what a plain simple thing it is, it has no more life and spirit in it, I'gad, than a Hobby-horse;

and his *Mice* talk so meanly, such common stuff, so like *meer* '
Mice, that I wonder it has pleas'd the world so long. But now
will I undeceive *Mankind,* and teach 'em to *heighten,* and
elevate a Fable . . .[76]

Prior even gives us a sample of the imagined version (based on lines
90–2 of *Satires,* II, vi):

> Leave, leave . . . this hoary Shed and lonely Hills,
> And eat with me at *Groleau's,* smoak at *Will's,*
> What Wretch would nibble on a Hanging-shelf,
> When at *Pontack's* he may *Regale* himself?
>
> (p. 49)

Dryden's major satires were written during a period of political
ferment caused partly at least by the Stuart hankering for
Catholicism. The Anglican Commons excluded Catholics from
civil and military office in the Test Act of 1673. In 1678, violent
anti-Catholic feelings were unleased by Titus Oates's fraudulent
'revelation' of a 'Popish Plot' to kill the King. A vain attempt was
made to exclude the King's Catholic brother, James, Duke of York,
from the throne. The Exclusion crisis culminated in the arrest of
the Whig leader, Shaftesbury, for his part in the Exclusion
campaign. The rancorous and declamatory tone of Oldham's
Satires upon the Jesuits (1678–81) were designed to inflame feelings
rather than mollify them. Dryden, in *Absalom and Achitophel*
(1681), had a quite different effect in view. Writing on behalf of the
Court party, he aimed to be both *partisan* and *moderate.* This was
achieved by the production of a 'new heroic idiom'[77] which
combined heroic satire and 'fine raillery'. The political allegory,
involving a parallel between Absalom's conspiracy against King
David (II Samuel) and Monmouth's rebellion, is presented in a
suitably elevated style which is carefully leavened with a Horatian
conversational reasonableness. The choice of heroic action and
heroic style might easily have resulted in Marlovian rant, but
Dryden places great emphasis upon the delicacy of his stance:

> If I happen to please the more Moderate sort, I shall be sure of
> an honest Party; and, in all probability, of the best Judges; for,
> the least Concern'd, are commonly the least Corrupt: And, I
> confess, I have laid in for those, by rebating the Satyre, (where
> Justice would allow it) from carrying too sharp an Edge. (*Works,*
> II, 3)

The Horatian allegiance is overt: 'I have but laught at some mens
Follies, when I coud have declaim'd against their Vices; and, other

mens Vertues I have commended, as freely as I have tax'd their Crimes.' Dryden's reasonableness is expressed in the balanced but unforced rhetoric of the prose, and in the repeated parenthetical qualifications and reservations which cumulatively identify Dryden as himself a representative of 'the more Moderate sort'.

The political and ideological function of Dryden's moderate stance is evident. The seditious activities of Shaftesbury (Achitophel), especially his suborning of Monmouth (Absalom), are treated in a consciously non-antagonistic spirit. Despite the potentially dire consequences of their actions, the protagonists are fools and not knaves. Dryden is probably the first English satirist to call a man Satan without raising his voice in anger. In his treatment of Absalom, Dryden combines deadly *ad hominem* accusations (for example, in the reference to 'Amnon's Murther') and a flexible Horatian moral tone:

> What faults he had (for who from faults is free?)
> His Father coud not, or he woud not see.
> (35–6)

Dryden's presentation of the Civil War, the Restoration and the plot is coloured throughout by this politically potent Horatian stance. 'The sober part of *Israel*', we read, looked back 'with a wise afright' at the 'ugly Scars' inflicted during the Civil War:

> The moderate sort of Men, thus qualifi'd,
> Inclin'd the Ballance to the better side.
> (75–6)

The same rational values of sober discrimination and judicious good sense are expressed in the imagery of Dryden's account of the Popish Plot, which was

> Rais'd in extremes, and in extremes decry'd . . .
> Not weigh'd, or winnow'd by the Multitude;
> But swallow'd in the Mass, unchew'd and Crude.
> (110,112–13)

The poem opens with a tactically brilliant use of the satire of 'fine raillery'. The dubious morality of the Court made it difficult for a Juvenalian satirist to defend the King with anything resembling righteous indignation. Dryden adopts an ironic libertine stance in an effort to laugh away his hero's well-known weakness:

> In pious times, e'r Priest-craft did begin,
> Before *Polygamy* was made a sin:

> When man on many, multiply'd his kind,
> E'r one to one was, cursedly, confind:
> When Nature prompted, and no law deny'd
> Promiscuous use of Concubine and Bride;
> Then, *Israel's* Monarch, after Heaven's own heart,
> His vigorous warmth did, variously, impart
> To Wives and Slaves: And, wide as his Command,
> Scatter'd his Maker's Image through the Land.
>
> (1–10)

A controlled and decorous heroic idiom is here deployed in the manner of the heroic drama: there is a strong sense of the incongruity of style and perception; the heroic language and stance clash with the libertine perspective. The effect is complicated by a witty allusion to Burnet's discussions of polygamy,[78] which gave the King's libertinism a kind of noble legitimacy. Having thus wittily conceded a point to the opposition without diminishing Charles's dignity, Dryden is free to allow a growing seriousness to culminate in the closing passage of unadulterated Virgilian grandeur:

> He said.Th'Almighty, nodding, gave Consent;
> And Peals of Thunder shook the Firmament.
> Henceforth a Series of new time began,
> The mighty Years in long Procession ran:
> Once more the Godlike *David* was Restor'd,
> And willing Nations knew their Lawfull Lord.
>
> (1026–31)

The mock-heroic is thus superseded by the heroic; the poem opens with a witty and slightly blasphemous use of the grand style, and ends by drawing up Charles to the level of the style.

The essentially flexible satiric stance enables Dryden to adopt a wide range of satiric tones from the heroic ridicule of Absalom and Achitophel through the delicate raillery of the portrait of Zimri (Buckingham) to the harsher and more scurrilous treatment of Shimei (Bethel) and Corah (Titus Oates). However, it is the allegorical framework and the pattern of imagery which sustain the poem as an essentially heroic satire. The surface parallel between biblical history and contemporary Restoration history is less important in this respect than the deeper structural analogy between the actions of the protagonists in the Exclusion crisis and the protagonists of Milton's greater and lesser epics.[79] In his prose remarks 'To the Reader', Dryden lays the foundation of this sublime parallel by referring to Adam's temptations and Achitophel's satanic cast. In the poem, there is an underlying allusion to Satan's rebellion in *Paradise Lost,* both in the conspiracy against Charles

and in the temptation of Monmouth by Shaftesbury. The temp-
tation scenes are modelled initially on the temptation of Christ in
Paradise Regained: Achitophel refers to Absalom's 'Nativity', and
speaks of him as 'Saviour' and 'Their second *Moses*'. We remem-
ber that Christ too was a son of David. Later, as Absalom
weakens, Achitophel tempts him as Satan tempted Eve:

> Him Staggering so when Hells dire Agent found
> While fainting Vertue scarce maintain'd her Ground,
> He pours fresh Forces in, and thus Replies:
>
> (373–5)

The allusion to Milton here includes the use of a Miltonic inversion
in line 373. Unlike Juvenal's Virgilian allusions, Dryden's are
sustained and border more closely on the genuinely heroic. The
protagonists, too, are closer to the heroes of Senecan and
Shakespearean tragedy in their overweening and misdirected
energy. Absalom's greatness of soul is contradicted by his meanness
of birth, which can only be overcome by an objectification of
the contradiction in a linguistic form:

> My Soul Disclaims the Kindred of her Earth:
> And Made for Empire, Whispers me within;
> Desire of Greatness is a Godlike Sin.
>
> (370–2)

The satirist himself explores the full implications of the oxymoron
('Godlike Sin') in an earlier passage:

> Desire of Power, on Earth a Vitious Weed,
> Yet, sprung from High, is of Caelestial Seed:
> In God 'tis Glory: And when men Aspire,
> 'Tis but a Spark too much of Heavenly Fire.
>
> (305–8)

The first metaphor ('Weed . . . Seed') seems to damn Absalom's
aspirations utterly and to mark a clear boundary between divine
greatness and Tamburlaine-like hubris. But the second metaphor
('Spark . . . Fire'), by reminding us of Prometheus, permits a more
generous assessment of Absalom's 'mounting Spirits'. It is as
though Dryden was able to tap some of that ambivalent grandeur
which makes Satan such a magnificent sinner in *Paradise Lost*.

Dryden cunningly encircled his enemies with an elaborate net-
work of high-style allusion, typological imagery and incipient
allegory. The opening of *The Medal* (1682) is a masterpiece in
this respect. The failure to influence the trial of Shaftesbury

moved Dryden to abandon 'fine raillery' for an unqualified Juvenalian vehemence. He no longer laughs at foolish court peccadilloes, but castigates vicious inclinations to sedition. After Shaftesbury's acquittal, the Whigs arranged to have a medal struck to commemorate the occasion. The reverse side shows a view of London and a rising sun with the legend *Laetamur*. The engraved face of Shaftesbury is Dryden's first object of attack:

> Never did Art so well with Nature strive;
> Nor ever Idol seem'd so much alive:
> So like the Man; so golden to the sight,
> So base within, so counterfeit and light.
>
> (6–9)

The coin displays three likenesses: a representational likeness of Shaftesbury, a likeness between the coin's baseness and the man's spiritual baseness, and the likeness ('Idol') of a false god and false king. The last of these establishes a typological significance: Shaftesbury is the type of the false god (or golden calf) and the antitype of the true Lord. *Laetamur* ('let us rejoice') is a blasphemous parody of the true worship of God. The denigration of Shaftesbury is more venomous than in *Absalom,* but the same web of Miltonic and biblical allusion gives the poem its moral authority. For example, an allusion to *Paradise Lost,* III, 636, is sustained between lines 31 and 81 where Shaftesbury, like Satan, puts on 'Hypocritique Zeal' and becomes 'A Vermin, wriggling in th'Usurper's Ear' only to be exposed ('shows the Fiend confess'd') as a rebel. Shaftesbury is the obverse of the Messianic Charles of *Astraea Redux*. The poetics of panegyric and satire are interdependent and, in a sense, interchangeable. Satire inverts the images of panegyric like those in a *camera obscura*.

Dryden wrote his most densely wrought mock-heroic satire against the unfortunate Shadwell. In *Mac Flecknoe* (1682) the narrative structure is that of a mock coronation procession (compare *To His Sacred Majesty*) in which the vulgar landscape of the city parodies the heroic world:

> From its old Ruins Brothel-houses rise,
> Scenes of lewd loves, and of polluted joys;
> Where their vast Courts the Mother-Strumpets keep,
> And, undisturb'd by Watch, in silence sleep.
>
> (70–3)

Part of Cowley's description of Hell in *The Davideis*[80] reads:

> Where their vast Court the Mother-waters keep,
> And undisturb'd by Moons in silence sleep.

Dryden's fondness for stylistic incongruity is evinced particularly in the description of the coronation route:

> No *Persian* Carpets spread th' Imperial way,
> But scatter'd Limbs of mangled Poets lay:
> From dusty shops neglected Authors come,
> Martyrs of Pies, and Reliques of the Bum.
>
> (98–101)

The heroic image of crucified saints ('Limbs', 'Martyrs', 'Reliques') lining the imperial route is brilliantly overlaid with the vulgar imagery describing the undignified fate of Shadwell's unsold books.

Flecknoe's coronation speech is modelled on the Sibyl's prophecies in Book VI of the *Aeneid* when the future dimensions of the Roman Empire are foretold. The classical allusion is interwoven with biblical echoes and references to Shadwell's plays in a most potent satirical mixture:

> . . . long he stood,
> Repelling from his Breast the raging God; }
> At length burst out in this prophetick mood:)
>   Heaven bless my Son, from *Ireland* let him reign
> To farr *Barbadoes* on the Western main;
> Of his Dominion may no end be known,
> And greater than his Father's be his Throne.
> Beyond loves Kingdom let him stretch his Pen;
> He paus'd, and all the people cry'd *Amen*.
>
> (136–44)

The reader will not fail to notice that the stretch of empire between Ireland and Barbados is an empire of fishes! The echo of Isaiah is mixed with references to the title of a play by Flecknoe (*Love's Dominion* or *Love's Kingdom*). The satiric victim is thus effectively sunk beyond trace in a flood of high-style locutions and allusions.

The use of *figura* (or biblical 'types') reappears in *Mac Flecknoe*, in a manner which closely resembles its use in panegyric, where the exemplary lives of past heroes illuminate the present and give it a heightened semi-religious significance.[81] Dryden traces Shadwell's dramatic ancestry in a brilliant parody of biblical typology:

> *Heywood* and *Shirley* were but Types of thee,
> Thou last great Prophet of Tautology:
> Even I, a dunce of more renown than they,
> Was sent before but to prepare thy way.
>
> (29–32)

Not only is Shadwell the antitype of Christ, but Flecknoe is later linked in typological fashion with Satan and Aeneas in a passage of complex epic allusion:

> High on a Throne of his own Labours rear'd.
> At his right hand our young *Ascanius* sate,
> *Rome's* other hope, and pillar of the State.
> His Brows thick fogs, instead of glories grace,
> And lambent dullness plaid around his face.
>
> (107–11)

The passage is not only complex in its allusions, but also illustrates three modes of epic reference. In the opening couplet there are two incipient allusions, one Miltonic ('High on a Throne'), the other biblical ('At his right hand'). The subsequent allusion to Aeneas' son Ascanius is in part an imitation of lines which appear later in Dryden's *Aeneid*, XII, 253–4:

> A lambent Flame arose, which gently spread
> Around his Brows, and on his Temples fed.

The Miltonic reference depends for its satiric effect on an irony residing in the epic context (Satan's grandeur). The initial analogy between Shadwell and Ascanius operates through ironic incongruity. The final couplet works by explicit deflation of the epic context.

The treatment of Shadwell in the *Second Part of Absalom and Achitophel* (1682) is more Juvenalian in tone:

> With all this Bulk there's nothing lost in *Og* [Shadwell]
> For ev'ry inch that is not Fool is Rogue:
> A Monstrous mass of foul corrupted matter,
> As all the Devils had spew'd to make the batter.
> When wine has given him courage to Blaspheme,
> He Curses God, but God before Curst him;
>
> (462–7)

In all three poems, Dryden developed that combination of Juvenalian invective, 'fine raillery' and Miltonic and biblical allusion which Pope perfected in *The Dunciad*.

Dryden's use of Christian and Old Testament allusion is part of a sustained attempt to establish what Bernard Schilling called 'the Conservative Myth', that body of ideas and assumptions which sustained a particular world-view. Dryden's blackening, in *The Medal*, of the Exclusionist Whigs, the Dissenters and the City interests has a mythical power beyond anything in Juvenal's satires; the Roman's conservatism is more cynical and less coherent. Dryden succeeded in carving out a new territory for the heroic poem in which there was room for the comic, the satanic, the realities of social and political struggle, and the characterisation of living individuals.[82] By entangling contemporary political events in a rich web of high-style language, allusion, metaphor and allegory, without infringing the neoclassical norms of 'common sense' rationality, elegant plainness and good humour, Dryden achieved a form of satiric writing which reaches beyond the traditions of Roman and Elizabethan satire.

Chapter 4

The 18th-Century Horace: Pope and Swift

After the constitutional settlement of 1688, following the expulsion of the Catholic James II and the accession of William and Mary, a new generation of writers revived the classicism of moderation. The polite circle of Garth, Congreve, Walsh, Granville and Wycherley cultivated the arts of translation and imitation of the classics, following the direction taken by Dryden during the 1690s. Satire was neglected in favour of more sober poetic kinds in a spirit of conformity to a new regime, whose establishment marked the final stilling of the echoes and reverberations of the Civil War. George Granville (Lord Lansdowne) registered the group's reaction against the stylistic excesses of the early Restoration theatre:

> Our King [Charles II] return'd, and banish'd Peace restor'd,
> The Muse ran mad, to see her exil'd Lord;
> On the crack'd Stage the Bedlam Heroes roar'd,
> And scarce cou'd speak one reasonable Word.

Dryden himself, says Granville, was a victim of the popular rage, but finally, descending from these dizzy heights, ' . . . in each elab'rate Piece/He vies for Fame with ancient *Rome* and *Greece*'.[1] During the last decade of his life, Dryden abandoned polemical and personal satire, preferring to devote himself to translations of Juvenal, Persius and Virgil, and to imitations of Chaucer. A similar sobering change occurs in comedy: Congreve argued, in the Prologues to *The Way of the World* (1700) and *Love for Love* (1695), that social disapproval and 'ill-natured' satire were no longer necessary elements in social comedy.

The polite circle which dominated poetic taste during the 1690s produced no major poetry, but exerted an important influence on the neoclassical poets of the eighteenth century, especially Pope, whose talents were first recognised by Walsh. Pope regarded his early mentors as a group of men of taste very like the circle of Maecenas to whom Horace appealed in the tenth satire of Book I. Pope echoes this passage in *An Epistle to Dr Arbuthnot*:

> *Granville* the polite,
> And knowing *Walsh,* would tell me I could write;
> Well-natur'd *Garth* inflam'd with early praise,
> And *Congreve* lov'd, and *Swift* endur'd my Lays;[2]
> (135–8)

Like the Roman Scipionic Circle, this coterie cultivated refinement and correctness in diction and prosody, and consolidated the development of a rigorously plain-style classicism. Within the literary world, this development marks a new stage in the history of Augustan poetry and separates the satirists of the Restoration period from those of the age of Pope. After 1690, the tradition of Juvenal and the satyr-satirist is eclipsed by the voice of Horace.

The resurgence of the Horatian tradition was prefigured in the classical revival in France, specially in René Rapin's *Reflections* and André Dacier's 'Préface sur les satires d'Horace'. Following Casaubon, Dacier established the derivation of 'satire' from *satura* (not from *satyrus*). By emphasising the Roman origin of satire (*satura* means 'miscellaneous') the French critics were trying to play down the primitive image of the genre and to stress its civilised accomplishments and its stylistic variety. Dryden was not entirely in agreement with the speculations about etymology, but was deeply influenced by the French preference for Horace's refinement and 'delicacy'.[3] In his earlier satiric practice, Dryden had permitted himself very little scope for Horatian 'fine raillery'; his preference was for the 'majestic way' of Juvenal, which was vehement without being uncivilised. After Dryden's *Discourse,* in which neither Horatian delicacy nor Juvenalian 'spleen' are endorsed unequivocally, the balance inclines towards Horace.

An aspect of Dacier's discussion of Horace which is of importance for an understanding of eighteenth-century satire is his insistence that satire's moral purpose has both a negative and a positive side: it should teach by portraying not only knaves and fools, but also men of reason and good sense. Satire, in his view, is not simply the reverse of panegyric but contains within its own formal design a balance of *praise* and *blame*. This analysis leads Dacier to question the distinction between Horace's 'satires' and 'epistles', both of which fall within the satiric genre differing only in the *proportions* of the elements of praise and blame within the formal design.[4] Dryden not only follows Dacier's lead in the

Discourse, but also embodies the new theory of satire's formal design in his own satires, notably in *Absalom and Achitophel*. The implications of Dacier's theory are fully worked out in Pope's work: his 'satires' and 'epistles' converge more than Horace's on a single structural pattern. The epistles *To Dr Arbuthnot* and *To Augustus* are more satiric than Horace's, while the satires addressed to Mr Fortescue and to Mr Bethel (both imitations of Horace) contain more elements of praise than Horace's.

An interesting barometer of the changing neoclassical taste in satire is William Wollaston's preface to *The Design of Part of the Book of Ecclesiastes* (1691), which looks at the Roman satirists through the new spectacles of Lockean rationalism. Both Horace and Juvenal, he suggests in the 'Epistle to the Reader', have qualities which appeal to the age. Despite his tendency to '*Mirth and Drollery*', Horace is more concerned with 'truth' than with 'jest', and with what is '*rational*' than with what is 'risible'. Conversely, 'Juvenal . . . is not so *hot* and *violent,* as some would make him . . . Nay, sometimes he abates so much of his seriousness, as to be even merry.' The truth is that the various tones ('drolling', 'pleasantness', 'gravity' and 'inveighing') are not absolutes but 'modes' of satire, 'and to be used as occasion requires'. The Horatian recipe – a mixture of *triste* and *iocosum* ('gravity' and 'gaiety') – became the Augustan norm and reinforced the reasonableness which underlay Dacier's conception of the *balance* of 'praise' and 'blame'.

Both the revival of orthodox classicism and the final taming of the woodland 'satyr' were part of a general tendency in the literary world between 1690 and 1720, towards a narrowing of the spectrum of styles within which it was possible (that is, considered acceptable) to write. The plain style conquered the centre ground and controlled the whole range of poetic kinds. Locke successfully brought philosophy 'into well-bred company and polite conversation', and superseded the more radical and divisive philosophy of Hobbes, whose presence overshadowed the drama and poetry of the early Restoration period. Idealist philosophy, mysticism and political radicalism lost their position of challenge.[5] In satire, the most important verse satirists of the early eighteenth century, Pope, Swift and Young, are more 'rational' and 'polite' than their Restoration counterparts. Pope's style is plainer in general than Dryden's; Swift tempers the doggerel of Butler and the obscenity of Rochester. The dominant literary elite, who cultivated the polite conversation of gentlemen, believed that the rational qualities of the best 'prose' formed the basis of the best 'verse'. Such a view favoured the *sermo pedestris,* which conformed to Pope's poetic ideal of 'What oft was thought, but ne'er so

well expressed'. According to Thomas Sprat, Cowley captured
the gentlemanly qualities of Horatian satire in his imitations:

> I know some Men disapprove it, because the Verse seems to
> be loose, and near to the plainness of common Discourse. But
> that which was admir'd by the Court of *Augustus* never ought
> to be esteem'd flat or vulgar. And the same judgements should
> be made of Mens styles as of their behaviour and carriage:
> wherein that is most courtly and hardest to be imitated, which
> consists of a Natural easiness and unaffected Grace, where
> nothing seems to be studied, yet every thing is extraordinary.[6]

Sprat's recognition of the neoclassical qualities of Horace's 'plain-
ness' anticipates the attitudes of Pope and Swift, and reminds
us that Dryden's distaste for Horace's 'grovelling' style sets him
apart from Augustan orthodoxy. Wollaston expressed better than
Dryden the appeal of Horace to the new generation of Augustans
when he wrote: 'For his thoughts are generally rational, and yet
modified with a sort of newness and delicacy almost proper to
himself. And in this it is that he excels *Juvenal*' (*Design*, p. 17).

GOOD-HUMOURED SATIRE: YOUNG'S 'LOVE OF FAME'

Critics tend to assume that Pope and Swift held a position of un-
challenged ascendancy in the field of verse satire during the
early eighteenth century. The puny dunces, it seems, were con-
temptuously brushed aside like so many flies. While there is no
doubt that Pope's verse satires were unequalled, his view of satire
was not unchallenged. The early years of the century witnessed
the rise of an enlightened middle-class conception of humour,
comedy and satire. The old classical preference for the 'liberal
jest'[7] is revived in a new form. Following the lead given by
Anglican preachers like Tillotson (in 'The Folly of Scoffing in
Religion') and Glanvill (in 'Reflections on Drollery and Atheism'),
Addison and Steele were largely responsible for establishing the
new ideal of humour and raillery, which was deeply hostile to the
aristocratic wit of the Restoration satirists.[8] In this they were
supported by the Earl of Shaftesbury whose *Charactericks* (1711)
was widely read. According to the earl, happiness was attainable
by following the dictates of 'Reason', which always took the
middle path, avoiding extremes. A reasonable mind was also a
good-humoured mind. Gravity, melancholy, fanaticism and en-
thusiasm led inevitably to irrational behaviour. Ridicule might be
used in defence of reason and morality, but only if employed
responsibly and without malice.

Addison is unequivocal in his condemnation of scurrilous satire in the *Spectator, no. 23*:

> Lampoons and Satyrs, that are written with Wit and Spirit, are like poison'd Darts, which not only inflict a Wound, but make it incurable . . . If, besides the Accomplishments of being Witty and Ill-natured, a Man is vicious into the bargain, he is one of the most mischievous Creatures that can enter into a Civil Society.[9]

Everywhere Addison and Steele emphasise the importance of social cohesion and universal good will. Good-natured raillery is inoffensive and leavened with kindness. The best satires are those in which 'the Satyr is directed against Vice, with an Air of Contempt of the Fault, but no ill Will to the Criminal'.[10] It was not surprising that Horace was regarded as the model of good nature and sociability. Dacier had described Horace in language which might have been written for the *Spectator*: 'In a word, he [Horace] endeavours to make us happy for our selves, agreeable, and faithful to our Friends, easie, discreet and honest to all, with whom we are oblig'd to live.'[11]

The cultural potency of the *Spectator* (1711–12) and *Tatler* (1709–11) periodicals stemmed largely from their successful pursuit of the role of arbitrator between sectional interests. Sir Roger de Coverley and Sir Andrew Freeport represent the Tory and Whig interests in benign and moderate form.[12] Addison and Steele acted as mediators between urban middle-class values and aristocratic and genteel Augustan values. Middle-class and Puritan attitudes to satire were expressed in Sir Richard Blackmore's *Essay upon Wit* (1716), which attacks the Augustan 'wits' for their ridicule of 'the industrious Merchant, and grave Persons of all Professions' and their failure to 'promote Prudence and Sobriety of Manners'.[13] Addison, replying in the *Freeholder, no. 45* (1716), gives general support to Blackmore's moral tone, but adds a rider to the effect that raillery, if based on morality, is socially beneficial, for it 'unbends the mind from serious studies and severer contemplations, without throwing it off from its proper bias'. The wit of a Roger de Coverley, implies Addison, is perfectly consistent with 'politeness and good humour'.[14]

The ideals of the *Spectator* were invoked by Edward Young in his *Love of Fame, The Universal Passion: In Seven Characteristical Satires* (1725–8).[15] Young is usually remembered for his preromantic poetry in *Night Thoughts* and his attack on Augustan orthodoxy in *Conjectures on Original Composition* (1759). In the Preface to the *Love of Fame*, Young attempts to define a genteel and amiable theory of satire; without abandoning the classical touchstones, he reassesses their value in the light of Addisonian and Shaftesburian ideals. He favours *'laughing Satire'* which avoids personal malice and is addressed to 'the general conduct of mankind'. Dryden's analysis of the differences between Horace and Juvenal is accepted, but Young alters the overall evaluation:

> Moreover, *laughing Satire* . . . only has any delicacy in it. Of this delicacy *Horace* is the best master: He appears in a good humour while he censures; and therefore his censure has the more weight, as supposed to proceed from Judgement, not from Passion. Juvenal is ever in a Passion; he has little valuable but his Eloquence, and Morality. (sig. A4)

The over-riding value placed upon 'good humour' separates Young from his neoclassical predecessors and contemporaries. He questions that mingling of raillery and spleen which Dryden inherited from Boileau: *'Boileau* has joyn'd both the *Roman* Satirists with great success; but has too much of *Juvenal* in his serious Satire on Women, which should have been the gayest of all' (sig. A4ᵛ). Nevertheless, like Addison, Young is anxious to include neoclassical values within his good-humoured satire. The first satire invokes the names of a wide range of humorists: Donne, Dorset, Dryden, Rochester, Congreve, Addison, Steele and Pope. An anonymous author, writing in the *Gentleman's Magazine,* captured accurately the mingling of traditions achieved by Young:

> Good-natur'd YOUNG, well-leaned and well bred,
> Studies to lay prevailing folly dead.
> How gently he the well-turn'd Satire deals,
> Smiles while he strikes, and while he wounds he heals![16]

The paradoxes in the final line capture well Young's attempt to combine two apparently incompatible attitudes. The general willingness to accept Young's 'good-natured' claims at their face value underlined the dominance of the Addisonian/Shaftesburian culture of the feelings in the early eighteenth century.

Two conflicting strains of feeling, associated with pre-romantic subjectivism, can be discerned in Young's satire. The first, which became associated with Horatian satire, is the benign strain of Shaftesburian good nature. The second, associated with Juvenalian satire, is a mixture of Miltonic sublimity and egotistical sublime. Later in the century, the two strains are expressed separately in the nerveless satires of William Whitehead and in the unrelenting rhetorical flood of Charles Churchill's satires. Young's satires are fraught with at least two contradictions: first, the rhetorical commitment to good nature is in conflict with a stance of righteous indignation; secondly, fulsome panegyric is often negated by absolute pessimism.

The seven satires describe various social groups, in public and in private life, all of whom are guilty of the universal passion for fame. The satires are organised in a series of character-portraits of general types in the tradition of La Bruyère, Boileau and Addison. The portraits of women in the fifth and sixth satires anticipated and influenced Pope's.[17] Young's desire for advancement gave him a strong motivation to offend no one and to please the establishment. To this end he inserted fulsome panegyrics on George I ('Satire VII'), Walpole ('Satire VII'), Queen Caroline ('Satire IV' and 'Satire VI') and Lady Elizabeth Germain (Satire VI'). Swift observed that Young 'must torture his Invention,/ To flatter *Knaves* or lose his *Pension*'.[18] In his poem on the satires, Swift brilliantly captures the central contradiction which vitiates the whole series: on the one hand, Young paints a picture of a nation blessed with leaders who are imbued with 'Godlike Virtues'; on the other hand, he depicts a nation cursed 'With ev'ry *Vice*'. Swift enacts the total disjunction between 'praise' and 'blame' in the form of his poem, which consists of two unrelated paragraphs without resolution.[19] A desire to combine Augustan wit and Addisonian good humour results in an unsatisfactory blunting of both stances. Rejecting scurrilous, personal satire for the generalised character-sketch, Young loses the incisiveness of Pope and Rochester without achieving Johnson's grandeur of generality. The reflections on wisdom and on the opportunities for satire lack both Horace's delicacy and Juvenal's splenetic vigour:

> No man is blest by *accident* or *guess*
> True *wisdom* is the price of *happiness*:
> Yet few without long discipline are sage;
> And our *youth* only lays up sighs for *age*.
>   But how, my Muse, canst thou resist so long
> The bright temptation of the Courtly throng,
> The most inviting Theme? The *court* affords
> Much food for Satire; it abounds in Lords.
>
>   (p. 15)

The sententiousness lacks the conversational wit of Horace. The allusion to Juvenal's impatient 'How can I not write satire . . .' is blunted by pre-romantic fancy ('bright temptation', 'most inviting theme').

The two satires on women contain some of Young's best lines and also reveal the contradictions in his satire most clearly. The

brief character-portraits alternate with passages of heightened
didacticism. The satiric thumbnail sketches sometimes have the
gaiety and sophisticated wit of Pope:

> Some ladies are too beauteous to be wed,
> For where's the man that's worthy of their bed?
> If no disease reduce her pride before,
> *Lavinia* will be ravisht at threescore.
> Then she submits to venture in the dark;
> And nothing, now, is wanting – but her spark.[20]
>
> (p. 126)

> Here, might I sing . . .
> How two red lips affected *zephyrs* blow,
> To cool the *bohea* [tea], and inflame the *beau*:
> While one white *finger*, and a *thumb*, conspire
> To lift the *cup*, and make the *world* admire.
>
> (p. 142)

The sketch of Fulvia, whose 'passion for the town' breeds in her
distaste for the country –

> Green fields, and shady groves, and chrystal springs,
> And larks, and nightingales are odious things.
>
> (p. 98)

– resembles Pope's 'Epistle to Miss Blount on her leaving the
Town after the Coronation', but the brief sketch is followed by
a long pre-romantic effusion on the virtues of retirement. In
'the world' we suffer the afflictions of '*thorny* care, and *rank* and
stinging hate', which 'wound the firmest temper of our soul'. In the
'private scene' we are blessed:

> O sacred solitude! divine retreat!
> Choice of the prudent! envy of the great!
> By thy pure stream, or in thy waving shade,
> We court fair Wisdom, that celestial Maid:
> The genuine off-spring of her lov'd embrace,
> (Strangers on earth!) are *innocence* and *peace*.
>
> (p. 99)

By contrast, Horace's lyrical effusion *(o rus quando te aspiciam!)* in
the sixth satire of Book II, is well-integrated and entirely relevant
to the central theme of the poet's love of retirement.

Throughout the satires, Young filters in gestures of a Juvenalian
rhetoric which are quite at odds with his commendation of
'laughing' satire. He talks of the satirist's 'rage', 'censure', 'fury',

'our spleen', and 'our invectives', but only rarely does he actually employ invective, except in a few brief references to the general madness of the times. In the course of 'Satire VII', Young suddenly embarks on a long invective against women who now, we are told, threaten the fabric of society. The shift is justified logically as a shift of attention from fools to knaves and from folly to vice:

> Nor to the *glass* [alcohol] alone are nymphs inclin'd,
> But every bolder vice of bold mankind.
> O *Juvenal!* for thy severer rage!
> To lash the ranker follies of our age.
> Are there among the females of our isle,
> Such faults, at which it is a fault to *smile?*
> There are. Vice, once by *modest nature* chain'd,
> And *legal ties,* expatiates unrestrain'd.
>   (pp. 143–4)

But the change of stance is unconvincing, especially when we discover that the final retreat of female vice is the card-table! It is hard to see how Juvenalian apostrophes –

> Such dissolution through the whole I find,
> 'Tis not a world, but Chaos of mankind.
>   (p. 145)

– belong with Popean wit:

> *Flavia,* at lovers false *untouch'd,* and *hard,*
> Turns pale, and trembles at a *cruel* card.
>   (p. 154)

   The contradictory satiric strategy produces an unstable tone and weakens the credibility of the ethical norms which the poems project. The Addisonian good-humour of the Preface is not only at odds with the Augustan wit of the sketches, but also clashes with passages of pre-romantic invective in which Young indulges that Juvenalian 'passion' referred to unfavourably in the Preface. The *Dunciad*-like chaos which threatens the land is suddenly banished by a magical 'flood of light,/That bursts o'er gloomy Britain' in the form of Queen Caroline's 'Excess of goodness'. Once again, fulsome praise overbalances despairing blame. In the second 'Epistle to Mr Pope', Young discusses satire in a manner which indicates that his methods were consciously devised:

> Do boldly what you do, and let your page
> Smile, if it smiles, and if it rages, rage . . .

> Let satire less engage you than applause;
> It shows a gen'rous mind to wink at flaws: . . .
> Satire recoils whenever charg'd too high;
> Round your own fame the fatal splinters fly.
> As the soft plume gives swiftness to the dart,
> Good breeding sends the satire to the heart.

The alternation of praise ('applause') and blame ('rage') is recommended but only to be qualified by an Horatian preference for well-bred satire. A pre-romantic sublimity is constantly being displaced by an Addisonian good nature. Young's satires failed from an over-reaching comprehensiveness of ambition: he wanted to be both a public scourge and a man of feeling, but only succeeded in undermining the credibility of both roles.

POPE AND SWIFT

The temptation to call Pope the eighteenth-century Horace and Swift the eighteenth-century Juvenal should be resisted. A more flexible description is called for. Both admired Horace's Augustan urbanity, and both were capable of Juvenalian bitterness and personal animosity. Swift's anti-romantic attitudes resemble Juvenal's, but his regular use of Butler's 'boyish' decasyllabic verse prevented him from taking the Roman's 'majestic way'. Pope's satires range from the playfully ironic to the 'tragic' and declamatory. Nevertheless, both Pope and Swift are predominantly Horatian. Despite his low-style 'realism' and his philosophical bitterness, Swift upheld the essential Horatian satiric and literary values. In 'To Mr Delany' (1717), Swift declares his stylistic allegiance:

> To you the Muse this Verse bestows,
> Which might as well have been in Prose;
> No Thought, no Fancy, no Sublime,
> But simple Topicks told in Rime.
> (p. 215)

Pope, also, frequently acknowledged the Horatian plain-style values. For example, in his imitation of Horace's Epistle I, vi, Pope opens the poem with 'Plain Truth, dear MURRAY, needs no flowers of speech'.

During the early eighteenth century, Horace became a medium through which the Augustan writers filtered their experience, not only in satire but in the whole range of kinds. The cultural domination of the plain style is amply expressed in Reuben Brower's generalisation that: 'Pope and his friends – writers, statesmen, artists, country gentlemen of many degrees of grandeur – often saw their own world through Horace's eyes and to a surprising degree tried to shape the actuality to fit the dream.'[21]

Pope's mastery of satiric styles in verse was unprecedented. He wrote mock-heroic *(The Rape of the Lock),* heroic satire *(The Dunciad,* Book IV), satiric epistles, epistolary satires, Lucilian satire ('To Bethel') and satiric moral essays. Even formally non-satiric poems, such as *An Essay on Criticism* and *An Essay on Man,* are full of incisive satiric passages. Pope's rejection of the *Spectator's* good-natured satirist, and his refusal to write general satires rather than personal satire, has resulted in a generally bad press for his satiric tactics. Thackeray attacked Pope for being a 'ruthless little tyrant', who revelled 'in base descriptions of poor men's want'.[22] After 1945, the new rhetorical approach to Augustan satire overcame the prevailing biographical approach to produce a more satisfactory account, which gave full weight to the *variety* of Pope's voices. Maynard Mack separated the 'satirist' from the 'author', and pointed out Pope employed three voices: first, the plain-living, self-amused voice; secondly, the voice of the *naïf* or *ingénu* (a voice which permitted irony); and thirdly, the heroic voice of the public defender.[23] The biographical critic's argument, that the various voices represent various moods or aspects of Pope's personality, can be neither endorsed nor refuted. But it is surely simpler, if less heady, to talk in terms of Pope's deployment of 'voices' than in terms of the refractions of an imputed 'personality'.

All three voices can be heard in Horace's *Satires* and *Epistles*, but, in Pope's satires, the third voice – of the heroic defender of public morals – is far more elevated than in Horace, and owes something to the tradition of Juvenal's sublime indignation. Pope insisted that satire depended on the personal nature of its attack for its salutary effects:

> I am afraid that all such Writings [satires] . . . as touch no Man, will mend no Man. The *Good Natured* indeed are apt to be alarmed at any thing like Satire; and the *Guilty* readily concur with the *Weak* for a plain Reason, because the Vicious look upon Folly as their Frontier.[24]

Pope insisted that 'to chastise is to reform':

> To reform and not to chastise, I am afraid is impossible . . . To attack Vices in the abstract, without touching Persons, May be safe fighting indeed, but it is fighting with Shadows . . . Examples are pictures, and strike the Senses, nay raise the Passions, and call in those . . . to the aid of reformation.[25]

But the satirist elsewhere makes it clear that by 'personal satire' he did not intend 'libel'. There is no licence for the uncontrolled savagery of a Marston or the naked malice of a Rochester. Pope's concern for moral seriousness was so great in his later work that he considered renaming his satires 'epistles'. Writing to Swift in 1733, Pope argued that moral discourse outweighs invective in his satires:

> I have not the courage however to be such a Satyrist as you, but I would be as much, or more, a Philosopher. You call your satires, Libels; I would rather call my satires, Epistles: They will consist more of morality than wit, and grow graver, which you will call duller.[26]

In his *The First Satire of the Second Book of Horace Imitated* (1733), Pope defends his satires against Fortescue's legal warnings. Horace had argued that his verses are not 'bad' (sc. libellous) but 'good'. Pope neatly translates:

> *Libels* and *Satires!* lawless Things indeed!
> But grave *Epistles,* bring Vice to light . . .
> (150–51)

Pope's disclaimer should be carefully examined; we should not assume that he is making concessions to the good-natured Muse. The word 'grave' should remind us that Pope's most serious and 'moral' satires are often intensely vehement and elevated in tone. Pope's *adversarius* in *Epilogue to the Satires, Dialogue I* (1738), unlike Fortescue and Arbuthnot, is a true 'adversary', whom Pope calls 'an impertinent Censurer'. His complaints about Pope's new 'moral' tone must be rejected by the reader:

> You grow *correct* that once with Rapture writ,
> And are, besides, too *Moral* for a Wit.
> (3–4)

Pope gives full rein to his moral indignation in the closing lines, in which the satirist, lamenting the inversion of moral values, rises to a declamatory grandeur which anticipates the tragic satire of *The Dunciad,* Book IV:

> 'Tis Av'rice all, Ambition is no more!
> See, all our Nobles begging to be Slaves!
> See, all our Fools aspiring to be Knaves!
> The Wit of Cheats, the Courage of a Whore,
> Are what ten thousand envy and adore . . .

While Truth, Worth, Wisdom, daily they decry –
'Nothing is Sacred now but Villany.'
(162–6, 169–70)

The avoidance of 'Libel', then, does not mark a capitulation to the good-natured satirist. The style of generalised declamation is a new version of the Juvenalian voice, one which is chastened by Augustan 'correctness' and which is elevated by a deep moral seriousness. Dr Johnson was to develop this new 'tragic' voice in his imitations of Juvenal.

The *Imitations of Horace* involve a considerable complication of Horace's style and tone.[27] They cover a wide spectrum of satiric styles, from the Lucilian harshness of *The Second Satire of the First Book of Horace Imitated* (1734) to the amiable plainness of *The Sixth Epistle of the First Book of Horace Imitated* (1738). The distinction between satires and epistles, which is not absolute in Horace, is further eroded by Pope, who sometimes includes Juvenalian invective in epistles, and sometimes extends the epistolary qualities in the satires. Above all, Pope shows great skill in enriching and complicating the satiric persona, especially by introducing irony and indirection.

Pope's imitation of Horace's key programmatic satire (II, i), illustrates the complexity of his method. Horace asks Trebatius' advice on the problem of the satirist's role. Trebatius recommends that Horace should abandon satire and write epic, reminding him of the laws against libel. Horace's replies are full of wit, irony and mock-seriousness. Pope, however, deepens the irony, introducing *ad hominem* satire in the opening lines. Where Horace simply declares 'Some think that I am too bitter in satire', Pope elaborates and particularises:

> There are (I scarce can think it, but am told)
> There are to whom my Satire seems too bold,
> Scarce to wise *Peter* complaisant enough,
> And something said of *Chartres* much too rough
> (1–4)

The ironic 'wise' immediately undermines Horace's neutrality of stance and implies that satiric roughness and boldness is justified against the financial speculation of Peter Walter and the profligacy of Francis Chartres. Even Fortescue, Pope's legal adviser, is implicated in Pope's ironic wit. Trebatius suggests that great rewards will be gained if Horace praises Caesar's exploits. Fortescue declares:

> Of if you needs must write, write CAESAR's Praise:
> You'll gain at least a *Knighthood*, or the *Bays*
> (21–2)

The hits against Sir Richard Blackmore and Colley Cibber which are developed in the subsequent lines, transform Horace's delicate and amused tone into something more astringent. On the other hand, Pope is equally anxious to develop Horace's brief allusion to the epistolary 'sincerity' of Lucilius, whose 'whole life is open to view, as if painted on a votive tablet'. Pope elaborates the celebration of plain-style values by heightening the poetic language –

> I love to pour out all myself, as plain
> As downright *Shippen,* or as old *Montagne.*
> In them, as certain to be lov'd as seen,
> The Soul stood forth, nor kept a Thought within . . .
> (51–4)

and by interpolating references to the golden mean ('this impartial glass', 'Like good *Erasmus* in an honest Mean,/In Moderation placing all my Glory'). Perhaps the most significant change is Pope's self-identification with Lucilius. While Horace looks backward nostalgically to Lucilius' free-ranging moral invective, Pope throws aside the qualifying effects of Horatian detachment and embraces the role of moral scourge:

> What? [Shall I be kill'd?] arm'd for Virtue when I point the Pen,
> Brand the bold Front of shameless, guilty Men,
> Dash the proud Gamester in his gilded Car,
> Bare the mean Heart that lurks beneath a Star . . .
> (105–8)

Thus Pope superimposes the 'voice' of public defender on the 'voice' of plain honest man. There is a strong implication in *Dialogue I* that Pope found Horace's 'sly, polite, insinuating stile' too tame for his own age. Pope rejects the role of 'artful Manager', and with bitter irony pretends to abandon his own ideal of satire:

> Adieu Distinction, Satire, Warmth, and Truth!
> Come harmless *Characters* that no one hit . . .
> (64–5)

In *Dialogue II*, Pope eloquently extols the satirist's role as public defender, whose essential motivation is moral ('Antipathy of Good to Bad'), and whose mission gives heightened significance to the lowly style of satire:

> Truth guards the Poet, sanctifies the line,
> And makes Immortal, Verse as mean as mine.
> (246–7)

Pope's financial independence evidently permitted him a more uncompromising stance than Horace could afford to adopt. Horace could not boast that he was 'Above a Patron'.

It is difficult in a short space to do justice to the variety and subtlety of Pope's satiric verse. So much has been written on Pope in recent years that a brief account can concentrate only on a few distinctive and innovatory features of his satire. Here we shall consider Pope's mastery of tone (his 'fine raillery'), his metaphoric exuberance and his 'realism'.

To say that Pope mastered Horatian delicacy is not to say that he was never the heroic declaimer or the ill-natured lampooner, but it is to say that his central achievement as a satirist was his perfection of that plain-style Horatian voice. It is an achievement of tone – a muscular tension of wit which does not depend on outright aggression or explicitness. The indirection of Pope's satire is not the sign of a Swiftian sublimation and concealment of aggressive drives, but of the assured irony of a sophisticated and genteel Augustan wit.

His best-known satire, *The Rape of the Lock* (1714), is a masterpiece of 'fine raillery'. It is Pope's only 'good-natured' satire. The dedication to Arabella Fermor, the original of Belinda, is itself written with subtle raillery. Throughout Pope sustains a delicate balance between gallantry, flattery, mockery and wit. Pope introduces the technical notion of 'Machinery' as follows:

> The *Machinery, Madam*, is a Term invented by Criticks, to signify that Part which the Deities, Angels, or Daemons, are made to act in a Poem: For the ancient Poets are in one respect like many modern Ladies; Let an Action be never so trivial in itself, they always make it appear of the utmost Importance. (p. 217)

The hit at Arabella's own inflation of a triviality (the rape of the lock) is pleasingly softened by the parallel hit at critics and poets. Pope assumes that playful tone which prevents offence and flatters by its refined attentions.

The same delicacy is sustained throughout the poem, in the gentle mockery of the *beau monde* of Queen Anne's day, a mockery which touches the margin of flattery. The management of the mock-heroic device permits a simultaneous elevation and ridicule of Belinda and of her social world. There is both beauty and triviality. In the description of Belinda's toilet preparations, she is both a goddess and an epic hero arming for combat, and, at the same time, a vain young lady and a predatory siren. The delicacy lies in the achievement of apparent congruence between the heroic and mundane levels:

> First, rob'd in White, the Nymph intent adores
> With Head uncovere'd, the *Cosmetic* Pow'rs.
>
> (I, 123–4)

We hardly notice the bathos in *'Cosmetic'*, which passes itself off as 'Cosmic'.

Pope's ridicule of 'modern Ladies' is conducted with a very light touch. Ariel, appearing to Belinda, in epic fashion, in a 'Morning-Dream', explains the history and function of the Rosicrucian spirits, and interjects:

> What tho' no Credit doubting Wits may give?
> The Fair and Innocent shall still believe.
>
> (I, 39–40)

The ridicule of female credulity could not be phrased in a more winning manner. The description of Belinda on the Thames (modelled on Aeneas' voyage up the Tiber) draws ironic attention to her flirtations and fickle nature, but concludes with a disarming piece of flattery:

> If to her share some Female Errors fall,
> Look on her Face, and you'll forget 'em all
>
> (II, 17–18)

Pope frequently uses a mock-Petrarchan mode of flattery which is not entirely ironic: *'Belinda* smil'd, and all the World was gay' (II, 52). This flattery is wittily inverted when the gnome, Umbriel, visits the Cave of Spleen to ask the Goddess for assistance:

> Hear me, and touch *Belinda* with Chagrin,
> That single Act gives half the World the Spleen.
>
> (IV, 77–8)

Pope's delicacy here is partly derived from the superimposition of heroic and Petrarchan hyperboles; the former mode deflates Belinda, the latter elevates her. The result is a poetically productive ambiguity of tone.

By the final canto, the force of satire and moral commentary has begun to overturn Belinda's precarious dignity. Pope skilfully introduces a counterbalance by turning the satire against the defeated Baron and 'Beaus' in general: their 'Wits' weigh light in Jove's balance compared with the 'Lady's Hair'. The final apotheosis of the lock, after the manner of Catullus' *Lock of Berenice,* completes the counter-movement and at the same time combines the flattery of Belinda and the conventional dedication of the poem to posterity:

> *This Lock,* the Muse shall consecrate to Fame,
> And mid'st the Stars inscribe *Belinda's* Name!
> (V, 149–50)

Pope's control over tone in the *Rape* is particularly evident in his exploitation of the devices of bathos and paraprosdokian (departure from normal expectation). Sometimes the effects are cutting and even savage; sometimes there is a genuine sadness or pathos. Pope's application of the *topos* of the inevitability of Fate to the lock's demise at the hands of 'The conqu'ring Force of unresisted Steel' does not have an entirely deflating effect. The opening of Canto IV is remarkable for its tonal nuances:

> But anxious Cares the pensive Nymph opprest,
> And secret Passions labour'd in her Breast.
> Not youthful King's in Battel seiz'd alive,
> Not scornful Virgins who their Charms survive,
> Not ardent Lovers robb'd of all their Bliss,
> Not ancient Ladies when refus'd a Kiss,
> Not Tyrants fierce that unrepenting die,
> Not *Cynthia* when her *Manteau's* pinn'd awry,
> E'er felt such Rage, Resentment and Despair,
> As Thou, sad Virgin! for thy ravish'd Hair
> (IV, 1–10)

The allusion to Dido's suffering in the *Aeneid,* IV, leaves Belinda a good deal of dignity (despite the mild bathos of 'Nymph'). The comparisons are grouped in pairs. The first of each pair has a tragic or heroic connotation, the second has a bathetic effect. There are also a number of patterned echoes and antitheses between the couplets which give the whole passage a pleasing formal integrity. The 'Kings' and 'Virgins' are linked by survival in contrast to the 'Tyrants' (as opposed to 'Kings') who 'die'. The *'youthful* Kings' are the antithesis of the *'ancient* Ladies', and the *'scornful* Virgins' are similarly paired with *'ardent* Lovers'. Thus the opening epithets of lines 3–6 form a chiasmic pattern:

> 'youthful'
> 'scornful'
> 'ardent'
> 'ancient'

The third couplet contains the strongest bathos, intensified by the mythological connotations of *'Cynthia'*. The overall effect is evidently one of ridicule, but we do not simply link Belinda with Cynthia: the rape is not as trivial as Cynthia's momentary loss of elegance. Nor do we regard Belinda as sunk beneath the weight of genuine heroic dignity: the 'Kings', 'Lovers' and 'Tyrants' are themselves absurd, fustian cut-out stereotypes. In a sense, only Belinda survives the passage.

Pope began to make literary and social enemies early in his career. Some remarks in *An Essay on Criticism* (1711), written when Pope was only twenty-three, offended the professional critic John Dennis, who wrote a vitriolic reply in *Reflections Critical and Satirical, upon a Late Rhapsody, call'd an Essay upon Criticism*. Despite efforts to remain neutral, Pope found himself, by 1712, supporting the Tory coffee-house elite against its Whig rival. The Scriblerus Club (Pope, Gay, Swift, Parnell, Dr Arbuthnot and Harley) was founded in order to defend classical values and aristocratic cultural standards against both the pedantry and dry scholarship of the traditional critics (Bentley, Theobald) and the incursions of the alternative culture associated with the rising middle classes and the City business interests. Pope's *Dunciad* (1728 and 1742) is the club's most powerful attack upon the new class of poets, journalists and publishers, collectively known as 'Grub Street', who challenged the dominance of the aristocratic culture.[28]

In *The Dunciad* and in 'An Epistle to Dr Arbuthnot', Pope developed the tradition of satire against literary dunces inaugurated by Horace, Persius and Juvenal and continued by Butler, Oldham and Dryden. The immediate historical context was the final phase of the quarrel between the 'Ancients' and the 'Moderns' described in mock-heroic prose in Swift's *Battle of the Books*. Swift and Pope joined the Scriblerus Club in order to combat what they regarded as the radical cultural threat embodied in the moderns' rejection of the authority of the classics. Pope's conservativism has been regarded by a recent critic as a severe limitation: 'Pope does not seem to me to have penetrated beyond the vocabulary and specific concerns of his own culture, despite the vigour, thoughtfulness, and skill with which he investigates them.'[29] But, one must reply, a writer may achieve a cultural significance either by surpassing his cultural situation in some way, or, as Pope does, by *crystallising* those cultural concerns – by giving the reader a sharper and more fully realised embodiment of those concerns. Pope's reactionary attack on the new bourgois culture involved the fullest poetic *development* of the essential structure of Augustan values. Pope's most distinctive stylistic achievement in this field in his extraordinary figurative vitality. His central metaphors are not new and can be found in the poetry of Cowley, Oldham, Rochester and Dryden. But Pope was able to sustain and develop metaphoric imagery for satiric purposes to a degree which was unprecedented. In many ways we are reminded of the figurative exuberance of Donne, two of whose satires, despite their un-Augustan abstruseness, were imitated by Pope. Far from removing Donne's conceits, Pope fondly elaborated them in a more 'rational' form.

The central metaphors of Pope's later satires are developed from the antitheses of Augustan orthodoxy. Sanity, Reason and Wit confront Madness, Folly and Dullness, while Order, Nature and Light oppose Anarchy, Chaos and Night. The post-revolutionary rigidities of Augustan ideology facilitated the deployment of these bold and simplified formulae. Pope's originality lies in the metaphoric elaboration and recombination of these commonplaces.

'An Epistle to Dr Arbuthnot' (1735) turns upon the two metaphors of madness and sickness. The poem's opening lines set them in motion:

> Shut, shut the door, good *John!* fatigu'd I said,
> Tye up the knocker, say I'm sick, I'm dead,
> The Dog-star rages! nay 'tis past a doubt,
> All *Bedlam*, or *Parnassus,* is let out:
> Fire in each eye, and Papers in each hand,
> They rave, recite, and madden round the land.
>
> (1–6)

The playfully desperate 'say I'm sick, I'm dead' is later neatly transformed into a metaphoric instrument of satire:

> What *Drop* or *Nostrum* can this Plague remove?
> Or which must end me, a Fool's Wrath or Love?
> A dire Dilemma! either way I'm sped,
> If Foes, they write, if Friends, they read me dead.
>
> (29–32)

In both passages, Pope sets up a poetic interaction between the metaphors and the offending literary activities. The couplets are tightly organised in related antitheses (*Bedlam – Parnassus,* Fire – Papers, rave – recite), culminating in 'madden round the land', in which the interaction is completed in a fused image of the universal fury of scribblers. In the other passage, fusion is achieved in the metaphoric/literal play on 'Plague' and in the syntactic daring of 'write' and 'read me dead'. The metaphoric pattern is developed throughout the poem in passages of vigorous wit and inventiveness:

> Is there, who lock'd from Ink and Paper, scrawls
> With desp'rate Charcoal round his darken'd walls.
>
> (19–20)

> Of all mad Creatures, if the Learn'd are right,
> It is the Slaver kills, and not the Bite.
>
> (105–6)

The metaphor of sickness is poignantly restored to its literal level
in a Horatian passage of autobiography in which Pope refers to
'this long Disease, my Life', to his father's enviable death ('His
Death was instant, and without a groan'), and to his mother's
illness. The tribute to Mr Pope enables the poet to complete the
antithesis of madness and sanity ('Stranger to Civil and Religious
Rage'), falsehood and honesty (he spoke 'No language but the
language of the heart'). Praise of the father not only echoes Horace's
sixth satire of the first book, but fulfils the structural design of
the epistle in which 'blame' is to be fully balanced by 'praise'. The
'autobiography' stands as an oasis of positive values in a degenerate
world of sickness and madness.

The stereotyping of Pope as the greatest poet of Reason leads
one to expect a poetry of denotation, prose values and discursive-
ness. However, *The Dunciad* (1728, 1742) is one of the densest
metaphoric poems in the English language. Almost all the poetic
effects deriving from imagery can be understood in terms of
incongruity or contradiction. The essential mock-heroic in-
congruity, involving the comparison between an epic action and a
series of mundane literary actions, is complicated by a contradictory
infusion of diminishing imagery.

The goddess, Dullness, 'Daughter of Chaos and eternal Night'
labours to restore 'her old Empire'. The new 'order' established
in Book III is a grotesque parody and inversion of the ideal of
Nature embodied in *An Essay on Man*.[30] *The Dunciad* is the mirror
reverse:

> Thence a new world to Nature's laws unknown,
> Breaks out refulgent, with a heav'n its own:
> Another Cynthia her new journey runs
> And other planets circle other suns.
>
> (III, 241–4)

In *An Essay on Man,* only God can

> Observe how system into system runs,
> What other planets circle other suns.
>
> (I, 24–5)

The 'new World' of Dullness is a world of merely metaphoric
grandeur. Pope often dissolves the grandeur by running to the
opposite metaphoric pole, for example, when the goddess observes

the dunces' abortive poetic creations emerging from the 'Cave of
Poverty and Poetry':

> Here she beholds a Chaos dark and deep,
> Where nameless Somethings in their causes sleep,
> 'Till geneal Jacob, or a warm Third day,
> Call forth each mass, a Poem, or a Play:
> How hints, Like spawn, scarce quick in embryo lie,
> How new-born nonsense first is taught to cry,
> Maggots half-form'd in rhyme exactly meet,
> And learn to crawl upon poetic feet.
>
> (I, 55-62)

The sublime images of cosmogony and the allusions to the Genesis
story ('Chaos', 'Third day') degenerate into images of sexual
reproduction and unnatural creation. The inflation and diminution
form a simultaneous impression of incongruity and instability.
Characteristically, Pope brings the literal and metaphoric levels
together in the pun on 'feet' (metrical and anatomical). Through-
out the poem, the dunces are both grandiose subversives and
insignificant busybodies. Bacon's diminishing comparison of false
wit and cobwebs is extended to include bugs (I, 130), silk-worms
(IV, 253) and flies (IV, 454). The philosophical significance of the
diminishing metaphor is summed up in Pope's comment on textual
critics:

> The critic Eye, that microscope of Wit,
> Sees hairs and pores, examines bit by bit.
>
> (IV, 233-4)

Like Oldham, Dryden and Swift, Pope generates a good deal of
poetic vitality from the use of scatology. But unlike his pre-
decessors, Pope's refinement forced him to make his wit less
pungent, less overt. Indeed, much of the metaphoric play is derived
from the incongruous decorum of Pope's periphrases:

> Renew'd by ordure's sympathetic force,
> As oil'd with magic juices for the course,
> Vig'rous he rises; from th' effluvia strong
> Imbibes new life, and scours and stinks along.
>
> (II, 103-6)

The competition for 'Who best can send on high/The salient spout,
far-streaming to the sky' concludes with a scurrilous reference to
Curl's venereal infection couched in epic terms: 'His rapid waters
in their passage burn' (II, 184). Pope comments on a similar
passage justifying this 'lowness' of the action with quotations from
Homer and Virgil. He draws attention to Dryden's practice of

mentioning vulgar incidents, but wittily distinguishes between Dryden's obscenity and his own more decorous scurrility: 'But our author is more grave, and . . . *tosses about his* Dung *with an air of Majesty*' (*Variorum,* II, 71n). The playful wit does not invalidate the essentially serious recognition of Pope's 'politeness'. Dryden had struck out for the extremes of style in his description of Shadwell's coronation route, littered with unsold books: 'Martyrs of Pies, and Reliques of the Bum.' Pope describes Cibber's library where books retire 'And 'scape the martyrdom of jakes and fire', especially twelve which are 'Redeem'd from tapers and defrauded pies' (I, 144, 155). Where Dryden goes for *stylistic* incongruity, Pope sustains a polite style and elects to confine the effect of incongruity to that between style and subject-matter. Far from weakening the metaphoric intensity of *The Dunciad,* Pope's sustained 'politeness' demands invention of more and more ingenious metaphoric transformations of the vulgar and mundane. In the *Rape* Pope had already developed the metaphoric possibilities of epic periphrasis: the card-table is metamorphosed into a 'verdant Field', a 'velvet Plain' and a 'level Green'; the deadly scissors became a 'fatal Engine' (Virgil's *fatalis machina,* the Trojan horse), a 'glittering Forfex', and a 'two-edged Weapon' (biceps, an axe). The innate precariousness of Augustan poetic diction, its tendency to lapse from dignity to bathos, is fully exploited in *The Dunciad.*

Pope often generates satiric effects by allowing the fullest possible play of ambiguity in his use of imagery. Mist or fog had played an honourable role in classical and Miltonic epic as instruments of divine protection or as garments of invisibility. Dullness, 'the cloud-compelling Queen', beholds her creation 'thro' fogs, that magnify the scene' (I, 79–80). The epic connotations (we recollect cloud-gatherer Zeus) appear to be reinforced by the wicked word 'magnify', but we remember Pope's remark in *Essay on Criticism*:

> As things seem *large* which we thro' *Mists* descry,
> *Dulness* is ever apt to *Magnify*
> (392–3)

The essential mock-epic device is thus frequently extended in further metaphoric variations:

> O! ever gracious to perplex'd mankind,
> Still spread a healing mist before the mind.
> (I, 173–4)
> So spins the silk-worm small its slender store,
> And labours till it clouds itself all o'er.
> (IV, 253–4)

Pope displays a similar inventiveness in his variations on the image of 'lead'. The epic connotation of Dullness's 'new Saturnian age of Lead' is neatly turned to satiric advantage by the substitution of 'lead' for the expected 'gold'. The footnote points out, 'The ancient Golden Age is by Poets stiled *Saturnian;* but in the Chymical language, *Saturn* is Lead' (*Variorum,* I, 26n). It is appropriate that bathos should be introduced with a reference to the dunces' beloved experimental science. Pope exploits the images of 'lead' relentlessly, drawing on its connotations of dullness (colour), weight (ponderousness), mechanical motion, and its tendency to fall (bathos).

The apparent disorder of the poem is partly an objectification of the dunces' disorder; but, underlying the appearance of chaotic redundancy, there is a formal order which was first properly recognised by Aubrey Williams.[31] The action of the poem embodies the charge that the dunces were undoing the entire accumulated tradition of Western culture. By transferring the kingdom of Dullness from the City (Smithfield) in the east, the centre of bourgeois values, to the polite world of the Court in the west, the dunces were enacting a debased version, a parody, of the action of the *Aeneid,* in which ancient cultural values are preserved by Aeneas' transference of the ruined kingdom of Troy (in the east) to Rome (in the west). Thus, parody extends not only to diction and formulaic features, but even to the heroic *action* itself. *The Dunciad* is Pope's re-enactment of the heroic poem in Augustan terms. In Book IV, Pope allows the cosmic heroic style to prevail in the tragic vision of the final chaos in which all civilised values are obliterated:

> *Religion* blushing veils her sacred fires,
> And unawares *Morality* expires.
> Nor *public* Flame, nor *private,* dares to shine;
> Nor *human* Spark is left, nor Glimpse *divine!*
> Lo! thy dread Empire, CHAOS! is restor'd;
> Light dies before thy uncreating word:
> Thy hand, great Anarch! lets the curtain fall;
> And Universal Darkness buries All.
>
> (IV, 649–56)

The mock-heroic is finally superseded by the heroic satire, not in its Restoration baroque mode nor the ironic Virgilian mode, but in the fully-fledged Augustan heroic style, which is characterised by a tendency to allegorical abstraction, a carefully controlled, almost spare, use of the couplet form, and an elegiac tone which preserves a Roman dignity. Dr Johnson developed and perfected the style in *The Vanity of Human Wishes.* This is the fully evolved

Augustan equivalent of Juvenal's bitter manner. It reflects that Tory pessimism which links the gloomy vision of *The Dunciad* and the reactionary sourness of Juvenal. Both satirists shared a deep unease about the state of their societies. Both diagnosed a sick patient and a dying culture. Pope's satire, however, is distinguished by the certainty and clarity of its Augustan values, which are strongly implied in the account of their subversion. Juvenal lacks the positive vision. The moral fervour of Pope's Juvenalian voice is nowhere more clearly expressed than in the *Epilogue to the Satires, Dialogue II,* in which Pope transforms the Horatian 'apology' into a sublime celebration of the satirist's high calling:

> O sacred Weapon [satire]! left for Truth's defence,
> Sole Dread of Folly, Vice, and Insolence!
> To all but Heav'n-directed hands deny'd,
> The Muse may give thee, but the Gods must guide.
>
> (212–15)

Here we have an invocation to what one might call the baptised muse of satire. John Peter's arguments about the 'immiscibility of *Satura* and Christianity' seem quite inapplicable to Pope's late writings. Here surely we have Juvenal *moralisé*!

'Realism' is not a term normally attributed to Augustan poets. However, satire had always tended towards realism in one of its senses: according to the classical 'separation of styles', satire, as a low-style genre, was concerned with ordinary mundane existence. Horace's abandonment of the title *poeta* and his adoption of the humbler 'pedestrian Muse' permitted him a greater 'realism', that is, a more direct engagement with the 'real' world of ordinary men, a non-heroic world of human folly, domestic triviality and familiar conversation. Adopting an Auerbachian view, we would have to deny such satire a sense of the serious, the problématic and the creatural. Nevertheless, even acknowledging the limitations of Pope's world-view, we can still discern a peculiar dimension of the 'real' which the Augustan poet is able to realise.

Georg Lukács uses the word 'typical'[32] to describe a central feature of realism: a 'typical' character combines generality and particularity. Realism in this sense achieves a sense of particular lived experience with a sense of characteristic general experience, avoiding the extremes of naturalism and pure subjectivity. The Augustans were apt to become abstract in the commitment to the universal, and were incapable of the historical concreteness required by Lukács, but Pope sometimes succeeds in producing the 'typical'. In the 'Epistle to Miss Blount, on her leaving the Town, after the

Coronation', Pope describes Zephalinda's unhappy retirement from the pleasures of the town:

> She went, to plain-work, and to purling brooks,
> Old-fashion'd halls, dull aunts, and croaking rooks,
> She went from Op'ra, park, assembly, play,
> To morning walks, and pray'rs three hours a day:
> To pass her time 'twixt reading and Bohea,
> To muse, and spill her solitary Tea,
> Or o'er cold coffee trifle with her spoon,
> Count the slow clock, and dine exact at noon;
> Divert her eyes with pictures in the fire,
> Hum half a tune, tell stories to the squire;
> Up to her godly garret after sev'n,
> There starve and pray, for that's the way to heav'n
>
> (11–22)

The first couplet is a finely realised vision of domestic tedium; the sense of tedium is intensified by the poetic conventionality of 'purling brooks' which reflects the lady's jaundiced view of the country. 'Croaking rooks' adds further monotony (assonance, symmetry). The satirist moves quickly from establishing Zephalinda's perspective to an ironic depiction of her rural purgatory. The realism is strongly envinced in the irony (compare Jane Austen's). The fineness also resides in the observations of inaction which are both psychologically and socially exact. The metrical control adds a further precision: in 'To muse, and spill her solitary Tea', the tedium and an appropriate irregular movement are enacted in the versification. In 'Count the slow clock, and dine exact at noon', the movement from boredom to mechanical activity is also registered metrically. The 'realism' enacted in the 'typical' description, the ironic tone, and the prosodic control of the passage is not felt in the last couplet in which a more abstractly satiric presentation supervenes. The subjective dimension of the realism is lost in a general satire on rural asceticism.

Realism of this kind is most often used to illuminate the female world from within. Sometimes there is sympathetic empathy as in the account of Belinda's morning in the *Rape*. In the 'Epistle to Miss Blount: with the Works of Voiture', the general theme, that happiness does not reside in 'false shows, or empty Titles', is saved from cliché and abstraction by a concise illustration:

> The Gods, to curse *Pamela* with her Prayers,
> Gave the gilt Coach and dappled *Flanders* Mares,
> The shining Robes, rich Jewels, Beds of State,
> And to compleat her Bliss, a Fool for Mate.

> She glares in *Balls, Front-boxes* and the *Ring,*
> A vain, unquiet, glitt'ring, wretched Thing!
> Price, Pomp, and State but reach her outward Part,
> She sighs, and is no *Dutchess* at her Heart
> (49–56)

The 'realism' does not come from particularity (only *'Flanders'*
departs from pure generality), but from a convincingly composed
nexus of subjective and objective facets of an experience. The
appurtenances and the social setting of a duchess's life-style are
compactly presented together with an unsentimental evocation of
human disappointment and loss. The structural antitheses upon
which the irony is built are focused in the antithesis between
'She glares' and 'She sighs': the contradictory aspects of Pamela's
plight are thus given an effectively unemotive expression. There is
a *moral* effect of distance which is effected through the irony. This
ironic detachment is Horatian, not Juvenalian. Cleanth Brooks's
remarks on the *Rape* are apposite here: 'The tone is ironical, but
the irony is not that of a narrow and acerb satire; rather it is an
irony which accords with a wise recognition of the total situation.'[33]
The ideological strength of such a wise realism should be recognised;
it is 'common sense' raised to the highest pitch.

Swift's satiric verse declares its low-style orientation in several ways.
The poems are almost all in Hudibrastic verse.[34] Almost all are
anti-romantic in purpose. Swift's commitment to 'laughing'
satire is more clear and consistent than Young's. In 'An Epistle to a
Lady' (1733), Swift refuses to 'suspend' his 'paultry Burlesque
Stile' and to sing the lady's 'Praise in strain sublime'. It goes against
his 'nat'ral Vein', which inclines him to merry satire:

> Like the ever-laughing Sage [Democritus],
> In a Jest I spend my Rage:
> (p. 635)

Swift declares that he 'Hardly can be grave in Prose'. He associates
the heroic style with contentious and angry satire, and quotes
Horace to support his preference for 'raillery':

> . . . . For, as
> It is well observ'd by HORACE,
> Ridicule has greater Pow'r
> To reform the World, than Sour.
> (p. 636)

Swift thus evades the Augustan demand that satire should involve
both 'praise' and 'blame'. By failing to quote Horace's remarks

about the alternation of the 'grave' (*triste*) and the 'gay' (*iocosum*), Swift places his emphasis exclusively on 'blame', which he considered incompatible with gravity. Like Butler and Rochester, Swift used the high style only in fun:

> His Vein, ironically grave,
> Expos'd the Fool, and lash'd the Knave:
>
> (p. 565)

Swift's favourite satiric form is the mock-poem. Every serious poetic kind, including the elegy, the pastoral, the rural ode, the panegyric and the progress poem, is mocked with irony or in doggerel verse. In 'Phillis, Or, the Progress of Love', Phillis marries a respectable man, only to elope with John, the butler. Swift ruthlessly satirises Phillis's romantic protestations, and describes the sordid degeneration of the couple's married life:

> How oft she broke her marriage Vows
> In kindness to maintain her Spouse;
> Till Swain's unwholesome spoyld the Trade,
> For now the Surgeon must be paid;
> To whom those Perquisites are gone
> In Christian Justice due to John.
>
> (p. 225)

Swift ridicules by incongruous use of circumlocution and poetic diction. Prostitution ('broke her marriage vows'), venereal disease ('Swain's unwholesome'), and the profits of a pimp ('Perquisites') are ironically dignified in decorous terms.

It would be wrong to give the impression that Swift's poetry is simply a reversion to the tradition of Butler. His obvious indebtedness to *Hudibras* hides a profound difference of sensibility. 'Jocoseness'[35] is certainly the dominant tone in the poems, but we should not forget that *saeva indignatio* which so often disturbs the sober Augustan surface of Swift's prose. Swift has a kinship with Juvenal which is not shared by Butler. Scott's remarks on this subject are extremely suggestive:

> Sometimes . . . the intensity of the satire gives to his poetry a character of emphatic violence, which borders upon grandeur. Yet this grandeur is founded, not on sublimity either of conception or expression, but upon the energy of both; and indicates rather ardour of temper than power of imagination. *Facit indignatio versum.*[36]

The Juvenalian 'grandeur' which can be found in the fourth book of *Gulliver's Travels* can also be found in the poems. In the mock-

Ovidian 'The Progress of Beauty' (1719), Swift describes the sordid cosmetic art by which Celia gives 'form' to the 'matter' of her face. The account of her physical decay is compared with the waning moon:

> Yet as she [the moon] wasts, she grows discreet,
> Till Midnight never shows her Head;
> So rotting Celia stroles the Street
> When sober Folks are all a-bed.
> (p. 229)

The macabre starkness of 'rotting Celia' is highlighted by the native realism which underlies the simplicity of the last line. The low-style realism,[37] which Swift inherits from Butler and Ben Jonson, acts as a foil to the macabre image and gives the satire its intensity.

Sometimes a savage *animus* transforms a rollicking satire into something closer to Rochester's low-style indignation. In 'The Progress of Marriage', Swift describes a barren marriage between a Dean (Dean Pratt in life) and a 'Nymph Coquette' (Lady Philippa Hamilton in life), which results in the Dean's demise and the widow's enrichment. The poem concludes with a bitter prayer reminiscent of Rochester's cursing of Corinna in 'A Ramble':

> Oh, may I see her soon dispensing
> Her Favors to some broken Ensign.
> Him let her Marry for his Face,
> And only Coat of tarnish't Lace;
> To turn her Naked out of Doors,
> And spend her Joynture of his Whores:
> But for a parting Present leave her
> A rooted Pox to last for ever.
> (p. 295)

There is a gratuitousness in the concluding couplet which supports the traditional accusation that Swift is misanthropic. The misanthropy goes beyond that materialistic view of human nature which he shared with Hobbes. One has to admit that Swift's disgust is sometimes pathological in comparison with Rochester's, which is generally consistent with his unorthodox ethical views. On the other hand, there is consistency in Swift's attitude towards the satirist's ethical role. He is the only Augustan satirist to doubt the moral efficacy of satire:[38]

> For, let Mankind discharge their Tongues
> In Venom, till they burst their Lungs,
> Their utmost Malice cannot make
> Your Head, or Tooth, or Finger ake
> (p. 414)

The resulting overflow of undirected indignation is a phenomenon which we have seen, in different forms, in Juvenal and in Marston. The Juvenalian satirist is always in danger of allowing the indignant voice a disturbing autonomy, especially in the absence of a secure moral framework.

Swift's disgust is often expressed in the language of scatology and obscenity. Like a great deal of obscenity in Restoration verse, Swift's stems from that essentially Christian and Neo-platonic tradition of thought which finds a source of paradox or irony or disgust in the dual nature of man. The Platonist laments the soiling flesh in which the soul is temporarily housed. The Christian accepts the paradox, and sanctifies the body in the ennobling myth of the Resurrection. The naturalistic libertine (Rochester) demands a full recognition of our animal nature. In 'A Satyr against Reason and Mankind', Rochester declares that if he could choose

> What case of flesh and blood I pleased to wear,
> I'd be a dog, a monkey, or a bear,
> Or anything but that vain animal
> Who is so proud of being rational.
>
> (4–7)

We are so proud of being more than animals, that we forget that 'Huddled in dirt the reasoning engine lies'.

Swift's sensitive awareness of man's duality gives some of his scatological poems a remarkable modernity and relevance. In Yeats's 'Crazy Jane Talks With the Bishop', the Bishop gives the traditional Pauline argument:

> Those breasts are flat and fallen now,
> Those veins must soon be dry;
> Live in a heavenly mansion,
> Not in some foul sty.

Crazy Jane's reply is a kind of Swiftian assertion of the Christian incarnational conviction:

> But Love has pitched his mansion in
> The place of excrement;
> For nothing can be sole or whole
> That has not been rent.

Freud acknowledged the psychic shock which accompanies the realisation that man is born *inter urinas et faeces*. Scatological obscenity can be understood either as a symptom of neurosis or as a gesture aimed at the exorcism of neurosis. Donald Greene argues[39] that, far from displaying his own pathological obsession, Swift criticises Cassinus' and Strephon's obsessions with the fact that 'Caelia shits'. Greene concludes:

> Strephon . . . is the victim of his 'foul imagination' and 'vicious Fancy', which in the first place demanded for his inflated ego a super-human partner, . . . and now, when his fantasy world collapses, makes him see in every woman *only* her excretory functions . . . *This* is madness; this is obsession; this is the 'excremental vision', which makes a fetish of the routine, trivial, and harmless fact of human excretion . . .

Greene may have overstated Swift's equanimity in the face of 'the place of exrement', but his arguments are a useful corrective to the relentlessly Freudian interpretations of Aldous Huxley, D. H. Lawrence and Norman O. Brown. We may reject a psychological explanation of Swift's preoccupation with scatology, but there remains a traditional basis for it: the image of the death's-head, the *memento mori*. When Donne wrote of women 'At their best/Sweetness and wit, they'are Mummy possest', he was play-fully drawing on that storehouse of imagery in which Shakespeare and the Jacobean dramatists were so prolific: we remember Hamlet's vision of man as 'this quintessence of dust', his realisation that 'Imperious Caesar' is reduced to clay and to stopping 'a hole to keep the wind away', and we remember Bosola's grim words to the Duchess of Malfi: 'Thou art but a box of worm seed, at best, but a salvatory of green mummy.'

To dwell exclusively on Swift's Juvenalian qualities would give a quite false impression of his satiric verse. Swift shares with Rochester and Pope an ability to create a strong impression of autobiographical immediacy.[40] The Augustan 'I' is unexpectedly well realised in satiric poetry. The conventions of the 'Honest Muse', the epistolary tradition of Montaigne and Erasmus, and the example of Horace, are evidently formative. In Pope and in Swift the presentation of personality has a vividness which has been described as 'romantic'. But one should remember that this vividness can be found earlier in Wyatt, in Ben Jonson, in Cowley and in William Temple. Wesley Trimpi writes of Ben Jonson's poems: 'They have the curious personal quality of the author's continued and unchanging presence coming through the lines.'[41] In Swift's imitation of Horace (*Satires*, II, vi, 1714), the account of Maecenas' levee hour is elaborated in poignantly personal terms:

> I get a Whisper, and withdraw,
> When twenty Fools I never saw
> Come with Petitions fairly pen'd,
> Desiring I would stand their Friend.

> This, humbly offers me his Case –
> That, begs my Interest for a Place –
> A hundred other Men's Affairs
> Like Bees, are humming in my Ears . . .
> Thus in a Sea of Folly tost,
> My choicest Hours of Life are lost:
> (pp. 200, 202)

Our sense of an intensely personal realisation of Horace's predicament is supported by the fact that Swift used the same Horatian allusion in a letter to Archbishop King in 1707:

> The World may contradict me if they please; but
> when I see your Palace crowded all day to the
> very Gates with suitors, sollicitors, Petitioners,
> who come for Protection, Advice and Charity . . .
> I cannot forbear crying out with Horace, Perditur
> interea misero lux.[42]

The passage immediately preceding in the imitation describes Swift's attempts to gain access to Harley on his levee-day:

> Another in a surly Fit,
> Tells me I have more Zeal than Wit,
> 'So eager to express your Love,
> 'You ne'er consider whom you shove,
> 'But rudely press before a Duke.'
> I own, I'm pleas'd with this Rebuke,
> And take it kindly meant to show
> What I desire the World should know
> (p. 200)

Horace is delighted to admit to the bystander that, in his enthusiasm, his mind does indeed absent-mindedly run on Maecenas; but Swift introduces a new emphasis on private friendship as against public respect. His lack of concern for social precedence ('rudely press before a Duke') is an indiscretion he is pleased to have made public. A letter to Harley, written only a few weeks before the poem's completion, establishes clearly the personal nature of Swift's projection of the Horatian persona. Swift declares 'I always loved you just so much the worse for your Station'. He respects and loves Harley not in his 'publick Capacity', but 'as a private man'. Swift can claim that 'it was never in the Power of any publick or concealed Enemy to make you think ill of me, though Malice and Envy were often employd to that End'. As if he were writing the letter and the poem in conjunction, Swift concludes: 'I have said enough, and like one at your Levee having made my Bow, I shrink back into the Crowd.'[43]

Swift's 'autobiographical' poems are full of satiric stories about himself or against himself. His narrative ingenuity alone repays study. His favourite strategy is to write in an ironic third-person voice, which enables him to attack others while appearing to mock himself. In 'An Apology to the Lady Carteret', the apparent apology masks a satire on the lady's courtly pretentions. Swift depicts himself as a socially gauche but learned divine who, when invited to dinner by Lady Carteret, appears to be overawed by the occasion:

> He trembles at the Thoughts of State;
> For, conscious of his Sheepish Gait,
> His Spirits of a sudden fail'd him,
> He stop'd, and cou'd not tell what ail'd him
>
> (p. 376)

The lady is offended when, coming late for the appointment, she finds the 'Doctor' gone. Summoning him again, she accepts *his* apology and invites herself to lunch, on the understanding that he tells her 'the real Truth in Rhime'. With some irony, the 'Doctor' promises her suitably plain fare:

> But first resolv'd, to shew his Taste
> Was too refin'd to give a Feast,
> He'd treat with nothing that was Rare,
> But winding Walks and purer Air;
> Wou'd entertain without Expence,
> Or Pride, or vain Magnificence;
> For well he knew, to such a Guest,
> The plainest Mails must be the best:
> To Stomachs clog'd with costly Fare,
> Simplicity alone is rare;
> Whilst high, and nice, and curious Meats,
> Are really but Vulgar Treats:
> Instead of Spoils of *Persian* Looms,
> The costly Boast of Regal Rooms,
> Thought it more courtly and discreet,
> To scatter Roses at her Feet;
> Roses of richest Dye, that shone
> With native Lustre like her own;
> Beauty that needs no Aid of Art,
> Thro' ev'ry Sense to reach the Heart.
>
> (378–9)

The satiric raillery is nicely controlled. Swift adopts the tone and idiom of a courtly refinement which is at the same time rejected by the Horatian theme of 'simplicity'. The lady is apparently praised for her artless natural beauty which wins an un-Swiftian romantic tribute ('To Scatter Roses at her Feet'). The poem's satiric sting comes from this ironic identification of the lady's beauty and the beauty of nature. She finds 'the purer Air' of Swift's rural retreat unbearably fatiguing, whereupon the doctor tells 'the real Truth' by arguing that her distaste for the country cannot match his distaste for the sneering pomposity of the Court. If she flees 'this Majestick Eye' of the sun, how much more forgivable is it for him to fly 'the living Lusture' of her eyes, especially when he fights his way through 'Crowds of Coxcombs & of Coaches', only to be told that the lady is out! The poem shows many of Swift's strengths: the management of irony, the subtle use of allusion, and the masterly control of point of view.

In 'Lady Acheson, Weary of the Dean', Swift slyly satirises the lady's ungracious hospitality by showing her inverting the classical values of 'good housekeeping' in her complaints to her husband about the Dean's visit:

> The House Accounts are daily rising
>   So much his Stay do's swell the Bills;
> My dearest Life it is surprising,
>   How much he eats, how much he swills.
>
> (p. 860)

In 'The Humble Petition of Frances Harris' and 'Mary the Cook-Maid's Letter to Dr Sheridan', Swift constructs perceptions of himself from a lower-class angle. In the former, a young working girl in Lady Berkeley's employ loses her purse. She asks Swift for his advice, doubly offending by calling him 'Parson' and by implying he is a 'conjurer':

> With that, he twisted his Girdle at me like a Rope,
>   as who should say,
> Now you may go hang your self for me, and so went away.
>
> (p. 72)

We see only the young girl's innocent view of Swift's behaviour: he doesn't come out of it well. In the other poem, Swift gives us an account of a quarrel with his friend Dr Sheridan through the eyes of his cook, who defends the Dean in forthright terms:

> Well; if ever I saw such another Man since my Mother bound
>   my Head,
> You a Gentleman! marry come up, I wonder where you were
>   bred?
>
> (p. 985)

In both poems, Swift uses an irregular doggerel verse which some-how avoids mocking the speakers. The naivety and simplicity of their point of view is realised in an amused but empathic manner. It would be an exaggeration to claim that Swift anticipates Browning here, but he shares something of Browning's fascina-tion with unorthodox or atypical voices. In these poems the self is seen at a distance with an ironic and an unromantic eye. Swift's exploration of the self and of his 'roles' as poet, priest, friend and politician extends the scope of the autobiographical Horatian voice by multiplying points of view and by introducing an existen-tial bitterness into the Horatian candour.

The early eighteenth-century verse satirists complicate the laughing satirist's voice in different ways. If Horace may be said to have dominated the fifty years between 1690 and 1740, the same cannot be said of the final decades of the Augustan period when the voice of Juvenal is revived for the last time in the poetry of Dr Johnson and Charles Churchill.

Chapter 5

The 18th Century Juvenal:
Dr Johnson and Churchill

The periodisation of literary history is a notoriously imprecise art. We use the label 'Augustan', recognising that its effectiveness as a catch-all is severely limited. The 'Age of Reason' turns out to have been an 'Age of Feeling' and even an 'Age of Passion'. We no sooner recognise a distinctive feature which expresses a historical moment than we perceive its 'opposite' lurking in embryonic form waiting for the moment of contradiction. We tend to identify the 'Age of Pope' with firmly established neo-classical attitudes, with a belief in the priority of reason, art and social life over feeling, nature and individual personality. But, even in Pope's work, these choices are not made so exclusively. In the *Essay on Criticism,* for example, nature and art are unified in brilliantly dialectical fashion ('Nature and Homer were he found the same'). The seeds of contradiction may be found in more potent form in Addison's essays, in which many of the attitudes we now consider 'romantic' or 'pre-romantic' can be found. By developing the latent emphasis on subjective experience to be found in Locke's philosophy, Addison laid the foundation of romantic aesthetics.[1] This interest in the individual's experience raised doubts about neoclassical views on 'imitation' and the nature of 'Truth'. Ideas later to be developed by Edward Young and Joseph Warton can be found in the work of Addison, John Dennis and Leonard Welsted early in the century. The influence of the Greek critic Longinus's *On the Sublime* reinforces the pre-romantic rejection of servile classicism:

> Imitation is the Bane of Writing, nor ever was a good Author, that entirely form'd himself on the Model of another . . . to imitate is purely mechanical, whereas to write is a Work of Nature . . .[2]

The adoption of a Longinian attitude did not entail a complete rejection of imitation, but only of 'servile' imitation. Edward Young insists that the classics cannot pre-empt poetic progress: the ancients should be regarded not 'as masters . . . but as hard-match'd rivals for renown'. The modern writer may 'emulate' the ancients and 'feed on' their 'Understandings', but only so long as his own genius is not annihilated.[3] One might argue that English classicism at its best had always observed this essentially Baconian requirement. Nevertheless, there is no doubt that the seeds of contradiction were germinating vigorously in Joseph Warton's *Essay on the Genius and Writings of Pope* (1756), in which his demotion of Pope in the poetic hierarchy is based upon the preromantic assumption that 'The Sublime and the Pathetic are the two chief nerves of all genuine poesy'.[4]

The emerging pre-romanticism of the mid-eighteenth century led to further revaluation of the Roman Satirists. In the Preface to his translation of Horace (1743), Philip Francis draws attention to Horace's insistence that satire was not 'poetry':

> . . . he really thought a satirist and a poet were extremely different characters; that the language of poetry was as un-natural to the morality of satire, as a low, familiar style to the majesty of an epic poem . . . In Juvenal the vices of his age are shown in all their natural horrours. He commands his readers in the language of authority, and terrifies them with images drawn in the boldness of a truly poetic spirit.[5]

Francis goes on to indicate a preference for Horace's conversational manner, but this does not entirely remove the force of the phrase 'truly poetic spirit' from our minds. The truth is that, while paying lip-service to Augustan orthodoxies, many writers, especially after 1740, were allowing Longinian rhetoric to colour their theories and even to modify their practice in a direction which favoured the Juvenalian manner in satire.

Boileau's translation of Longinus's *Peri Hupsous* was available in England during the 1670s, and probably exercised an influence on Dryden's development of a new, more classical, heroic style in *All for Love* and *Absalom and Achitophel*. The translation of Boileau's version by John Pulteney, *A Treatise of the Loftiness or Elegancy of Speech* (1680), in which Dryden had a hand, had some importance in the history of the development of an Augustan heightened style. In its Chapter 27 it is argued:

> . . . that which is extraordinary [sic] Great and Lofty, cannot have that naturall purity, that which is plain and easie, for that a too great care of being Polite and Elegant, does oftentimes degenerate into lowliness . . . (pp. 121–2)

The kinds of 'loftiness' attempted in the period of Pope and Dr Johnson are very different from those in the period of Cowley and Dryden. The metaphysical *frisson* and the baroque grandiloquence which survives in Cowley and in Dryden virtually disappear in Pope.[6] The Longinian vogue generates a new conception of 'elevation' which includes a more subjective and affective element.

A *general* change in the dominant conception of Juvenal was clearly related to Longinian ideas – for example, in the work of John Dennis, who regards the greatest poetry as 'religious' and 'throughout pathetick':

> And in Poetry, they who write with a great deal of Passion, are generally very harmonious; whereas those who write with but little are not so musical. *Horace* is an illustrious Example of this. No Man, who has read his Odes can doubt of the fineness and the Delicacy of his Ear; and therefore his Satires are often harsh and rugged, because the Spirit in them is mean and little. No Man can believe that *Juvenal* had a finer ear than *Horace,* but yet his Satires are more musical, because they have a greater Spirit in them.[7]

While the resemblance between the 'enthusiastic' Dennis and the sober Dr Johnson is slight, they are related by a Longinian current of ideas. What marks the difference between Pope and Johnson as neoclassical satirists is, to a large extent, the pervasive *pathos* of Johnson's tone. Johnson is a 'religious' satirist in the sense that he elevates a rational plain style with a Christian emotional depth. In this he belongs in the tradition of Ben Jonson, Henry Vaughan and Abraham Cowley.

In the first thirty years of the century, a number of poems were written which conform to a more serious and dignified conception of Juvenal. Samuel Cobb was an important early Longinian critic,[8] who brought in a new attitude to 'sublime' satire. His admiration for the Juvenalian Oldham knows no bounds:

> He [the Sun] set him out insufferably bright,
> And sow'd in every part his beamy light.

'Low' kinds of humour are anathema:

> For Raillery, and what creates a Smile
> Betrays no lofty Genius, nor a Style.[9]

Cobb's poem 'Of Vain Wishes' puts into practice the elevated view of Juvenal, which had been expressed long before in theory. The opening lines shadow forth the language of Dr Johnson's *Vanity of Human Wishes*:

> By error led, Unwary Minds pursue
> Imagin'd Pleasure, and Neglect the True;
> Things far remote from solid Good desire,
> And what's Destructive, to themselves require.
> They gain their Wish, but curse the false Embrace,
> And find a Cloud in Royal *Juno's* Place.
> (p. 280)

Cobb's account of vain desires is expressed in a style, which combines a tight neoclassical balance and a generalising economy of language with a heightened pathos, which anticipates Johnson's tone and even his locutions: 'perish in the mad Pursuit of Gain'. 'The painful Pagentry of Scepter'd woe'. Compare Johnson:

> Then say how Hope and Fear, Desire and Hate,
> O'erspread with Snares the clouded Maze of Fate,
> Where wav'ring Man, betray'd by vent'rous Pride,
> To tread the dreary Paths without a guide,
> As treach'rous Phantoms in the Mist delude,
> Shuns fancied Ills, or chases airy Good.[10]

What was incipient in Cobb's work was developed during the next thirty years into a distinctly formal and elevated version of the Augustan couplet. The most significant stylistic features which elevate the Augustan plain style are abstraction, personification (incipient allegory) and sublime metaphor. Thomas Brewster's translations of Persius' satires reveal the changes in Augustan couplet style which had occurred since Dryden's translation. Brewster's version of the second satire (1733), a poem closely related to Juvenal's tenth, is distinctly less colloquial, and more 'sublime' than Dryden's version. For example, Persius' Stoic conclusion is treated very differently in the two versions:

> A Soul, where Laws both Humane and Divine,
> In Practice more than Speculation shine;
> A genuine Virtue, of a vigorous kind,
> Pure in the last recesses of the Mind.
> (Dryden, 130–33)

> A *Soul,* where settled Virtue reigns enshrin'd:
> Where Justice dwells, with Sanctity combined:
> Within whose inmost close Recesses lie
> Tinctures of generous Honour's deepest Dye.
> (Brewster, 158–61)

While Dryden writes discursively, in balanced antitheses ('Humane', 'Divine', 'Practice'/'Speculation'), Brewster heightens the passage with abstract personifications ('Virtue reigns', 'Justice dwells') and extended metaphors. Dryden's avoidance of Persius' terse metaphoric idiom *(incoctus)* is in the interests of rational lucidity. In the *Discourse* he boldly rejects Casaubon's justification of Persius' metaphors:

> In defence of his boisterous metaphors, he [Casaubon] quotes Longinus, who accounts them as instruments of the sublime; fit to move and stir up the affections, particularly in narration. To which it may be replied that where the trope is far-fetched and hard, 'tis fit for nothing but to puzzle the understanding; . . .[11]

Brewster evidently took Casaubon's view of Persius' metaphors, which he expands for the sake of Augustan clarity. Dr Johnson, who disliked the 'unnatural' conceits of metaphysical poetry, cultivated a controlled metaphoric sublimity which resembles Brewster's.

Several eighteenth-century poets who exhibit pre-romantic leanings wrote satires which aspire to the 'sublime' rather than the conversational style. Mark Akenside's *An Epistle to Curio* (1744) is written with a Juvenalian moral indignation, purged of Juvenal's demeaning realism: the 'grandeur of generality' subdues invective and irony. Johnson singled out the *Epistle* for praise, and declared that it was 'written with great vigour and poignancy'. The vigorous and egoistic Richard Savage, whose imaginative flair was admired by Johnson, wrote a satire, dedicated to Young, *The Authors of the Town* (1725), in which Johnson's trenchant couplet style is anticipated:

> Views and Reviews, and wild Memoirs appear,
> And Slander darkens each recorded Year . . .
> A lying Monk on Miracles refines,
> And Vengeance glares from violated Shrines . . .
> Thus from feign'd Facts a false Reflection flows,
> And by Tradition Superstition grows.[12]

The style is weighty and generalising in its abstractness. The couplets are solemn and carefully measured. The particular slips relentlessly into the general by means of personification. The weight of meaning is carried by the verbs ('darkens', 'refines', 'glares', 'flows', 'grows') which are vigorous and often emotive in tone. The satiric manner is declamatory and subjectively intense. Johnson was to refine upon this mature Augustan satiric style and to infuse a cooler impersonality of stance without displacing the emotive qualities.

DR JOHNSON'S IMITATIONS OF JUVENAL

Until recently, Johnson's imitations of Juvenal's third and tenth satires have been viewed from an inappropriate critical perspective. Confusions about the nature of his achievement have arisen partly as a result of an unsatisfactory reading of Juvenal, and partly from an unsympathetic attitude towards imitations as a form.

Ian Jack was right in drawing attention to the Augustan belief in Juvenal's moral seriousness,[13] but mistaken in concluding that an ethical affinity actually exists between model and version. H. Gifford saw that Johnson exaggerates the 'stateliness' of Juvenal, and that his imitation of the tenth satire is far removed in attitude and manner from its model: 'It moves us as an original poem, and the feelings it moves are different from those stirred by Juvenal.'[14] Paul Fussell summarised the conclusions of modern criticism as follows: 'Juvenal's poem is vigorous and on occasion indecent; ... Johnson's is frightened and dark, for he has enforced his argument with an imagery rich in connotations of conflict, excitement, and even horror.'[15]

Even when they recognised a disparity between Johnson and Juvenal, critics have often assumed that the disparity is a sign of Johnson's failure. T. S. Eliot began by regarding Johnson as the pure satirist, whose moral seriousness brought him 'nearer in spirit to the Latin' than either Dryden or Pope. But in 1944, Eliot changed his mind in deciding that Johnson lacked 'a certain divine levity'[16] which belonged to satire. P. O'Flaherty argued that Johnson made 'an ill-advised effort to imitate an author who differed from him in temperament and outlook'.[17] Such approaches neglect Johnson's deeply interesting literary transformation of Juvenal, which tells us so much about the poetic currents in the 1730s and 1740s.

Like Addison, Young and Warton, Johnson did not have a high opinion of the art of imitation, which, he considered, displayed 'industry' and 'observation' but not 'genius'.[18] But, in his own imitations, he not only modernises Juvenal but introduces a new and independent poetic ordering of his model. In fact, the metaphoric vitality of the poems threatens to break the structural link between model and version. Johnson frequently introduces imagery which embodies his own reflective habits of mind rather than Juvenal's. Juvenal's ironic presentation of the horrors and dangers of urban life are given a more pathetic treatment by

Johnson, who adds a more subjective dimension by alluding to
the mental life of the victims. Before Umbricius (Johnson's Thales)
commences his Stoic diatribe on the 'thousand perils of this terrible
city', the poet reflects on the changed topography of Rome.
Johnson takes this opportunity to allow the narrator and Thales a
moment of rapt reverie:

> We kneel, and kiss the consecrated Earth;
> In pleasing Dreams the blissful Age renew,
> And call BRITANNIA'S Glories back to view . . .
> A transient Calm the happy Scenes bestow,
> And for a Moment lull the Sense of Woe.
> (24–6, 31–2)

The sad gap between dream and reality is evoked again in later
passages:

> The sober Trader at a tatter'd Cloak,
> Wakes from his Dream, and labours for a Joke.
> (162–3)

> Rais'd from some pleasing Dream of Wealth and Pow'r,
> Some pompous Palace, or some blissful Bow'r,
> Aghast you start, and scarce with aking Sight
> Sustain th' approaching Fire's tremendous Light.
> (184–7)

Johnson's evocation of man's existential plight, of his tortured and
tragic disappointment, totally transforms Juvenal's sceptical bitter-
ness. It is significant that there is no equivalent in the Latin for
these passages. For Johnson, man is always the dupe of 'that hunger
of the imagination which preys incessantly upon human life'. As
Imlac says in *Rasselas*: 'The truth is that no mind is much em-
ployed upon the present: recollection and anticipation fill up
almost all our moments.' The imagination and the dream help us
to forget, 'And for a Moment lull the sense of Woe'.

Juvenal's account of the burning of the rich man's house is
treated in very different ways by Oldham and Johnson. Oldham
captures the racy naturalistic detail of the Latin and modernises
it in the manner of Boileau. The style resembles Ben Jonson's
in its colloquial simplicity and directness:

> But if the fire burn down some Great Man's House,
> All strait are interested in the loss:
> The Court is strait in Mourning sure enough, . . .
> Nay, while 'tis burning, some will send him in
> Timber, and Stone to build his house agen;

> Others choice Furniture; here some rare piece
> Of *Rubens,* or *Vandike* presented is;
> There a rich Suit of *Mortlack* Tapestry,
> A Bed of Damask, or Embroidery;
> One gives a fine Scrutore, or Cabinet,
> Another a huge mighty Dish of Plate,
> Or Bag of Gold: thus he at length gets more
> By kind misfortune than he had before;
> And all suspect it for a laid Design,
> As if he did himself the Fire begin.
> (pp. 191–2)

Johnson is less concerned with explicit modernisation and more
with preserving and enhancing the dignified poetic qualities in
the Latin at the expense of particularity and mock-heroic effect:

> Should Heav'n's just Bolts *Orgilio's* Wealth confound,
> And spread his flaming Palace on the Ground,
> Swift o'er the Land the dismal Rumour flies,
> And publick Mournings pacify the Skies;
> The Laureat Tribe in servile Verse relate,
> How Virtue wars with persecuting Fate;
> With well-feign'd Gratitude the pension'd Band
> Refund the Plunder of the beggar'd Land.
> See! while he builds, the gaudy Vassals come,
> And crowd with sudden Wealth the rising Dome; . . .
> *Orgilio* sees the golden Pile aspire,
> And hopes from angry Heav'n another Fire.
> (194–203, 208–9)

Very little of Juvenal's wit remains: the irony of Orgilio's re-
covered wealth borders on the tragic. Great intensity of feeling is
evoked in the contrast between the human cost of the production
of wealth ('the Plunder of the beggar'd Land', 'The price of
Boroughs and of Souls') and the gratuitous re-enrichment of
Orgilio ('crowd with *sudden* Wealth the rising Dome').

David Garrick thought that *The Vanity of Human Wishes,*
Johnson's second imitation of Juvenal, was 'as hard as Greek. Had
he gone on to imitate another satire, it would have been as hard
as Hebrew.'[19] The 'difficulty' of this poem lies in its ruthless
economy of syntax and diction, and the sheer pressure of abstrac-
tion. Sometimes paraphrase is required:

> Now Kindred Merit fills the sable Bier,
> Now lacerated Friendship claims a Tear.
> (303–4)

For 'Kindred Merit', read 'a virtuous relation'; for 'lacerated

Friendship', read 'the loss of a friend'. Usually the abstractness has
a 'weight' which does not exclude 'concreteness'.[20] The abstrac-
tions are animated and articulated by powerful verbs:

> Time *hovers* o'er, impatient to destroy,
> And *shuts* up all the Passages of Joy . . .
>
> (259–60)

> Stern Famine *guards* the solitary Coast,
> And Winter *barricades* the Realms of Frost.
>
> (207–8)

The personified abstractions are not intended to 'puzzle the under-
standing' but to function as 'instruments of the sublime'.

Two passages from Juvenal's Latin in which a heightened epic
tonality is manifested, provide a sure test of the translator's or
imitator's stylistic leanings. The first describes the fateful outcome
of Sejanus' hubris:

> . . . nam qui nimios optabat honores
> et nimias poscebat opes, numerosa parabat
> excelsae turris tabulata, unde altior esset
> casus et inpulsae praeceps inmane ruinae.
>
> (104–7)

Compare the versions by Johnson and Dryden:

> For why did *Wolsey* by the Steeps of Fate,
> On weak Foundations raise th' enormous Weight?
> Why but to sink beneath Misfortune's Blow,
> With louder Ruin to the Gulphs below?
>
> (Johnson, 125–8)

> For he who grasp'd the World's exhausted Store,
> Yet never had enough, but wish'd for more,
> Rais'd a Top-heavy Tow'r, of monst'rous height,
> Which Mould'ring, crush'd him underneath the Weight.
>
> (Dryden, 168–71)

In the Latin the first clause establishes a strongly rhetorical and
declamatory mood – '*nimios . . . nimias*', '*optabat . . . poscebat*',
'*honores . . . opes*' – which lends a cooling formality to the epic
description of the ruinous fall. Dryden's version retains something
of the formality, perhaps achieves a simpler dignity by eliminating
the particularity of Juvenal's '*numerosa . . . tabulata*', and intro-
duces an added elegance in 'the World's exhausted Store', changes
which justify Dryden's claim that he 'made him [Juvenal] more

Sounding, and more Elegant, than he was before in English'. In Johnson's imitation the dignity is tragic in tonality: the metaphor of the tottering building is made more impressionistic and therefore more awful. 'Steeps', 'sink' and 'Gulphs' add an emotive fatalism which is characteristic of the recasting of tonality in the poem as a whole.

The second passage describes the bitter outcome of Xerxes' Greek expedition:

> . . . nempe una nave, cruentis
> fluctibus ac tarda per densa cadavera prora,
> has totiens optata exegit gloria poenas.
> (185–7)

Compare the versions of Dryden and Johnson:

> In a poor Skiff he pass'd the bloody Main,
> Choak'd with the slaughter'd Bodies of his Train.
> For Fame he pray'd, but let th' Event declare
> He had no mighty penn'worth of his Pray'r.
> (Dryden, 297–300)

> Th' insulted Sea with humbler Thoughts he gains,
> A single Skiff to speed his Flight remains;
> Th' incumber'd Oar scarce leaves the dreaded Coast
> Through purple Billows and a floating Host.
> (Johnson, 237–40)

The Latin is cool and detached in its grim heroics: the ironic and deflating *nempe una nave* dissolves any sense of dignity. Dryden, whose satiric theory was an attempt to synthesise the 'comic' and 'tragic' traditions of Horace and Juvenal, exaggerates the mock-heroic possibilities in the Latin. He begins by quietly registering irony in 'poor Skiff . . . bloody Main'. But the second couplet is pure mock-heroic:[21] the high style is deflated by 'penn'worth', a bathos unwarranted by Juvenal's *poenas*. In Johnson's lines the pure generalizing diction and the inclusion of pathetic images, which have no equivalents in the Latin ('humbler Thoughts', 'th' incumber'd Oar scarce leaves the dreaded Coast'), dissolves the grim detachment of Juvenal's irony, leaving an effect of tragic dignity.

Johnson's consistent heightening of Juvenal's style is felt not only in the addition of a tragic dimension, and in the omission of Juvenal's low-style detail, but also in the frequent infusion of pre-romantic impressionistic modifiers. Between two hyperbolic and declamatory passages, near the beginning of the satire, Juvenal placed four lines of more subtle irony in which the heightened third line is gently deflated by the surrounding succinct plainness, especially by the epigrammatic fourth line:

> pauca licet portes argenti vascula puri
> nocte iter ingressus, gladium contumque timebis
> et motae ad lunam trepidabis harundinis umbram:
> cantabit vacuus coram latrone viator.
> (19–22)

Johnson replaces irony with pathos:

> The needy Traveller, serene and gay,
> Walks the wild Heath, and sings his Toil away.
> Does Envy seize thee? crush th' upbraiding Joy,
> Encrease his Riches and his Peace destroy,
> Now Fears in dire Vicissitude invade,
> The rustling Brake alarms, and quiv'ring Shade,
> Nor Light nor Darkness bring his Pain Relief,
> One shews the Plunder, and one hides the Thief.
> (37–44)

The empty-handed, unencumbered traveller is no longer simply a carefree vagrant, but a Stoical labourer, 'needy', but 'serene and gay'. The irony of *pauca licet portes* is transformed into an element in the pathos of the traveller's Stoical serenity: we have no cause to envy him his serenity, since it depends upon his continued poverty: 'Encrease his Riches and his Peace destroy'. The empty-handed traveller's singing loses its carefree connotation and is associated with his 'need': 'sings his Toil away'. The passage is scattered with emotive epithets: 'needy', 'serene and gay', 'wild', 'upbraiding', 'rustling', and 'quiv'ring'. Shadwell's version offers a remarkable contrast:

> Though Journying you but little *Silver* bear
> By Night, a Sword, or Quarter staff you fear;
> And a Reeds motion in a Moon light Night
> Shall make you quake and tremble with the fright.
> While the poor man void of all precious things
> In Company with Thieves jogg's on and Sings.
> (V, 298)

Despite its closeness in rendering the sense of the Latin, Shadwell's translation modifies Juvenal quite perceptibly; there is intensification of the low style which is the counterpart of Johnson's heightening of the Augustan plain style. Shadwell's 'poor man' has no Stoic dignity about him; he 'jogg's on and Sings'.

Despite Johnson's endorsement of Democritus' comic vision, there is little doubt that Johnson's vision is more akin to the lachrymose Heraclitus' tragic view of man, which seemed absurd to Juvenal. But Johnson's tragic tone is heavily qualified by the satire's conclusion, in which Juvenal's half-ironic Stoicism is transformed into an otherworldly Christian *consolatio*. The prospects within this world are tragically bleak, but, if we admit 'the Sense of sacred Presence', our prospects are altered by virtues which transform the pain of both recollection and anticipation:

> Pour forth thy Fervours . . .
> For Patience sov'reign o'er transmuted Ill;
> For Faith, that panting for a happier Seat,
> Counts Death kind Nature's Signal of Retreat . . .
>
> (359, 362–4)

The betrayal of hopes and the disappointment of ambitions are transformed by the divine perspective:

> With these celestial Wisdom calms the Mind,
> And makes the Happiness she does not find.

The conclusion does not diminish the force with which Johnson *realises* the tragic bleakness of the human prospect without religion. In the *Idler,* no. 41, Johnson vividly evokes the mental landscape of bereavement:

> The loss of a friend upon whom the heart was fixed, to whom every wish and endeavour tended, is a state of dreary desolation in which the mind looks abroad impatient of itself, and finds nothing but emptiness and horror.

No human 'philosophy', even Stoicism, can do more than distract or conceal our sorrow; only religion can give 'Patience'. For Johnson, the frustration of human ambitions and the vanity and restlessness of the imagination are not viewed with scorn or sceptical detachment but with a melancholy and sympathetic omniscience. In the *Vanity* there is a fruitful tension between Augustan rationality and pre-romantic pathos, which is embodied in a style which combines intellectual density and economy with emotive imagery and an elegiac sonority.

CHARLES CHURCHILL

It is a generally accepted view that formal satire declines sharply after Pope's death. The standard histories allow Charles Churchill a brief notice, but do not consider his work as more than a late and undistinguished revival. C. W. Previté-Orton declared: 'On the whole we have arrived at the unhonoured senility of a once great satiric style.'[22] During this period, verse satire was under some strain and stress as a literary form. New 'bourgeois' pre-occupations were being superimposed on classical forms, often with incongruous and inorganic results. Young's arguments against imitation of the classics were more romantic and individualistic in emphasis than Addison's earlier views. The satirists themselves asserted the new rhetoric of 'originality' and 'genius'. These gestures inevitably encouraged the abandonment of direct formal imitation of Horace and Juvenal, but did not prevent a renewal of Juvenalian and Horatian voices at other levels. Indeed, in the last phase of the Augustan period, the most extreme formulations of the 'laughing' and the 'indignant' satiric voices were developed. The final breakdown of the neoclassical principle is marked by the pre-romantic experimentation of William Whitehead and Charles Churchill.

Whitehead, successful playwright, Poet Laureate and faithful advocate of 'good nature', embodies in much of his work the liberal Horatianism of Addison, Steele and Young. *On Ridicule* (1743) is unequivocally optimistic and complacent in its view of human nature, concluding with a tribute to the Horatian tradition as it is interpreted by a mentor of middle-class culture:

> We, like Menander, more discreetly dare,
> And well-bred satire wears a milder air . . .
> Then let good-nature every charm exert,
> And, while it mends it, win the unfolding heart.
> Let moral mirth a face of triumph wear,
> Yet smile unconscious of th'extorted tear.
> See, with what grace instructive satire flows . . .
> So, in our age, too prone to sport with pain,
> Might soft humanity resume her reign;
> Pride without rancour feel th' objected fault,
> And folly blush, as willing to be taught;
> Critics grow mild, life's witty warfare cease,
> And true good-nature breathe the balm of peace.[23]

Whitehead's conception of the satiric mode is connected by a tenuous thread to the Horatian dictum *ridiculum acri . . . melius . . . secat res,*[24] but the allusion to the mild Menander directly contradicts Horace's derivation of satire from the scurrilous Old Comedy. Edward and Lillian Bloom rightly consider that Whitehead 'would remove so much of the acidity that satire would remain as little more than a handbook on human good will'.[25] In Whitehead's work, preoccupations, which elsewhere were informing the novel and the essay, were straining the confines of classical forms.

In *An Essay towards Fixing the True Standards of Wit* . . . (1744), Corbyn Morris made an interesting attempt to construct a theory of comic tone by distinguishing modes ranging from the most 'generous' and good-humoured to the most indignant. Addison's Sir Roger de Coverley represents the generous type of humour, which is the product of 'a warm universal *Benevolence'*. Morris describes four main modes: humour, raillery, ridicule and satire. According to his classification, Horace's satire on the bore is not 'satire', 'as the Subject is not *Vice* or Immorality' but *'slight* Foibles'. The distinction between 'raillery' and 'satire' corresponds to the Horace/Juvenal antithesis:

> It is a just Maxim upon these Subjects, that in *Raillery* a good-natur'd Esteem ought always to appear, without any Resentment or Bitterness; In *Satire* a generous free Indignation, without any sneaking Fear or Tenderness: . . . It is from hence that *Juvenal,* as a *Satirist,* is greatly superior to *Horace* . . .[26]

According to Morris's definitions, Whitehead wrote 'raillery' and Churchill wrote 'satire'. Indeed, each writer thought of the other as the worst type of satirist. Whitehead, the son of a rich baker, was a respectable establishment figure, who was made Poet Laureate in 1758 and became David Garrick's play-reader during the 1760s. It is hardly surprising that he found Churchill's life and writings offensive. Churchill's meteoric rise to fame following the success of his *The Rosciad* (1761) enabled him to abandon his career in the Church and to lead a rather dissipated personal life. His brief career as satirist (he died in 1764) has a Byronic or even Rochesterian flavour; his reputation has been similarly dominated by biographical questions.

In his fragmentary verses 'On Churchill', Whitehead adopts a complacently self-righteous tone as he calls his enemy back into the orbit of rational normality:

> Churchill had strength of thought, had power to paint,
> Nor felt from principles the least restraint; . . .
> That I'm his foe, ev'n Churchill can't pretend,
> But – thank my stars – he proves I am no friend:
> Yet, Churchill, could an honest wish succeed,
> I'd prove myself to thee a friend indeed;
> . . . I [would] bridle thy eccentric soul,
> In reason's sober orbit bid it roll:
> Spite of thyself, would make thy rancour cease.
>
> (p. 276)

Churchill's lines on Whitehead, in *The Ghost,* appear to be a re-joinder to these very verses:

> Thee, WHITEHEAD, Thee I now invoke,
> Sworn foe to Satyr's gen'rous stroke,
> Which makes unwilling Conscience feel,
> And wounds, but only wounds to heal.
> Good-natur'd, easy Creature, mild,
> And gentle as a new-born Child, . . .
> O may thy sacred pow'r controul
> Each fiercer working of my soul,
> Damp ev'ry spark of genuine fire,
> And languors, like thine own, inspire,
> Trite be each Thought, and ev'ry Line
> As *Moral,* and as *Dull* as THINE.[27]

The derogatory use of '*Moral*' is a significant departure from neoclassical practice, and is part of Churchill's profound modification of the tradition of Dryden and Pope. Churchill strains the confines of the Augustan style, which he so completely assimilated, by introducing an intense egotistical sublimity which has affinities with Marston and even with Byron. He preferred Dryden, whose satires he considered endowed with 'strong invention' and 'noblest vigour', and whose 'ennobling numbers' flow 'in varied force'. Churchill refused to emulate the 'correctness' of Pope or to 'refine/ Th' gen'rous roughness of a nervous line'. Dryden was equivocal in his admiration for Oldham's 'roughness', but he had more sympathy for the Juvenalian vigour of his friend than Pope had. It must be emphasised that Churchill's downright and un-Augustan championing of 'Satyr's gen'rous stroke' is primarily a *stance* and is not a confession of rough workmanship: he mastered the couplet form as perfected by Pope,[28] and in no sense returns to the metrical roughness of Elizabethan satire.

Nevertheless, Churchill's apparent Augustan orthodoxy is deceptive. He employs the concepts of neoclassical discourse with an almost glib facility. He champions common sense, judgement, nature, reason and good breeding. The binary pairs, art and nature, head and heart, order and chaos, wit and dullness, are deployed in predictable fashion. But there is also a marked shift of values, which gives romantic ideas predominance, and leaves the neoclassical machinery in a curious state of suspended animation. The account, in *The Rosciad,* of Garrick's character-acting is based on the neoclassical antithesis of outward nature and inward passion. But the balance inclines clearly towards an admiration for Garrick's portrayal of *ineffable* passion. Churchill is encouraging that cultivation of *personality* and *individuality* which was to be so important not only in the history of the drama but in the development of romanticism:

> When Reason yields to Passion's wild alarms
> And the whole state of man is up in arms;
> What, but a Critic, could condemn the Play'r,
> For pausing here, when Cool Sense pauses there?
> Whilst, working from the Heart, the fire I trace,
> And mark it strongly flaming to the Face;
> Whilst, in each sound, I hear the very man;
> I can't catch words, and pity those who can.
>
> (1055–62)

The ultimate values of reason and truth are transmuted into concepts more sublime than in their orthodox forms. The closing paragraph of *The Apology Addressed to the Critical Reviewers* (1761) elevates 'Reason' to a divine level by personification:

> To HER [Reason] I bow, whose sacred power I feel;
> To HER decision make my last appeal;
> Condemned by HER, applauding worlds in vain
> Should tempt me to resume the Pen again:
> By HER absolved, my course I'll still pursue:
> If REASON's for me, GOD is for me too.
>
> (pp. 416–21)

Churchill's use of personification and allegory as devices of the high style has none of Johnson's sober economy and elegiac resonance, but is intensely subjective in its effects.

The Prophecy of Famine (1763) is a virulent attack upon Scotland and upon the Scottish Lord Bute, who became George III's chief minister in 1763 and who openly declared his intention of restoring the King to autocratic powers.[29] Churchill was actively involved with John Wilkes in arguing the Whig case in the *North Briton,* and was lucky not to have suffered the persecution and imprisonment to which Wilkes was subjected for his opposition to the regime. The poem gives vent to a virulent chauvinism which is every bit as bitter as Juvenal's. The goddess Famine presides over the Scots in a 'barren corner of the isle'. Like Pope's goddess, Dullness, Famine describes her subjects as incomplete creations, bereft of the vital spark. The Scots are 'Consider'd as the refuse of mankind', a 'mass' which nature hesitated 'to stamp with life,' a people 'never enter'd in Creation's book'. But Churchill's goddess has none of Dullness's translucent biblical and epic connotations. Famine is personified with all the allegorical vividness of Spenser's most gothic creations (compare Despair in the *Faerie Queene,* I, ix, 35):

> Her hollow cheeks were each a deep-sunk cell,
> Where wretchedness and horror lov'd to dwell;
> With double rows of useless teeth supplied,
> Her mouth, from ear to ear, extended wide,
> Which, when for want of food her entrails pin'd,
> She op'd, and cursing swallow'd nought but wind ...
>
> (411–6)

Personification is a rhetorical device which the eighteenth-century critics regarded as belonging to the high style. Anthony Blackwall argued that 'Homer, Virgil, Shakespeare, Milton, and all our eminent poets have [by using personification] exceedingly animated their poems, and given sublimity, force and fire, to what would had been otherwise low, languid and cold'.[30] John Ogilvie remarked: 'The last, and principle source of real grandeur in Composition consists of bold and animated personifications.'[31] Just as Juvenal parodied the epic style of Virgil, and Pope the epic and cosmic imagery of the Bible and Milton, so Churchill was fond of parodying the popular eighteenth-century vogue of Spenserian personification, and, like his predecessors, often reached beyond mockery to a genuinely sublime effect. Churchill's bardic and prophetic voice is heightened and given emotional force by the use of such personification and allegory. This voice of moral absolutism pictures the world as full of knaves and fools in the manner of Juvenal's first satire. *The Author* (1763) opens with this familiar theme of universal folly:

> Accurs'd the man, whom fate ordains, in spite,
> And cruel parents teach, to Read and Write! ...
> Much are the precious hours of youth misspent,
> In climbing Learning's rugged steep ascent;
> When to the top the bold advent'rer's got,
> He reigns, vain monarch, o'er a barren spot,
> Whilst in the *vale* of *Ignorance* below,
> FOLLY and VICE to rank luxuriance grow;
>
> (1–2, 5–10)

The incipient Bunyanesque allegory gives the Juvenalian *topos* a note of portentousness and rhetoric extravagance.

Churchill's moral stance differs from that of earlier satirists, partly, at least, as a result of the presence of a new pre-romantic emphasis on authorial *personality*. Churchill's 'I' is more aggressively individualistic and even idiosyncratic than Pope's or Swift's. Unlike Swift's astringent and detached self-scrutiny, Churchill's is coloured by a cultivation of subjectivity which undermines the *social* orientation of the satirist. 'Self' is 'that darling, luscious theme' which prompts Churchill to ask, 'What Man can from himself divide?' – a question which marks a new stage in the prehistory of the 'egotistical sublime'.

In his later satires, Churchill develops the romantic side of his style, particularly in his emphasis upon the mysterious power of passion. In *The Farewell* (1764) the 'Poet' declares his intention of emigrating in order to find new material for satires. He acknowledges the force of patriotic feeling in an almost Wordsworthian vein:

> Howe'er our pride may tempt us to conceal
> Those passions, which we cannot chuse but feel,
> There's a strange Something, which without a brain
> Fools feel, and with one wise men can't explain,
> Planted in Man, to bind him to that earth,
> In dearest ties, from whence he drew his birth.
>
> (61–6)

An even more striking feature of the later poems is Churchill's abandonment of the Augustan rational mode of discourse in favour of a technique of inspired *digression* and *association* of ideas.[32] In *The Ghost* (1763), Churchill acknowledges his discipleship of Laurence Sterne, whose *Tristram Shandy* began to appear in 1759. Like Sterne's novel, *The Ghost* perversely mocks conventional narrative structure. The whole first book is a series of 'wild excursions', long parentheses and asides, which contribute little to rational communication, but vividly express the *movements of the speaker's mind*. In Book II the poet echoes Sterne's witty apology to the reader for the fact that the story is so little advanced after so many pages. Churchill confesses that, 'With nothing done, and little said', he has been misled by 'wild excursive FANCY' and needs the help of 'some GODDESS to descend,/And help me to my journey's end'. Churchill's indulgence of 'fancy' should be clearly distinguished from later romantic forms of subjectivity: his mode of perception is not imaginative and is evidently based, like Sterne's, on Locke's principles of association.

While it is true to say that Churchill's satires deviate strikingly from the classical and Augustan patterns, beneath the new surface can be discerned the familiar formal patterns of dialogue and of praise and blame, the use of satiric irony and the formal programmatic concerns of satire. Churchill often uses the dialogue form, but not in the manner of Horace or Pope. Churchill's dialogues are always heavily loaded in the poet's favour (except in *The Farewell*). *The Conference* (1763) is a Horatian dialogue, loosely related to Horace's Satire II, i, and to Pope's imitations of that poem, in which the satirist's freedom of expression is

questioned. But Churchill leaves his *adversarius* defenceless from
the very beginning:

> My Lord, in usual taste, began to yawn,
> And lolling backward in his Elbow-chair,
> With an insipid kind of stupid stare,
> Picking his teeth, twirling his seals about –
> CHURCHILL, You have a Poem coming out.
> You've my best wishes; but I really fear
> Your Muse in general is too severe . .
>
> (6–12)

Churchill's justification of his severity and his self-righteous tone
resembles Pope's in the *Epilogue to the Satires,* but the intensity of
animus goes beyond the public gestures of an Augustan poet.
There is an almost Jacobean disgust in his remarks on the outward
splendour of high birth and the glittering Order of the Garter
('the STAR'):

> Blazing without, whilst a base heart within
> Is rotten to the core with filth and sin; . . .
>
> (307–8)

Much of the *Epistle to William Hogarth* (1763) is taken up by a
pseudo-dialogue between 'Satire' and 'Candour'. The dialogue is
virtually a rehearsal of Churchill's debate with poets like William
Whitehead, who, like Candour, advocated 'Soul-smoothing
PANEGYRIC'S flowr'y way' and 'the sweet milk of human
kindness'. Churchill rests his defence upon a lofty conception of
satiric justice, which precludes attacks upon misfortune or personal
'foibles' (he alludes to Pope's characterisation of Addison). He then
proceeds, in Juvenalian fashion, to picture a land overwhelmed by
vice which even Candour must detest:

> Can Satire want a subject, where Disdain
> By Virtue fir'd may point her sharpest strain,
> Where, cloath'd with thunder, Truth may roll along,
> And CANDOUR justify the rage of song?
>
> (209–12)

The dialogue form soon gives way to an extended and powerful
attack on Hogarth, who is sunk beneath the weight of unrelenting
rhetoric:

> VIRTUE, with due contempt, saw HOGARTH stand,
> The murd'rous pencil in his palsied hand.
> What was the cause of Liberty to him,

> Or what was Honour? let them sink or swim,
> So he may gratify without controul
> The mean resentments of his selfish soul.
>
> (411–16)

The rhetoric, with its easy alliterative emphases, is rather cheap, and lacks the figurative vitality of Dryden's or Pope's invectives.

Churchill eventually achieved a high degree of sophistication, far removed from the virulent directness of the Hogarth portrait, in the art of ironic panegyric. In the early satires, notably in *The Rosciad,* irony is savage and over-explicit. But, in *The Candidate,* Churchill attempts a new kind of sustained and grandiloquent irony in an attack on Lord Sandwich, who was standing as the Tory candidate for the stewardship of Cambridge recently vacated by the death of the Whig Lord Hardwicke in March 1764. An ironic panegyric of Sandwich is prepared by a long series of elaborate rhetorical gestures by which Churchill discards all of his previous themes. Enough of actors, enough of authors, enough of critics, enough of Scotland, enough of states, enough of patriots, enough of Wilkes, enough of self(!), and enough of satire. Churchill then declares ironically that he has seen the error of his political ways, has changed sides and will now write in praise of Sandwich: 'Come PANEGYRIC'. On the whole, this sustained use of irony is confusing rather than satirically effective.[33] The grandiloquent style is used both in the panegyric of Sandwich ('*Hail* SANDWICH . . . SANDWICH, *All Hail*') and in the satiric portrait of Lothario, a shameless seducer in Nicholas Rowe's *The Fair Penitent:*

> Search Earth, search Hell, the Devil cannot find
> An Agent, like LOTHARIO, to his mind.
>
> (397–8)

After a long and tediously rhetorical accumulation of images of corruption, Churchill merges the characters of Lothario and Sandwich, pointing the irony of the panegyric in a sudden and awkward revelation:

> And, having brought LOTHARIO forth to view,
> To save her credit, [Nature] brought forth SANDWICH too.
>
> (413–4)

Far more impressive is the handling of irony in *The Dedication* (1765), which preceded Churchill's posthumously published sermons. The poem is a remarkably sustained piece of ironic panegyric at the expense of William Warburton, Bishop of Gloucester, an old ally of Pope's. Churchill establishes a con-

vincingly humble and sincere tone of address, which is marked
by a growing obsequiousness:

> Accept this greeting – nor let modest fear
> Call up one maiden blush – I mean not here
> To wound with flatt'ry – 'tis a Villain's art,
> And suits not with the frankness of my heart.
>
> (3–6)

The speaker is a subtle vehicle for irony: 'I mean not here/To
wound with flatt'ry' is, of course, the reverse of the poem's
intention, although, in the speaker's mouth, the words have an
innocent truthfulness: he will not offend Warburton's modest ear
with the calculated praises of a flatterer. A frank account would be
praise enough: 'But truth, *my Lord*, is panegyric here.' Churchill
proceeds, in characteristically expansive manner, to describe those
qualities ('Name', 'Title', 'Mitre', 'outward form', 'Birth', etc.)
which do not qualify for his approval. This is the traditional
neoclassical preamble to the praise of *true* nobility: but the account
of merely outward qualities becomes obtrusive; the reader begins
to notice their unprelate-like nature:

> Thy open front, thy Love-commanding eye,
> Where fifty Cupids, as in ambush, lie,
> Which can from sixty to sixteen impart
> The force of Love, and point his blunted dart;
>
> (47–50)

'Blunted dart' is a sharp reference to Warburton's well-known
profligacy. When finally the bishop's praises are sung, Churchill
skilfully shifts the focus to his own relationship with the 'saintly'
Warburton. Churchill wittily laments his own shortcomings in
the priestly vocation ('sacred Dullness ever in my view,/Sleep at my
bidding crept from pew to pew'), and remembers how he had
wished he had 'A Friend in him, who was The Friend of POPE'
(86). He longed to be instructed in literary scholarship and to be
told the secrets of Warburton's 'Taste':

> Instruct me, mingling profit with delight,
> Where POPE was wrong, where SHAKESPEARE was not right;
> Where they are justly prais'd, and where thro' whim,
> How little's due to them, how much to him.
>
> (93–6)

Here, in ironic form (the irony is shallow in the fourth line), we
have a reminiscence of Pope's celebrated attacks on Bentley and
Theobald as editors of Milton and Shakespeare. The sneering

rejection of scholarship, and especially of textual criticism, is characteristic of an Augustan humanism, but the voice of the satirist has become more sly, more romantic, more protean.

The speaker praises Warburton for refusing to help a mere poet. How could he neglect

> . . . the work of Grace
> And, idly wand'ring o'er The Muses' hill,
> Let the salvation of mankind stand still?
> (124–5)

Warburton's supercilious self-righteousness is subtly implied. The most damning ironic effects are drawn from a reference to Warburton's hypocritical attack on Wilke's *An Essay on Women*. We remember those 'fifty Cupids', when we read:

> Methinks I now
> See stern Rebuke enthroned on his brow,
> And arm'd with tenfold terrours – from his tongue,
> Where fiery zeal, and Christian fury hung,
> Methinks I hear the deep-ton'd thunders roll,
> And chill with horrour ev'ry sinner's soul –
> (133–8)

The use of Miltonic bombast and personification is more effective here than in the unironic Juvenalian savagery of *The Prophecy of Famine*. Not only is Warburton's hypocrisy devastatingly evoked, but the sincerity of his pastoral role ('The cure of souls, his duty and his joy') is ironically undermined by a savage hell-fire rhetoric which hardly becomes an orthodox Anglican bishop! The poem reduces Warburton to the same level as that of the profligate poet and lapsed priest (Churchill), who ironically pretends that they stand at opposite poles in fortune and in worth. The poem concludes with lines which almost drop the naïve irony of the speaker, when he warns the bishop of those dangers of pride which may threaten a man's reason:

> Let Him not, gorg'd with pow'r, and drunk with state,
> Forget what once he was, tho' now so high;
> How low, how mean, and full as poor as I.
> (178–80)

While Churchill clearly learnt something from Pope's brilliantly ironic 'Epistle to Augustus', he goes beyond Pope in his use of the naïve first-person voice, which is located somewhere between the Horatian/Augustan honest 'I' and the romantic dramatic speaker of the Browning monologue.

In a period when poets were seeking new models in Hebrew, Welsh and Norse poetry, Churchill's adherence to the Augustan tradition of verse satire in heroic couplets might appear an oddly conservative choice for a Whig radical. Richard Hurd, in *Letters on Chivalry and Romance* (1762), and Thomas Percy, in *Reliques of Ancient English Poetry* (1765), argued for a revival of those 'romantic' qualities, found in 'primitive' poetry of the Middle Ages, which had been partially transmitted through Chaucer, Spenser, Shakespeare and Milton. Poets like Gray, Collins and the Wartons strove for what Shenstone called 'the more striking effects of wild, original, enthusiastic genius'.[34] However, Churchill's admiration for 'Butler's wit, Pope's numbers, Prior's ease'[35] did not prevent him from absorbing the new experimental qualities of contemporary verse in a period immediately before the onset of Romanticism. Sterne's *Tristram Shandy* was not the only eccentric work written in the 1760s: Macpherson's medieval concoctions, Christopher Smart's bizarre *Jubilate Agno*, Walpole's *Castle of Otranto* and Chatterton's precocious Rowley poems all go beyond that modest sobriety of Augustan self-hood which rested upon a sense of a conveniently ordered universe. Churchill's satires possess that new mid-century awareness of self which Martin Price so well describes as 'the self-consciousness of a mind turned at once upon the world and upon itself, constantly surprised by what it discovers in the self'.[36] When Churchill describes 'self' as 'that darling luscious theme,/O'er which Philosophers in raptures dream', he is recognising, in a manner quite alien to Augustan satire, the presence of a new 'dominant' in verse satire, a new ordering principle, which points forward to Byron and not backward to Pope.

Verse satire survived the Augustan period, especially in the work of Burns, George Canning, Byron and the poetry of the Anti-Jacobin, but the classical models were superseded. The verse satirists between 1590 and 1765 worked adventurously within the space created by the Roman types. New combinations were found, and distinctive excursions were made into new territory. By the end of the eighteenth century, with the general and radical change in poetic consciousness, the classical models no longer provided a workable space: the 'dominant' had shifted.

This study has attempted to be both historical and evaluative, to understand both a 'tradition' and the 'individual talents' which compose it. The perspective of Roman satire is not the only one which might have thrown light on the development of verse satire, but it is, perhaps, the only one which is rich enough and flexible enough to provide a model capable of structuring the productions of such a long period without gross distortions and oversimplifications.

Notes and References

ABBREVIATIONS

Chalmers	Alexander Chalmers (ed.), *The Works of the English Poets from Chaucer to Cowper*, 21 vols (1810).
Kernan	Alvin B. Kernan, *The Cankered Muse* (New Haven, 1959).
Love	Harold Love (ed.), *Restoration Literature, Critical Approaches* (1972).
POAS	*Poems on Affairs of State, Augustan Satirical Verse, 1660–1714*, G.deF. Lord (gen.ed.), 7 vols (New Haven and London, 1963–75).
Gregory Smith	G. Gregory Smith, (ed.), *Elizabethan Critical Essays*, 2 vols (1904).
Spingarn	J. E. Spingarn (ed.), *Critical Essays of the 17th Century*, 3 vols (1908–9).
Watson	George G. Watson (ed.), *John Dryden's Of Dramatic Poesy and Other Critical Essays*, 2 vols (1962).

NOTES TO CHAPTER 1

1 Kernan, pp. 16, 19, 29.
2 'The Nature of Satire', *University of Toronto Quarterly*, vol. 14 (1944), pp. 75–89.
3 J. Bently, 'Satire and the rhetoric of sadism', *Centennial Review*, vol. 11 (1967), pp. 387–404.
4 *The Fictions of Satire* (Baltimore, 1967), ch. 1.
5 See N. Rudd, *The Satires of Horace: a Study* (Cambridge, 1966), pp. 222–3.
6 See Thomas E. Maresca, *Pope's Horatian Poems* (Ohio, 1966), p. 60.
7 *Critical Works*, ed. E. N. Hooker, 2 vols (Baltimore, 1939–43), II, 219–20.
8 There is a long history of controversy about the meaning of *Satura*. See C. A. Van Rooy, *Studies in Classical Satire and Related Literary Theory* (Leyden, 1965), and P. K. Elkin, *The Augustan Defence of Satire* (1973), pp. 26–43.
9 Quotations are from *Satires, Epistles, and Ars Poetica*, tr. H. R. Fairclough (Cambridge, Mass., 1942). Quotations from Juvenal and Persius are from *Juvenal and Persius*, tr. G. G. Ramsay (Cambridge, Mass., 1918). Translations are modified.
10 The differences between the plainness of Horace and that of Lucilius can be understood in the light of Cicero's distinction between the unpolished and the polished versions of the style. See *Orator*, section 20. See also W. S. Anderson's 'The Roman Socrates: Horace and his satires', in *Critical Essays on Roman Literature, Satire*, ed. J. P. Sullivan (1963), pp. 1–38.
11 A full account of the stylistic theories of the Scipionic Circle may be found in G. C. Fiske's 'The Plain style in the Scipionic Circle', *University of Wisconsin Studies in Language and Literature*, No. 3 (Madison, 1919), pp. 62–105.
12 Spingarn, I, 41.
13 *The Complete Poems*, ed. D. M. Vieth (New Haven and London, 1968), pp. 121–2.
14 For a discussion of satire and rhetoric, see I. G. Scott's *The Grand Style in the Satires of Juvenal* (Northampton, Mass., 1927), pp. 1–17.
15 For a useful account, see W. Trimpi's *Ben Jonson's Poems: A Study of the Plain Style* (Stanford, 1962).

16 *Horace* (Oxford, 1957), pp. 138–9.

17 *Alexander Pope: the Poetry of Allusion* (Oxford, 1959), p. 169.

18 cf. *Epistles*, I, 18: *asperitas agrestis*.

19 The quotations from Fawkes and Greene appeared in the second edition of W. and J. Duncombe's *The Works of Horace* in 4 vols. Smart's version appeared in his *The Works of Horace*.

20 Watson, II, 131–2.

21 A good refutation is to be found in N. Rudd's *The Satires of Horace* (Cambridge, 1966), pp. 269–72.

22 *Anger in Juvenal and Seneca*, University of California Publications in Classical Philology, vol. 19, No. 3 (1964), pp. 127–96.

23 G. Highet, *Juvenal the Satirist, a Study* (1954), p. 143. Ludwig Friedländer noted the inconsistency but did not explain it. See *Friedländer's Essays on Juvenal*, tr. J. R. C. Martyn (Amsterdam, 1969), p. 41.

24 *Divinae Institutiones*, 3.29 (PL, 6.443B). A full account of Juvenal's transmission and reception during the later Empire and after is given in Highet, *Juvenal the Satirist*, pp. 181–218.

25 *Fam.*, 3.15 and 3.17.

26 *De liberorum educatione*, tr. J. S. Nelson (Washington, 1940), p. 184.

27 Sir Robert Stapylton, *Mores Hominum: The Manners of Men, Described in sixteen Satyrs by Juvenal* (1660), sig. A7ʳ.

28 *A Modern Essay on the Tenth Satyr of Juvenal* (1687), Epistle Ded., sig. A3ʳ.

29 *Complete Works*, ed. M. Summers, 5 vols (1927), V, 294.

30 *The Tenth Satyr of Juvenal done into English Verse* (1693), Epistle Ded. For further discussion of Christianising of Juvenal, see my unpublished doctoral dissertation, *A Study of Formal Verse Satire . . . 1600–1770* (London, 1971), pp. 328–34.

31 For example, Duff offers two entirely different explanations in the 1927 and 1936 editions of his *A Literary History of Rome in the Silver Age*, pp. 617–18.

32 'Is Juvenal a Classic?', *Critical Essays on Roman Literature*, op. cit., pp. 93–176.

33 See Highet, *Juvenal the Satirist*, pp. 70–72.

34 *Reflections on Aristotle's Treatise of Poesie*, tr. Rymer (1674), p. 138.

35 e.g. *Georgics*, II, 103–4, Catullus, 6, and esp. Ovid, *Tristia*, V, vi, 37–41 (there is a slight verbal echo in Juvenal of Ovid's *me circumstat densorum turba malorum*).

36 The standard account of Juvenal's use of declamatory techniques is J. de Decker's *Juvenal's Declamans . . .* (Gand, 1913).

37 *Poetices Libri Septem*, Facsimile of the 1561 edn (Stuttgart, 1964), p. 20.

38 See Van Rooy, *Studies in Classical Satire . . .*, pp. 186–90, and below, p. 56.

39 *De Satyrica Graecorum poesi & Romanorum Satira Libri duo* (Paris, 1605).

40 *De Satyra Horatiana Liber*, appended to *Q. Horatii Flacci Opera* (Lugduni Batavorum, 1612), esp. pp. 8 and 43.

41 *De Artis Poeticae Natura ac Constitutione liber* (Amsterdam, 1647), III, ix, 5 (p. 41).

NOTES TO CHAPTER 2

1 *Pithy, Pleasant and Profitable Works* (1568, Scolar Press, 1970), sigs. O.iiʳ–Oiiᵛ.

2 See H. A. Mason, *Humanism and Poetry in the Early Tudor Period* (1959), pp. 255–89.

3 See P. J. Finkelpearl, *John Marston of the Middle Temple* (Cambridge, Mass., 1969), and J. Wilcox, 'Informal publication of late 16th-century verse satire', *HLQ*, vol. 13 (1949/50), pp. 49–50.

4 Kernan, pp. 1, 40–41.

5 See John D. Peter, *Complaint and Satire in Early English Literature* (1956), p. 9.

6   *The Selected Works*, ed. J. M. Cowper (1872) EETS, extra series 15 (1872), p. 20.
7   *Elizabethan Poetry* (Cambridge, Mass, 1952), p. 210.
8   See Peter, *Complaint and Satire . . .*, pp. 124–6, for a discussion of this poem.
9   *The Poems*, ed. A. Davenport (Liverpool, 1961).
10 *The Three Parnassus Plays*, ed. J. B. Leishman (1949), I, i, 84–9.
11 *The Collected Poems*, ed. A. Davenport (Liverpool, 1949), pp. 10, 96–8. cf. John Weever, *Faunus and Melliflora* (1600), ed. A. Davenport (1948): 'Satyres,/(So cald because they satisfide her ires), (p. 42).
12 ibid., p. 43. Similar criticisms were voiced by Nicholas Breton, Henry Fitzgeffrey and William Hornby.
13 See M. C. Randolph, 'The medical concept in English Renaissance satiric theory . . .', *SP*, vol. 38 (1941), pp. 125–57.
14 See Kernan, pp. 108–10.
15 See Thomas Drant's erroneous etymological connection between 'Satyre' and 'Saturn', *A Medicinable Morall* (1566), sig. a, iiii^v.
16 On this general subject, see L. Babb, *The Elizabethan Malady* (East Lansing, Mich., 1951); R. Klibansky, E. Panofsky and F. Saxl, *Saturn and Melancholy* (1964); T. Spencer, 'The Elizabethan malcontent', in *J. Q. Adams Memorial Studies*, ed. J. G. McManaway *et al.* (Washington, 1948); B. G. Lyons, *Voices of Melancholy* (1971); A. Stein, 'Donne and the satiric spirit', *ELH*, vol. 11 (1944), esp. pp. 271–82; G. B. Harrison, 'Essay on Elizabethan melancholy', in his edit. of Breton's *Melancholike Humours* (1929).
17 See A. Stein, 'Donne and the couplet', *PMLA*, vol. 57 (1942), pp. 676–96, and his 'Donne's harshness and the Elizabethan tradition,' *SP*, vol. 41 (1944), pp. 390–409.
18 'Satyre I' was written in 1593. See *The Satires, Epigrams and Verse Letters*, ed. W. Milgate (1967), p. 117.
19 *Works*, ed. Herford and Simpson, 11 vols (1925–52), VIII 585.
20 Thomas Warton dismisses it with 'But the darkness and difficulties of Persius arise in great measure from his own affectation and false taste. He would have been enigmatical under the mildest government.' (*The History of English Poetry*, ed. W. C. Hazlitt, 4 vols (1871, repr. 1968), IV, 383).
21 See A. Stein, 'Donne's obscurity and the Elizabethan tradition', *ELH*, vol. 13 (1946), pp. 98–118.
22 *Poems*, ed. P. B. Bartlett (New York, 1941), p. 49.
23 *Epigrames in the Oldest Cut and Oldest Fashion* (1599), ed. McKerrow (1911), p. 54.
24 C. Witke's bold claim that the classical satirists 'perpetually use the low, everyday, and humble to deal with the sublime, spiritual and ultimately significant' (*Latin Satire . . .*, Leyden, 1970, p. 198) is unproved.
25 On Donatus and Elizabethan satire, see O. J. Campbell, *Comicall Satyre and Shakespeare's Troilus and Cressida* (San Marino, Calif., 1938), pp. 24–5, and Kernan, pp. 54–6.
26 Thomas Lodge, *Defence of Poetry*, Gregory Smith, I, 80.
27 *The Workes of Master George Wither* (1620), p. 307.
28 See Horace, *Ars Poetica*, 220ff.
29 Spingarn, I, 205. See Irene Samuel, 'Milton on Comedy and Satire', *HLQ*, vol. 35 (1971–2), pp. 107–30. One wonders if Milton was familiar with the sixteenth-century French 'satyres', written under the influence of Donatus' false etymology. See the articles by C. A. Mayer, J. W. Jollife, and D. J. Shaw, on dramatic 'satyre' in vol. 13 (1951), pp. 327–33, vol. 18 (1956), pp. 84–95, and vol. 30 (1968), pp. 301–25 of *Bibliothèque d'humanisme et renaissance*.
30 Gregory Smith, I, 80.
31 *Complete Works*, Hunterian Club (1883), III, 44.
32 R. M. Alden, *The Rise of Formal Satire in England under Classical Influence* (Pennsylvania, 1899), p. 76.
33 See, for example, A. Stein, 'Donne's Obscurity', art. cit.

34 See K. J. Reckford, 'Studies in Persius', *Hermes*, vol. 90 (1962), pp. 476–504; W. S. Anderson, *The Satires of Persius*, tr. W. J. Merwin (Bloomington, Indiana, 1961), Introduction, p. 43; and C. Dessen, *Iunctura Callidus Acri: A Study of Persius' Satires*, Ilinois Studies in Language and Literature, No. 59 (Urbana, 1968), p. 10.

35 See, for example, Henry Eelbeck, *A Prosaic Translation of A. Persius Flaccus's Six Satyrs* (1719), p. 28; John Senhouse's *The Satires of A. Persius Flaccus* (1703), p. 63; and Edmund Burton's *The Satyrs of Persius* (1752), p. 52.

36 On Christian and classical usage, see *Satires of Persius*, ed. J. Conington (1893), p. 46; F. Villeneuve, *Essai sur Perse* (Paris, 1918), pp. 405–17; and Van Wageningen's *Auli Persi Flacci Saturae . . .*, 2 vols (Groningen, 1911), II, 38.

37 See my 'John Donne's "Incarnational Conviction"', *CQ*, vol. 17 (1975), pp. 55–73, and N. J. C. Andreason's 'Theme and structure in Donne's Satyres', *SEL*, vol. 3 (1963), p. 59.

38 H. Erskine-Hill stresses Donne's mingling of comedy and fear, in 'Courtiers out of Horace', *John Donne, Essays in Celebration*, ed. A. J. Smith (1972), p. 286. J. R. Lauritsen ignores the serio-comic in Donne's satires; see 'The Drama of Self-Discovery', *SEL*, vol. 16 (1976), pp. 117–30.

39 C. S. Lewis, *English Literature in the Sixteenth Century* (1954), pp. 469–70.

40 Peter, *Complaint and Satire . . .*, p. 22.

41 Milgate glosses the line 'The wealthiest heiress . . . you can think of among the families of the merchant princes of the City' (p. 123). Donne altered 'Infanta' to 'Infant'. Perhaps Donne saw the punning association with the previous analogy.

42 Peter, *Complaint and Satire . . .*, p. 135.

43 *History of English Poetry*, ed. Hazlitt, IV, 367–8.

44 The 'Prologue' (p. 33) is based on Horace, *Satires*, II, i, 1–3. The dialogue form in *Virg.*, III, iii, resembles Horace's. The dramatic form of III, v, is based on Horace, *Satires*, I, ix.

45 See A. Stein, 'Joseph Hall's imitation of Juvenal', *MLR*, vol. 43 (1948), pp. 315–26.

46 See Davenport's commentary for details of Hall's use of Nashe and Greene.

47 Cited by P. A. Smith, 'Bishop Hall, "our English Seneca",' *PMLA*, vol. 63 (1948), p. 1201.

48 See Davenport's notes on lines 1ff. and 67ff. (pp. 238–9, 242).

49 Robert Greene wrote a large number of prose satires of 'cony-catching' in the early 1590s.

50 See Davenport, pp. 7–10, and Morse S. Allen, *The Satire of John Marston* (New York, 1965), pp. 88–92. For the contrary view, see G. Gross, 'Marston's "Metamorphosis . . .": a mock-epyllion', *Études Anglaises*, vol. 13 (1960), pp. 331–6.

51 *Works*, IV, 306.

52 *History of English Poetry*, ed. Hazlitt, IV, 409.

53 The passage is parodied in *The Return from Parnassus*, II, 1343–4:
> Command his slymie spright to honour me
> For my high tiptoe-strowting poesye
> *(Parnassus Plays*, p. 305)

54 *The Satire of John Marston*, p. 94.

55 There are some similarities between these two satiric roles and the bifurcation of satiric roles embodied in the characters Asper and Macilente in Jonson's *Every Man Out of His Humour*. See also Kernan, pp. 136–8. Lyon's attempt to explain Marston's apparent vacillations by distinguishing between temperamental melancholy and philosophical melancholy is unconvincing (*Voices of Melancholy*, pp. 59–62).

56 See A. Caputi, *John Marston, Satirist* (Ithaca, 1961), pp. 27–9, and Kernan, p. 121.

57 *The Whipper Pamphlets*, ed. A. Davenport, Part II (Liverpool, 1951), pp. 22 and 25.

58 Wither's work was followed by R.C.'s *The Times' Whistle* (1615), John Taylor's *The Ripping or Snipping of Abuses* (1614), Henry Fitzgeffrey's *Satyres and Satyricall Epigrams* (1617), Henry Hutton's *Follie's Anatomie* (1619), and Richard Brathwait's *Natures Embassie* (1621).

NOTES TO CHAPTER 3

1   For example, Hodges *Vision from the Monument* (1675), and *Nostradamus's Prophecy* (1671). See Ruth Nevo, *The Dial of Virtue: A Study of Poems on Affairs of State in the 17th Century* (Princeton, NJ, 1963), pp. 180–83.

2   Individual satires were frequently translated or imitated. Horace's satire 'The Town Mouse and the Country Mouse' (II, vi) was attempted by Sir John Beaumont (1629), Wye Saltonstall (1637), John Smith (1649), Sir Richard Fanshawe (1652), Abraham Cowley (1666), and Thomas Sprat (1666). Juvenal's tenth satire was attempted by William Barksted (1617), Sir John Beaumont (1629), Henry Vaughan (1646), the anonymous author of *The Wish* (1675), Thomas Wood (1683), and Thomas Shadwell (1693).

3   Wesley Trimpi, *Ben Jonson's Poems: A Study of the Plain Style* (Stanford, 1962).

4   *Cynthia's Revels*, II, iii.

5   See *Discoveries, passim*, and *Poetaster*, V, i. Doris Powers *(English Formal Satire,* The Hague and Paris, 1971, p. 157) generalises: 'There are, then, links between Jonson's poems and all Augustan poems in which conceptual and explicit formal contrasts are made between the reasonable in idea and action, and the excessive on either side of the *via media.*'

6   *Iuuvenals Tenth Satyre Translated* (1646), in *Works*, ed. L. C. Martin (1957), p. 2.

7   See *Ben Jonson's Poems*, pp. 111–13, 121–35, and Jonson, *Works*, VIII, 184.

8   *D. J. Juvenalis and A. Persius Flaccus Translated . . .* (1673), and *Juvenal's Sixteen Satyrs* (1647), rev. edn; *Mores Hominum: The Manners of Men, Described in sixteen Satyrs by Juvenal* (1660).

9   See the essay on poetry written *c.* 1610–12, reprinted by L. A. Beaurline in his 'Dudley North's criticism of metaphysical poetry', *HLQ*, vol. 25 (1961–2), pp. 299–313.

10   See *Certain Selected Odes of Horace* (1621).

11   Beaumont's significance is recognised by W. J. Courthope, in *The History of English Poetry*, 6 vols (1895–1910), III, 197–8, and R. L. Sharp, in *From Donne to Dryden* (1940, rev. edn, Hamden, Connect., 1965); pp. 87, 102–3.

12   *Bosworth Field with A Taste of the Variety of other poems . . .* (1629), p. 110.

13   See S.-M. Røstvig, *The Happy Man, Studies in the Metamorphoses of a Classical Idea*, 2 vols (New York, 1954, rev. 1962 and 1958), I, 79–102.

14   Notice, for example, the interpolations (in lines 1 and 3) of elegant neoclassical generality in the following passage from Persius:

> The glorious name of gold hath put away
> The vse of *Saturnes* brasse, and *Numaes* clay.
> This glitt'ring pride to richer substance turnes
> The Tuscan earthen pots and vestall vrnes.

(p. 53)

> (aurum vasa Numae Saturniaque impulit aera
> Vestalesque urnas et Tuscum fictile mutat.)

15   On translation see T. R. Steiner, 'Precursors to Dryden: English and French theories of translation in the 17th century', *Comparative Literary Studies*, vol. 7 (1970), pp. 50–81. On imitation, see H. F. Brook's definitive 'The "Imitation" in English poetry especially in formal satire, before the age of Pope', *RES*, vol. 25 (1949), pp. 124–40, and H. D. Weinbrot's *The Formal Strain: Studies in Augustan Imitation and Satire* (Chicago, 1969).

16   See 'Preface', *The Destruction of Troy* (1656), and 'Remarks' prefixed to Fanshawe's *Pastor Fido* (1647).

17   *The Essays and Other Prose Writings*, ed. A. B. Gough (1915), p. 160.

18   Sprat renders Horace's account of the Stoic topics of after-dinner conversation with an emphasis on substantiveness ('which is more *material* to learn'), prudence and utility (Gough, p. 286).

19 *Hudibras*, ed. J. Wilders (1967).
20 Although Cleveland employs traditional cosmic and royalist imagery, his poetic method is Hobbesian in its mechanistic procedures. See my 'Hobbes and late metaphysical poetry', *JHI*, vol. 35 (1974), pp. 197–210.
21 *The Poems*, ed. B. Morris and E. Withington (1967), p. 29.
22 See 'On the Pouder Plot' (probably by Cleveland), *Poems*, p. 72:
> Satyrs run best when Classhing tearms do meet,
> And Indignation makes them knock their feet.
23 *Poems*, p. xix.
24 *POAS*, I, 5.
25 *Poems*, ed. J. Kinsley, 4 vols (1958), I, 369–70.
26 Cited by H. F. Brooks, in 'The Poems of John Oldham', Love, p. 182.
27 *The Works . . . Together with his Remains*, 4 Books (1698), sig. a3^v.
28 *Complete Works*, ed. M. Summers, 5 vols (1927), V, 293. John Harvey cites Oldham directly in attributing a 'Masterly roughness' to Juvenal *(The Tenth Satyr of Juvenal*, 1693, 'Epistle Ded.').
29 *From Concord to Dissent: Major Themes in English Poetic Theory, 1640–1700* (Menston, Yorks., 1973).
30 *The Honest Muse* (1967), pp. 102–3.
31 On the allegorical device, see E. D. Leyburn, *Satiric Allegory: Mirror of Man* (New Haven, 1956).
32 Spingarn, II, 61–2.
33 *The Art of the Satirist* (Texas, 1965), p. 59.
34 *Satires and Miscellaneous Poetry and Prose*, ed. R. Lamar (Cambridge, 1928), pp. 43–4.
35 See Earl Miner, *The Restoration Mode from Milton to Dryden* (Princeton, NJ, 1974), pp. 160–62.
36 Some helpful qualifications to my assessment can be found in R. Quintana, 'Samuel Butler: a restoration figure in a modern light', *ELH*, vol. 18 (1951), pp. 7–31.
37 V. de Sola Pinto, *Enthusiast in Wit* (1962).
38 *Etherege and the 17th-Century Comedy of Manners* (New Haven, 1957), pp. 10–40.
39 *Attribution in Restoration Poetry* (New Haven, 1963), ch. 4. Cf. P. C. Davies, 'Rochester: Augustan and explorer', *Durham Univ. J.*, vol. 30 (1969), pp. 59–64.
40 *Satires Against Man, The Poems of Rochester* (Berkeley, Calif. 1973), p. 5.
41 *Some Passages of the Life and Death of Rochester* (1680), repr. in *Rochester, the Critical Heritage*, ed. D. Farley-Hills (1972), pp. 47–92.
42 '"A Very Profane Wit": John Wilmot . . .', *The Sun at Noon: Three Biographical Sketches* (New York, 1939), pp. 269–306.
43 *Athenae Oxoniensis*, ed. P. Bliss (1813–20), III, 229.
44 See R. Wilcoxon's useful 'Rochester's philosophical premises: a case for consistency', *18th Century Studies*, vol. 8 (1974–5), pp. 183–201.
45 *The Complete Poems*, ed. D. M. Vieth (New Haven, 1968), p. 98.
46 See C. Fabricant, 'Rochester's world of imperfect enjoyment', *JEGP*, vol. 73 (1974), pp. 338–50.
47 Watson, II, 147.
48 Ibid., II, 136.
49 Spingarn, II, 290.
50 This comparison is also made in Griffin's *Satires Against Man*, pp. 258–9, but he compares the Sporus sketch with Rochester's lampoon style in 'My Lord All-Pride'. This comparison is less favourable to Rochester.
51 See Brooks, 'The "Imitation" in English poetry', art. cit., for the background, and Griffin, *Satires Against Man*, pp. 246–65, for a discussion of the poem and its influence on Pope.
52 In writings like 'A Celebration of Charis', Jonson develops what might called the tradition of Horatian dialectic, which presents an unresolved interplay of contradictory attitudes.

53 'Rochester and the traditions of satire', Love, p. 171.

54 R. P. Bond, *English Burlesque Poetry 1700–1750* (Cambridge, Mass., 1932). Bond's model is essentially binary: he has no category of 'low burlesque' or 'heroic satire'.

55 See Ruth Nevo, *The Dial of Vertue*. This paragraph is indebted to Nevo's book.

56 *On the Poetry of Pope* (1938), ch. 3.

57 *POAS*, I, 26–7.

58 cf. Korshin, *From Concord to Dissent*, pp. 96–9.

59 *Alexander Pope: the Poetry of Allusion* (Oxford, 1959), pp. 9 and 13.

60 See P. Harth's discussion of Dryden's scepticism in *Contexts of Dryden's Thought* (Chicago, 1968), pp. 1–31.

61 Watson, II, 125.

62 See J. Fowler's excellent 'Dryden and Literary Good-breeding', Love, pp. 225–46.

63 Watson, II, 22; cf. Spingarn, II, 136–7, 303. See also K. G. Hamilton, *John Dryden and the Poetry of Statement* (Michigan, 1969), esp. ch. 5.

64 *Dryden's Major Plays* (Edinburgh, 1966), p. 14. For an opposed view, see Ann Righter, 'Heroic tragedy', in *Stratford-upon-Avon Studies*, no. 6 (1965), pp. 134–57.

65 'All, all of a Piece Throughout', *Stratford-upon-Avon Studies*, pp. 158–76; cf. Jefferson's 'The significance of Dryden's heroic plays', *Proc. of the Leeds Philos. and Lit. Soc.*, vol. 5 (1940), pp. 125–39, repr. in *Restoration Dramatists*, ed. E. Miner (Englewood Cliffs, NJ, 1966), pp. 19–35. See also W. Myers, *Dryden* (1973), pp. 30–32.

66 Buckingham's *The Rehearsal* throws light on Restoration attitudes to the heroic plays. See *Burlesque Plays of the 18th Century*, ed. S. Trusler (1969), esp. pp. 31, 38, 41, 42, 52.

67 See my 'Juvenal and Restoration Modes of Translation', *MLR*, vol. 68 (1973), pp. 481–93.

68 Watson, II, 154.

69 See R. J. Smith, 'Shadwell's Impact upon John Dryden', *RES*, vol. 20 (1944), pp. 29–44, and D. R. Kunz, 'Shadwell and his Critics . . .', *Restoration & 18th-C. Theatre Research*, vol. 12 (1973), pp. 14–27.

70 *Works*, Calif. edn., vol. 4, ed. A. B. Chambers and W. Frost (1974), p. 221. Similarities in rhyme words between the seventeenth-century versions are noted in this edition's notes.

71 *Complete Works*, V, 308.

72 See above, p. 40.

73 Dryden is conscious of writing in the style of the heroic plays:

      Now what's the End, O Charming Glory, say
      What rare fifth Act, to Crown this huffing play.

                        (256–7)

74 *Poems*, ed. J. Kinsley (Oxford, 1958).

75 cf. D. Davie, *Purity of Diction in English Verse* (1952).

76 *Literary Works*, ed. H. Bunker Wright and Monroe K. Spears, 2 vols (Oxford, 1959), I, 39.

77 Ian Jack, *Augustan Satire: Intention and Idiom in English Poetry 1660–1750* (1952), p. 61.

78 See E. Miner, *Dryden's Poetry* (Bloomington, 1967), pp. 119–20.

79 See ibid., esp. pp. 130–34.

80 See A. L. Korn, '*Mac Flecknoe* and Cowley's *Davideis*', in *Essential Articles for the Study of John Dryden*, ed. H. T. Swedenberg, Jr (1966), pp. 170–200.

81 See W. L. Chernaik, *The Poetry of Limitation: A Study of Edmund Waller* (New Haven, 1968), p. 126. On *figura*, see E. Auerbach, *Scenes from the Drama of European Literature* (New York, 1959), pp. 11–76.

82 The recently discovered complete text of Cowley's *Civil War* enables us to see an early Augustan heroic poem very like Dryden's heroic satire in its combination of satire and epic. See A. Pritchard's edition (Toronto, 1973), esp. p. 51. See also W. Myers, *Dryden*, p. 90.

NOTES TO CHAPTER 4

1 'An Essay upon Unnatural Flights in Poetry', *Poems on Several Occasions*, (1712), pp. 176–7.
2 *Poems*, 1-vol. Twickenham text, ed. J. Butt (1963), p. 602; cf. Boileau, *Epistles*, VII.
3 See P. K. Elkin, *The Augustan Defence of Satire* (Oxford, 1973), pp. 26–31, 154. On Dacier's influence, see H. D. Weinbrot, *The Formal Strain: Studies in Augustan Imitation and Satire* (Chicago, 1969), pp. 62–5, and A. F. B. Clark, *Boileau and the French Classical Critics in England (1660–1830)* (Paris, 1925), pp. 286–8.
4 See Mary C. Randolph's germinal 'The structural design of the formal verse satire', *PQ*, vol. 21 (1942), pp. 368–84.
5 See the discussion of John Norris of Bemerton and John Mason in Christopher Hill's *Puritanism and Revolution* (1958), pp. 323–36.
6 'Life and Writings of Cowley', Spingarn, II, 136–7.
7 See Mary A. Grant's 'The ancient rhetorical theories of the laughable', *University of Wisconsin Studies in Language and Literature*, no. 21 (1924).
8 On this and on the 'good-natured' muse generally, see P. K. Elkin, *The Augustan Defence of Satire*, pp. 44–70 and 146–66; S. M. Tave, *The Amiable Humourist* (Chicago, 1960); E. N. Hooker, 'Humour in the Age of Pope', *HLQ*, vol. 11 (1947/48), pp. 361–85; C. S. Lewis, 'Addison', *Essays on the 18th Century, Presented to D. Nichol Smith* (Oxford, 1945), pp. 1–14, repr. in J. L. Clifford (ed.), *18th Century Literature* (New York, 1959), pp. 144–57; and T. Lockwood, 'The Augustan author-audience relationship: satiric vs. comic', *ELH*, vol. 36 (1969), pp. 648–58.
9 *Spectator*, ed. D. F. Bond, 5 vols (Oxford, 1965), I, 97.
10 *Spectator*, no. 422, in ibid., III, 585.
11 Tr. by Tom Brown as *Essay upon Satyr* in Charles Gildon's *Miscellaneous Poems upon Several Occasions* (1692), sig. B6^r.
12 See E. A. and L. D. Bloom, *Joseph Addison's Social Animal* (Providence, 1971), pp. 4–8.
13 *The Augustan Reprint Society*, Ser. 1, no. 1 (1946), pp. 195 and 219; cf. Jeremy Collier's attack on the Restoration stage in *A Short View of the Immorality and Profaneness of the English Stage* (1698).
14 ibid., pp. 325–6.
15 Quotations are from the 2nd edn (1728) in which the satires are first collected.
16 Vol. 1 (1731), p. 493, cited by H. D. Weinbrott, *The Formal Strain*, pp. 100–1; cf. Joseph Warton and William Boscawen, *The Progress of Satire* (1798), p. 12.
17 See Benjamin Boyce, *The Character-Sketches in Pope's Poems* (Durham, NC, 1962), pp. 54, 123–5, 128–30, and C. E. Crawford, 'What was Pope's debt to Edward Young?', *ELH*, vol. 13 (1946), pp. 157–67.
18 'On Poetry: A Rhapsody', *Poems*, ed. H. Williams, 3 vols. 2nd edit. (1958), p. 650.
19 Ibid., pp. 391–2.
20 cf. Pope:

> Rufa, whose eye quick-glancing o'er the Park
> Attracts each light gay meteor of a Spark . . .
>
> (*Poems*, p. 561)

21 *Alexander Pope: the Poetry of Allusion* (Oxford, 1959), p. 164.
22 *The English Humourists of the 18th Century*, 'Prior, Gay and Pope', in *The Works*, 13 vols (1895), X, 521.
23 'The muse of satire', *Yale Review*, vol. 61 (1951), pp. 80–92; cf. L. Feder, 'Sermo or satire: Pope's definition of his art', in *Studies in Criticism and Aesthetics 1660–1800*, Essays in Honour of S. M. Monk, ed. H. Anderson and J. S. Shea (Minneapolis, 1967), pp. 140–55.
24 *Correspondence*, ed. G. Sherburn, 5 vols (1956), III, 255.
25 ibid., III, 419.
26 ibid., III, 366.
27 On the Horatian poems, see A. L. Williams, 'Pope and Horace: the Second Epistle

of the Second Book', in *Restoration and 18th Century Literature*, Essays in Honour of A. D. McKillop, ed. C. Camden (Chicago, 1963), pp. 309–21; T. Maresca, *Pope's Horatian Poems* (Ohio, 1966); and P. Dixon, *The World of Pope's Satires: An Introduction to the Epistles and Imitations of Horace* (1968).

28 See Leslie Stephen, *English Literature and Society in the 18th Century* (1904), pp. 133–7. On Pope's relations with Grub Street, see George Sherburn, *The Early Career of Alexander Pope* (Oxford, 1934). On Grub Street, see P. Pinkus, *Grub Street Stripped Bare* . . . (1968); and Pat Rogers, *Grub Street; Studies in a Subculture* (1972).

29 M. J. B. Richards, 'Two Books on Pope', *Cambridge Quarterly*, vol. 7 (1977), pp. 198–9.

30 See Tony Tanner, 'Reason and the grotesque: Pope's *Dunciad*', *Cambridge Quarterly*, vol. 7 (1965), pp. 145–60.

31 *Pope's Dunciad* (1955).

32 e.g. *Studies in European Realism* (1950), p. 6.

33 *The Well-wrought Urn* (1947; Eng. edn, 1968), p. 82.

34 See C. L. Kulisheck, 'Swift's octosyllabics and the Hudibrastic tradition', *JEGP*, vol. 53 (1954), pp. 361–8.

35 See B. Dobrée, 'The Jocose Dean', repr. in *Swift Modern Judgements*, ed. A. N. Jeffares (1968), pp. 28–46.

36 *Miscellaneous Prose Works*, vol. 3, *Memoir of J. Swift* (1934), p. 434.

37 See I. Ehrenpreis's comments on *Baucis and Philemon* in *Swift, the Man, the Works, and his Age*, vol. 2 (1967), pp. 243–8; and G. Hill's interesting 'Jonathan Swift: the poetry of "reaction"', in *The World of Jonathan Swift*, ed. B. Vickers (Cambridge, Mass., 1968), pp. 195–212.

38 See P. K. Elkin, *The Augustan Defence*, pp. 86–8.

39 'On Swift's "Scatological" Poems', *Sewanee Review*, vol. 75 (1967), pp. 672–89.

40 See I. Jack, *Augustan Satire*, pp. 111–12; R. E. Hughes, 'Pope's *Imitations of Horace* and the ethical focus', *MLN*, vol. 71 (1956), pp. 569–74; and G. K. Hunter, 'The "Romanticism" of Pope's Horace', art. cit.

41 *Ben Jonson's Poems*, p. 154.

42 *Correspondence*, ed. H. Williams, 5 vols (1963–5), I, 59; cf. Cowley, 'Of Liberty', *Essays*, ed. Gough, p. 117. Swift often quotes Horace in this manner. See *Correspondence*, I, 142, 158, 421.

43 ibid., II, 44–5.

NOTES TO CHAPTER 5

1 See C. D. Thorpe, 'Addison's Contribution to Criticism', in *The 17th Century*, by R. F. Jones *et al.* (Stanford, 1951), pp. 316–29.

2 Welsted, 'A Dissertation concerning the perfection of the English Language', *Epistles, Odes, etc., Written on Several Subjects* (1724), pp. xxxvii–xxxviii.

3 *Conjectures on Original Composition* (1759), pp. 20, 71.

4 I, x. See P. F. Leedy, 'Genres Criticism and the Significance of Warton's Essay on Pope', *JEGP*, vol. 45 (1946), pp. 140–46.

5 Chalmers, XIX, 661.

6 Dr Leavis's 'The Line of Wit' argues that the metaphysical tradition ends in Pope. See *Revaluation* (1936), ch. 1.

7 *The Grounds of Criticism in Poetry* (1704), *Critical Works*, p. 364.

8 See Samuel H. Monk, *The Sublime, A Study of Critical Theories in XVIII-Century England* (1935, repr. Ann Arbor, 1960), p. 27.

9 *Poems on Several occasions* (1707) pp. 205 and 209.

10 *Poems,* ed. D. Nichol Smith and E. L. McAdam, 2nd edn (1974).

11 Watson, II, 121.

12 *Poetical Works,* ed. C. Tracy (Cambridge, 1962), p. 69.

13 *Augustan Satire,* pp. 135–45. See also J. W. Krutch, *Samuel Johnson* (1948); and D. Grant, 'Samuel Johnson: satire and satirists', *New Rambler,* n.s. no. 3 (1967), p. 14.

14 'The vanity of human wishes'. *RES,* vol. 6 (1955), pp. 157–65; cf. W. W. Robson, in *New Rambler* (June, 1965), p. 42, and Mary Lascelles, 'Dr Johnson and Juvenal', *New Light on Dr Johnson,* ed. F. W. Hilles (New Haven, 1959), pp. 35–55.

15 *The Rhetorical World of Augustan Humanism* (Oxford, 1965), p. 156; cf. S. I. Tucker and H. Gifford, 'Johnson's Poetic Imagination', *RES,* vol. 8 (1957), pp. 241–8.

16 *London, A Poem and The Vanity of Human Wishes,* ed. Eliot (1930), p. 15, and *On Poetry and Poets* (1957), p. 179.

17 'Johnson as Satirist: A New Look at The Vanity of Human Wishes', *ELH,* vol. 34 (1967), pp. 78–91.

18 *Lives,* III, 332–3; cf. Addison, *Spectator,* II. 129–30.

19 Boswell's, *Life of Johnson,* ed. G. B. Hill, rev. L. F. Powell, 6 vols (1934–50), I, 194.

20 F. R. Leavis, 'Johnson and Augustanism', *The Common Pursuit* (1952), p. 102.

21 cf. Dryden, *Aeneid,* V, 1051.

22 *Political Satire in English Poetry* (Cambridge, 1910), p. 136.

23 Chalmers, XVII, 208.

24 'Jest often cuts through the knot more effectively than bitterness.'

25 'The Satiric Mode of Feeling', *Criticism,* vol. 11 (1969), p. 131.

26 Augustan Reprint Society, Series One: *Essays on Wit,* no. 4 (1947), pp. 50–51.

27 *The Poetical Works,* ed. D. Grant (Oxford, 1956), pp. 109–10.

28 See W. C. Brown, 'Charles Churchill: a Revaluation', *SP,* vol. 40 (1943), pp. 405–24, and E. H. Weatherly, 'Churchill's Literary Indebtedness to Pope', *SP,* vol. 43 (1946), pp. 59–69.

29 See Wallace C. Brown, *Charles Churchill, Poet, Rake, and Rebel* (Lawrence, 1953), p. 91.

30 *Introduction to the Classics* (1718).

31 *Philosophical and Critical Observations* (1774), II, 164. See Earl R. Wasserman's excellent 'The Inherent Values of Eighteenth-Century Personification', *PMLA,* vol. 65 (1950) pp. 435–63.

32 See Yvor Winter's valuable 'The Poetry of Charles Churchill', *Poetry,* vol. 98 (1961), 44–53, 104–17. I. Simon warns against assimilating Churchill to Romanticism in 'An 18th-Century Satirist: Charles Churchill', *Rev. belge de philol. et d'histoire,* vol. 37 (1959), pp. 645–82. Contrast M. Golden, 'Sterility and Eminence in the Poetry of Charles Churchill', *JEGP,* vol. 66 (1967), pp. 333–46.

33 See Winter's 'The Poetry of . . . Churchill', p. 52.

34 Cited by Arthur Johnston, 'Poetry and criticism after 1740', in *Dryden to Johnson,* ed. R. Lonsdale (1971), p. 372.

35 Cowper, *Table Talk,* p. 764.

36 *To the Palace of Wisdom* (1964), p. 343.

A Reading List

GENERAL STUDIES

R. M. Alden, *The Rise of Formal Satire in England under Classical Influence* (Pennsylvania, 1899).
R. C. Elliott, *The Power of Satire: Magic, Ritual, Art* (Princeton, NJ, 1960).
M. Hodgart, *Satire* (1969).
D. C. Powers, *English Formal Satire, Elizabethan to Augustan* (The Hague, 1971).

CLASSICAL SATIRE

M. Coffey, *Roman Satire* (1976).
G. Highet, *Juvenal the Satirist, a Study* (1954).
N. Rudd, *The Satires of Horace* (Cambridge, 1966).
J. P. Sullivan, *Critical Essays on Roman Literature: Satire* (1963).

ELIZABETHAN SATIRE

O. J. Campbell, *Comicall Satyre and Shakespeare's Troilus and Cressida* (San Marino, Calif. 1938).
A. Caputi, *John Marston, Satirist* (Ithaca, Ill. 1961).
K. W. Gransden, *Tudor Verse Satire* (1970).
A. B. Kernan, *The Cankered Muse* (New Haven, 1959).
John Peter, *Complaint and Satire in Early English Literature* (1956).
Hallett Smith, *Elizabethan Poetry: A Study in Conventions, Meaning, and Expression* (Cambridge, Mass., 1952).

AUGUSTAN SATIRE

P. Dixon, *The World of Pope's Satires: An Introduction to the Epistles and Imitations of Horace* (1968).
P. K. Elkin, *The Augustan Defence of Satire* (1973).
D. H. Griffin, *Satires against Man: The Poems of Rochester* (Berkeley, Calif., 1973).
I. Jack, *Augustan Satire: Intention & Idiom in English Poetry 1660–1750* (1952).
H. Love, ed., *Restoration Literature: Critical Approaches* (1972).
T. E. Maresca, *Pope's Horatian Poems* (Ohio, 1966).
R. Nevo, *The Dial of Vertue: A Study of Poems on Affairs of State in the 17th Century* (Princeton, NJ, 1963).
B. Schilling, *Dryden and the Conservative Myth: A Reading of Absalom and Achitophel* (New Haven, Conn., 1961).
R. Trickett, *The Honest Muse: A Study in Augustan Verse* (1967).
H. D. Weinbrot, *The Formal Strain: Studies in Augustan Imitation and Satire* (Chicago, Ill. 1969).

Index

Addison, Joseph 122, 124, 125, 165
  on good humour 123
  pre-romantic elements in 153
  Spectator and *Tatler* 123
Aeneas Silvius:
  on Juvenal 32
Akenside, Mark:
  An Epistle to Curio 157
Allen, Morse:
  on Marston 70
Anderson, W. S.:
  on Juvenal 30, 31
Ashmore, John 77, 78
Augustan values 73–4, 77–8; *see also* neo-
    classicism
  vs middle-class values 73–4
  in Rochester 97, 99
  in Dryden 105
  poetic development of, by Pope 136,
    137, 142
  in Churchill 167, 175

Bacon, Francis 74, 77, 80, 89, 92
Beaumont, Sir John 77–8, 180
  'Happy Man' poems 78
  translations of Roman satires by 78, 180
  'To his late Maiesty . . .' 77
Bishops' prohibition of satire 51, 72
Blackmore, Sir Richard:
  Essay upon Wit 123
Blackwall, Anthony:
  on personification 169
Bloom, E. A. and L. D.:
  on Whitehead 165
Boileau, Nicolas 89, 94, 106, 124, 125, 159,
    183
  imitated by Rochester 97, 100
  translation of Longinus 154
Bond, R. P.:
  on burlesque 100, 182
Breton, Nicholas 72
Brewster, Thomas:
  translation of Persius 156
  compared with Dryden 156–7
Brome, Alexander 74
Brooks, Cleanth:
  on Pope's *Rape of the Lock* 144

Brower, Reuben:
  on Horace 25, 128–9
  on Dryden and Pope 105
Buckingham, George Villiers, 2nd Duke
    of:
  The Rehearsal 81, 182
Burnet, Gilbert:
  on Juvenal 32
  Rochester and 93, 95, 96
Butler, Samuel 13, **89–92**, 100, 104, 121
  anti-heroic outlook of 90
  neoclassical style of 91–2
  compared with Rochester 95–6
  compared with Swift 145, 146
  Hudibras: I, i 73, 80; I, iii 91; II, ii 80
  'Satyr upon the Licentious Age of Charles
    II' 92

Carew, Thomas 81
Casaubon, Isaac 51, 157
  theory of satire 43, 56
Chapman, George 53–4
Churchill, Charles 13, 29, 77, 124, 152,
    164–75, 185
  pre-romantic elements in 165, 167–70, 175
  his quarrel with Whitehead 166–7, 171
  his departures from Augustan values 167,
    170, 171, 175
  his preference for Dryden 167
  compared with Pope, 167 *et seq.*
  compared with Juvenal 168, 169, 171
  and Spenser 168–9
  authorial voice 169, 174
  compared with Sterne 170
  irony in 172–4
  on Warburton 172–4
  The Apology 168
  The Author 169
  The Candidate 172
  The Conference 170–1
  The Dedication 172–4
  Epistle to William Hogarth 171
  The Farewell 170
  The Ghost 167, 170
  The Prophecy of Famine 168, 174
  The Rosciad 166, 167, 172

Cleveland, John 73, 77, **81–4,** 89, 104, 181
  influence of Elizabethan satire on 81–3
  use of 'conceit' in 82–3
  'The Mixt Assembly' 82–3
Cobb, Samuel:
  compared with Johnson 156
  'Of Vain Wishes' 155–6
Complaint **47–50**
Congreve, William 86, 119
Cotton, Charles:
  Scarronides 100
Cowley, Abraham 74, 75, **79–81,** 83, 84,
    89, 90, 94, 102, 122, 148, 155
  'Happy Man' poems 78–81
  and imitation 79
  imitation of Horace by 79–81
  Civil War 182
  Davideis 79, 80, 115
  Essays 79
  The Mistress 79
  Pindaric Odes 101
Creech, Thomas 74
Crowley, Robert:
  'Of the Colier of Croydon' 48
  One and thyrtye Epigrammes 46

Dacier, André:
  on Roman satire 120, 123
  on 'praise' and 'blame' 120, 121
Davenant, Sir William 90
Davenport, A.:
  on Marston 71
Denham, Sir John 79, 81, 84, 102
Dennis, John 13, 153
  comparison between Horace and Juvenal
    41, 155
dialogue:
  Horace's use of 18, 24
  Rochester's use of 94
  Churchill's use of 170–1
Donatus, Aelius:
  on satire 56
Donne, John 46, **59–65,** 73, 81, 178, 179
  metre in his satires 52–3
  'mixed style' in 59–60
  compared with Horace 60, 63
  influence of *Complaint* on his satires 65
  imitated by Pope 137
  Satires: I 60–3; III 47; IV 63–4
Drant, Thomas:
  A Medicinable Morall 47, 49
Dryden, John 73, 77, 80, 83, 86, 89, 97–8,
  104, **105–18,** 119, 122, 155
  on Horace and Juvenal 28–9, 105–7, 110
  on Butler 96

  and heroic style 107–10, 113–18, 154,
    182
  on Virgil 107, 109, 119, 185
  translation of Juvenal's 10th satire 108–10,
    161–2
  and plain style 110
  Horatian element in 111
  allusions to Milton in 113–4, 115
  attacks on Shadwell 115–17
  and French classicism 120
  influence of Dacier on 120–1
  translation of Persius by 156–7
  compared with Brewster 156–7
  compared with Johnson 161–2
  Absalom and Achitophel 37, 74, 86, 100,
    107, 111–14, 122, 154
  Discourse . . . of Satire 105–7, 120, 157
  Mac Flecknoe 97, 100, 110, 115–17
  The Medal 114–15, 117
  Ovid's Epistles 89
  Of Dramatic Poesy 106
  'To the Memory of Mr Oldham' 84

Eliot, T. S.:
  on Donne 60
  on Johnson 158
Elizabethan satire **45–72,** 81, 84
  sadistic element in 52, 82
  metre in 52–3
  influence of Persius on 53
Epicureanism:
  Horace and 14, 20, 21, 27, 78
  Cowley and 79
  Rochester and 94
Erasmus 12, 148

Fraenkel, Edward:
  on Horace 25
Francis, Philip:
  on Horace and Juvenal 154
Frye, Northrop 12
Fuller, Thomas:
  on Cleveland, 83
Fussell, Paul:
  on Johnson 158

Garrick, David 166, 167
  on Johnson's style in *The Vanity* 160
Garth, Sir Samuel 119
  Dispensary 100
Gascoigne, George:
  The Steele Glas 46, 50
Gifford, H.:
  on Johnson 158
Glanvill, Joseph 89, 122

Gould, Robert:
on Oldham 85
'grand style', *see* heroic style
Granville, George, Lord Lansdowne:
on Dryden 119
Greene, Donald:
on Swift 147–8
Grey, Zachary:
on Butler 92
Griffin, D. H.:
on Rochester 93, 181
Guilpin, Everard 46, 67, 82

Hake, Edward:
Newes out of Powles Churchyarde 46, 50
Hall, Joseph 46, 51, 53, 55, **65–9**, 73, 179
influence of Horace and Juvenal on 66, 67, 68–9
Stoicism in 66–8
influence of Complaint on 68
attacked by Marston 70
Virgidemiarum Sixe Bookes (*'Virgidemiae'*) 46, 66; I, 'Prologue' 67; IV, vi 66
Heinsius, Daniel:
definition of satire 43, 44
heroic style:
Horace and 18
secularisation of 100–3
in the Restoration period 100–2
Waller and 102
Dryden and 110, 113
Higden, Henry:
on Juvenal 32
Highet, Gilbert:
on Juvenal 31, 177
Hobbes, Thomas 87, 89, 121, 146
anti-romantic theories of 90
and Rochester 94–5, 98, 100
Leviathan 94
Holyday, Barten 74, 76–7
Horace, **13–28**, 83
and Stoicism 13, 16, 19–20, 26–7, 28
and Epicureanism 14, 20, 21, 27, 78
as 'conservative' satirist 14, 28, 42
self-revelation in satires of 16
ethical stance of 16, 20, 42, 107
aversion to abuse in satire 17–18
commitment to plain style 18, 20, 21, 22, 23, 24, 27–8, 42, 77
and the 'grand style' 18
use of dialogue by 18, 24
imitation of Plautus 21
Dryden's comparison of, with Juvenal 28–9, 105–7, 110
compared with Juvenal 41–2

translated by Drant 49
influence of, on Donne 60, 63
translated by Beaumont 78
imitated by Cowley and Sprat 79–81
imitated by Rochester 97
influence of, on Dryden 111
influence of, on neoclassical satire 120–4
Wollaston on 121
compared with Young 125, 126
influence of, on Pope 128
influence of, on Swift 128
imitated by Pope 130, 131
imitated by Swift 148
Francis on, 154
translations of 180
Epistles: II, i 17
Epodes 106
Odes 19
Satires: I, iii 20; I, iv 16, 17, 18; I, v 21, 27; I, vi 22; I, viii 88; I, ix 23, 27; I, x 17, 18, 97; II, i 17, 170; II, iii 18; II, iv 21; II, vi 24–7, 58, 78–81, 148; II, vii 18, 19–20; II, viii 12
Hurd, Richard:
Letters on Chivalry and Romance 175

'imitation' 89, 180
Cowley and 79
Johnson and 158–64

Jack, Ian:
on Johnson 158
Jefferson, D. W.:
on Dryden 108
Johnson, Dr Samuel 77, 125, 152, 153, 157, **158–64**
his pathos 155, 158–9, 162
compared with Oldham 159–60
compared with Dryden 161–2
compared with Shadwell 163
Idler 164
London 159
Rasselas 159
The Vanity of Human Wishes 13, 75, 141, 156, 160–4
Jonson, Benjamin 12, 46, 53, 65, 74, 79, 92, 94, 148, 155, 159, 179, 181
Christian tone in 74
imitation of Juvenal 74–5
compared with Vaughan 76–7
Discoveries 15, 77
'Epode II' 74
Poetaster 63, 69
'To Penshurst' 67, 74
'To Sir Robert Wroth' 74–5

Juvenal **28–42,** 74, 89, 119, 153
  Dryden's comparison of, with Horace
    28–9, 105–7, 110
  as the indignant satirist 29–30, 31, 42
  immediacy of his satire 29–30
  and Stoicism 30, 31, 164
  inconsistencies in satiric voice of 31
  christianisation of 31–2, 74–6, 164
  moral stance of 32, 34–6, 42
  Petrarch on 32
  chauvinism of 36
  class-feeling in 36
  romantic critics and 37
  use of rhetoric by 37–9
  style in 39–40, 42, 107
  and epic style 41, 169
  compared with Horace 41–2
  and Complaint 49–50
  influence of, on Elizabethan satire **50–7**
  'mixed style' in 60
  translations of 74, 180
  imitated by Jonson 75
  translated by Vaughan 75–6
  translated by Dryden 108–10, 161–2
  translated by Shadwell 108–10, 163
  Wollaston on 121
  compared with Young 125, 126
  influence of, on Pope 128, 129
  influence of, on Swift 128
  Francis on 154
  Longinian view of 155
  imitated by Johnson **158–64**
  Satires: I 30, 41; II 35; III 36, 158–60;
    IV 36, 40; V 12; VI 41; X 22, 32–3,
    57–8, 108, 161–2; XI 41; XIII 30, 31;
    XIV 34

Kernan, Alvin 11
King, Bruce:
  on Dryden 108
Korshin, Paul:
  on Oldham 85

Langland, William 45, 46
Lewis, C. S.:
  on Donne and Horace 61
Locke, John 73, 121, 153, 170
Lodge, Thomas 46
  Defence of Poetry 57
  A Fig for Momus 57
  'Satyr 4' 57
  'Satyr 5' 58
Longinus:
  influence on 18th-century poetry 153–4
  Peri Hupsous 153–4

Love, Harold:
  on Rochester 99
Lucilius 11, 21, 97
  Horace's view of 14, 15, 16, 17
Lucretius:
  De rerum natura 89
Lukács, Georg 142

Mack, Maynard:
  on Pope 129
Marston, John 46, 50, 52, **69–72,** 73, 74,
    82, 88, 89, 94, 167, 179
  on obscurity in satire 55
  stylistic conflict in 55
  influence of Juvenal on 69
  attack on Hall 70
  Calvinistic stance of 71–2
  The Metamorphosis of Pigmalions Image 69
  'Reactio' (*Certain Satires,* IV) 70
  The Scourge of Villanie 57, 69, 70, 71
Marvell, Andrew 73, **103–5**
  'The Horatian Ode' 101
  Last Instructions to a Painter 100, 104–5
  Second Advice to a Painter 103–4
Mason, H. A.:
  on Juvenal 35–6, 37
Metre
  'roughness' 52–3, 84, 85
Milgate, W. 62, 179
Milton, John:
  on satire 56
  allusions to, in Dryden 113–14, 115
  Paradise Lost 91, 102
'mixed style':
  in Persius 59–60
  in Juvenal 60
  in Donne 59–60
mock-heroic 21, 80–1, 86–7, 89, 100, 104–5,
    108, 133, 138, 141, 162
Morgan, Edwin:
  on Dryden 107
Morris, Corbyn:
  on wit 166
Mulgrave, John Sheffield, Earl of 86, 96
  Rochester on 99
Murdock, Kenneth:
  on Rochester 93

Nashe, Thomas:
  Pierce Penilesse 46, 65
neoclassicism **77–81,** 119–21; *see also*
    Augustan values
North, Dudley 77

O'Flaherty, P.:
  on Johnson 158
Ogilvie, John:
  on personification 169
Oldham, John 73, 83
  satiric persona in 86–8
  Elizabethan satire and 88
  Cobb on 155
  compared with Johnson 159–60
  'Counterpart to the Satyr against Vertue' 87
  'Satyr against Vertue' 86
  Satyrs upon the Jesuits 85, **87–9**
  Some New Pieces 85

Paulson, Ronald 12
Percy, Thomas:
  Reliques 175
Persius 11, 52, 54, 119, 179
  influence of, on Elizabethan satire 53
  affinities with Donne 59
  proto-Christian style 59
  translated by Brewster and Dryden 156–7
Peter, John 50, 61
  on Donne 65
  on Pope 142
Petrarch:
  on Juvenal 32
Philips, John:
  Splendid Shilling 100
Pinto, V. de Sola:
  on Rochester 93
plain style:
  sermo 15, 18, 54
  classical 15, 22–3, 54
  Horace and 18, 20, 21, 22, 24, 27–8, 89, 176
  Juvenal and 39, 41
  Jonson and 75
  Vaughan and 76
  neoclassical 77–8, 121–2, 128, 156, 163
  Dryden and 110
  Pope and 119–21, 132, 133
Pope, Alexander 74, 77, 86, 89, 96, 99, 125, **128–44**, 155, 168, 169, 183–4
  as 'Horatian' satirist 12–13, 14, 120, 122, 128, 131–2, 138, 144
  and the plain style 119–21, 132, 133
  compared with Young 126
  influence of Juvenal on 128, 129, 142
  mastery of satiric styles 129, 133
  attacked by Thackeray 129
  'voices' employed by 129, 132
  insistence on personal satire 129, 131
  moral seriousness of 130–1, 132

  distinction between satires and epistles in 130, 131
  'fine raillery' in 133
  mock-heroic elements in 133, 138
  and the Scriblerus Club 136
  poetic development by, of Augustan values 136, 137, 142
  imitation of Donne's satires by 137
  his use of scatology 139–40
  compared with Dryden 140
  his 'realism' 142–4
  compared with Churchill 167–74
  The Dunciad 83, 92, 136, 138–42
  Epilogue to the Satires: Dialogue I 130, 132, 171; *Dialogue II* 132, 142
  'Epistle to Augustus' 174
  'An Epistle to Dr Arbuthnot' 60, 136, 137
  'Epistle to Miss Blount' 142–3
  An Essay on Criticism 136, 153
  An Essay on Man 138
  Horace, Satires and Epistles of, Imitated 121, 130, 131–2
  Rape of the Lock 99, 100, 133–6
Previte-Orton, C. W.:
  on Churchill 165
Price, Martin 175
Prior, Matthew:
  The Hind and the Panther Transversed 110
Pulteney, John 154

'raillery' 11, 44, 107, 112, 120, 123, 133, 144, 155, 166
Rankins, William 67
Rapin, René 120
  on Juvenal 37
Rochester, John Wilmot, 2nd Earl of 73, 86, 87, **92–100**, 106, 121, 125, 181
  his materialism 93
  Burnet on 93, 95, 97
  and Hobbes 94–5, 98, 100
  satiric persona in 94, 98–9
  compared with Butler 95–6
  and Elizabethan satire 96
  compared with Horace and Juvenal 97
  on Dryden 97–8
  and Horace 98
  'An Allusion to Horace' 16–17, 97
  'An Epistolary Essay from M. G. to O. B.' 99
  'A Letter from Artemisia in the Town to Chloe in the Country' 98–9
  'On Poet Ninny' 96
  'A Ramble in St James's Park' 95, 146
  'A Satyr against Reason and Mankind' 94, 98, 99, 147

'Timon' 97, 98
'A Very Heroical Epistle in Answer to Ephelia' 99
Rowlands, Samuel 72

satire:
    etymology of 43, 56, 57, 120, 176, 178
    definition of 43, 44
satirist:
    concept of 11, 17, 42–3, 94
Savage, Richard:
    The Authors of the Town 157
Scaliger, Julius Caesar:
    on the Roman satirists 43
    on satire 44
Scott, Sir Walter:
    on Swift 145
Scriblerus Club 136
Scroope, Sir Carr 96
Scudamore, James:
    Homer à la Mode 100
Seneca, *see* Stoicism
sermo, see plain style
Shadwell, Thomas 73, 74
    on Juvenal 32
    on rough satire 85
    and Rochester 97–8
    translation of Juvenal's 10th satire 108–10, 163
    attacked by Dryden 115–17
    compared with Johnson 163
Shaftesbury, 3rd Earl of:
    on good humour 122
Shenstone, William 175
Skelton, John:
    satires 45
Smith, Hallett 49, 68
    on Lodge 58
Soames, William:
    on Oldham 84
Spenser, Edmund 168
Sprat, Thomas 74
    on Cowley 79, 122
    imitation of Horace by 80, 180
Stapylton, Sir Robert 74, 76–7
Steele, Sir Richard 122, 123, 165
Sterne, Laurence:
    Tristram Shandy 170, 175
Stoicism:
    Horace and 13, 26–7, 28
    Juvenal and 30, 31
    influence of, on Hall 66–7
    Johnson and 164
Suckling, Sir John 81

Sutherland, W. O. S.:
    on Butler 90
Swift, Jonathan 74, 91, 121, 122, 128, 136, **144–52,** 184
    letters to Harley 14, 149
    on Young 125
    influence of Horace and Juvenal on 128, 144, 145
    low style in 144, 146
    compared with Young 144
    'raillery' in 144
    indebtedness to Butler's *Hudibras* 144, 145
    compared with Butler 145, 146
    compared with Rochester 145, 146, 147
    scatology and obscenity in 147–8
    his autobiographical voice 148–52
    imitation of Horace 148–9
    narrative strategies in his poetry 150–2
    compared with Browning 152
    'An Apology to the Lady Carteret' 150–1
    'An Epistle to a Lady' 144
    Gulliver's Travels 92
    'The Humble Petition of Frances Harris' 151–2
    'Lady Acheson, Weary of the Dean' 151
    'Mary the Cook-Maid's Letter to Dr Sheridan' 151–2
    'Phillis, Or, the Progress of Love' 145
    'The Progress of Beauty' 146
    'The Progress of Marriage' 146
    'To Mr Delany' 128
Sypher, Wylie 101

Temple, Sir William 86, 148
Thackeray, W. M.:
    attack on Pope 129
Tillotson, Geoffrey 101
Trickett, Rachel:
    on Oldham 89
Trimpi, Wesley 75
    on Jonson 148

Underwood, Dale:
    on Rochester 93

Vaughan, Henry:
    imitation of Juvenal 75–6
    compared with Johnson 75, 155
    Christian tone in 75–6
    compared with Holyday and Stapylton 76–7
Vieth, D. M.:
    on Rochester 93
Vossius:
    definition of satire 43
    on Horace and Juvenal 44